Strategic Career Management
Developing Your Talent

Jane Yarnall

ELSEVIER

AMSTERDAM • BOSTON • HEIDELBERG • LONDON • NEW YORK • OXFORD
PARIS • SAN DIEGO • SAN FRANCISCO • SINGAPORE • SYDNEY • TOKYO
Butterworth-Heinemann is an imprint of Elsevier

Butterworth-Heinemann is an imprint of Elsevier
Linacre House, Jordan Hill, Oxford OX2 8DP, UK
30 Corporate Drive, Suite 400, Burlington, MA 01803, USA

First edition 2008

British Library Cataloguing in Publication Data
A catalogue record for this book is available from the British Library

Library of Congress Cataloging-in-Publication Data
A catalog record for this book is available from the Library of Congress

ISBN: 978-0-7506-8369-2

For information on all Butterworth-Heinemann publications
visit our web site at books.elsevier.com

Typeset by Charon Tec Ltd (A Macmillan Company), Chennai, India
www.charontec.com

Printed and bound in Hungary

07 08 09 10   10 9 8 7 6 5 4 3 2 1

Contents

Foreword

Contemporary organisations face constant pressure to enhance levels of service and productivity whilst also improving levels of cost efficiency. The volatility of external environment and the rapid pace of technological change increasingly demand innovative means of improving business performance and securing competitive advantage. People are increasingly recognised as the prime source of competitive advantage and the need for effective people management is therefore more important than ever before. The responsibility for effective people management is shared between senior managers, HR professionals and line managers but the challenges facing today's organisations provide an ideal opportunity for the HR function to demonstrate its ability to contribute to organisational performance at a strategic level. To take advantage of this opportunity it is necessary to not only recognise the changes that are required but also to identify the steps to ensure that they can be implemented effectively.

Whilst much has been written about strategic human resource management and its contribution to organisational performance, real life examples of what works and what doesn't remain thin on the ground. We recognise that HR professionals and senior managers alike face a sometimes overwhelming pressure to follow trends or apply quick-fixes to a wide range of people management challenges and it can be difficult to get impartial advice about what to change and how to change it in order to create lasting results. We have therefore developed this series to bridge the gap between theory and implementation by providing workable solutions to complex people management issues and by sharing organisational experiences. The books within this series draw on live examples of strategic HR in practice and offer practical insights, tools and frameworks that will help to transform the individual and functional delivery of HR within a variety of organisational contexts.

Taking its rightful place in the series, *Strategic Career Management* focuses on the benefits to today's organisations of career strategies that facilitate the growth and retention of talent. Drawing on her extensive experience of organisational career management, the author provides clear insight into effective career strategies for the twenty-first century. Career strategies have long been on the back-burner in recent years. This book demonstrates the importance of a strategic approach to careers and links this to the current preoccupation with talent management. It provides a contemporary perspective on the key components of career strategy, i.e. succession planning, career acceleration and development opportunities, and discusses the potential implications of different approaches. The author is aware that demonstrating an appropriate return on investment in career management can be difficult, especially when competing priorities for scarce funding often put people-focussed initiatives at the back of the queue. Readers are clearly guided through the process of how to build a business case and how to measure success. Consideration is also given to the role of key stake-holders; HR specialists, line managers and the balances between organisational and individual responsibility for career management.

Whilst grounded in theory, the book is essentially a practical tool for HR professionals and line managers who wish to develop effective career management strategies. Rich in case studies, the book contains examples from diverse organisations covering a variety of sectors including travel, finance, legal, transport, manufacturing, IT and printing. In addition, clear models, tried and tested frameworks and the use of self-reflective questions facilitate the application of different approaches to specific organisational contexts. For HR professionals and managers seeking to bring about significant changes in the management of talent, we can think of few better models to follow than the approach mapped out in this book.

Julie Beardwell

Linda Holbeche

Associate Dean & Head of HRM

Director of Research & Policy

Leeds Business School

CIPD

Preface

I first got involved in the issues of organisational career management in the early 1990s, when I was tasked with project managing the introduction of a new career strategy and set of career initiatives aimed at supporting individuals in their own careers. To help me in this task, I scoured all available resources, attended conferences on the topic and joined various network groups – all in the vain hope that I would find some answers as to the practicalities of the process.

It soon became apparent that nearly all of the information available to me was either an academic perspective on careers in organisations or an individualistic approach aiming to help people with their careers across a range of opportunities and organisations. For me, two books stood out at that time, which I grasped hold of and held up as capturing best practice. They were Andrew Mayo's book *Managing Careers* and Liebowitz, Farren and Kaye's more American perspective *Designing Career Development Systems*. Thanks to these books and a strong network of contacts, I managed to implement what at the time was considered to be a leading edge set of initiatives.

But times have changed, and the nature of career management in organisations has moved on. Talent management is now very much on the agenda and organisations are starting to take more control of how their high potential employees develop and grow their careers. Alongside this, the values of the workforce are changing, with less commitment being shown to companies that are not willing to provide learning and development opportunities. As companies have become more global, leaders around the world have found that they lack the knowledge of who has the potential for what, and developing pools of talent as an approach to help them manage this, has come to the fore.

This book explores the current state of play in organisations and looks at how companies can and should implement career strategies in the 21st century to support the growth of their talent. It draws on case studies from a diverse range of companies to help illustrate the practical steps that are being taken and to help illustrate the points that are made.

Who is this book for?

This book aims to be first and foremost a practical tool. I would like to think that HR practitioners currently being tasked with career management will be able to use this text in the way that I used Andrew Mayo's many years ago, to help them understand the scope of the topic and get some practical insights into how to go about enhancing their own organisation's career strategies. This book is also written in such a way to be of interest to senior and line management looking to enhance their talent and motivate their own teams in their careers. As such, it will particularly appeal to people in roles such as:

- Talent Managers
- HR Business Partners
- Career Specialists
- Learning and Development Professionals
- Mentors and Coaches
- Talent Panellists
- Line Managers with an interest in developing the potential of those around them
- People studying HR strategy

Some of the many questions that this book will help to answer are:

- How do I go about developing a business case for career development in my organisation?
- How do I implement a talent management strategy that integrates with career development for all employees?
- How can I develop the key roles and skills needed to support an effective strategy?
- What processes do I need to put in place to make the strategy a success?
- What is the right balance between organisation-led strategies and individual-led careers?

What is different about this book?

There are various resources available on different aspects of career strategy and this book is not intended to replace the many informative books on topics such as mentoring, succession planning and assessment centres. However, few of these books look at the topic of career strategy as whole or focus on the difficult topic of integrating the component parts. Many of the career books take either a highly individual perspective, exploring what a person can do to grow their career, or they take more of an organisational research perspective, examining the topic in relation to career theory. Whilst this is all useful, it can be hard to draw out the implications for companies seeking to revitalise their career strategies.

The aim of this book is to bring together a lot of information under one roof and explore how career strategies work from an organisational perspective, taking account of the individual's needs and the implications from research in this field. It is full of practical advice and case study examples where practitioners are telling their story as it is, rather than as they would like it to be!

Readers are likely to be at different stages in their understanding, and the book is written in a way that will enable more experienced practitioners to dip into the parts that are relevant to them, or for people looking to build their HR toolkit, to gain a complete overview of the topic by reading the book from start to finish. Whichever way you choose to use it, I hope that you find the content useful and that it enables you to grow your own career alongside that of the organisations you are helping to drive forward.

The structure of this book

Chapter 1: An overview of career strategy

This chapter sets out the context of careers. It explores the different terminology and how definitions of what careers mean to individuals have changed over the last 20–30 years. It looks at the importance and benefits of career strategies and how this links to current thinking on talent management. This chapter explores the cultural influences and different business drivers that impact on career strategies and gives an indication of the different tools and techniques used by organisations to support these.

The *First Choice* case study at the end of this chapter is a nice example of a company starting out on the process of redefining their career strategy to focus more on growing high potential talent.

Chapter 2: Focusing in on your talent: getting the balance right

Talent management is the buzzword of all companies and this chapter explores what the concept of talent management means in practice and how this fits with the overall career strategy of a company. There are interesting debates about whether talent should be singled out and if so how you go about identifying and selecting high potential. The psychological contract and the need to balance organisational and individual needs is explored within this chapter, as well as the consequences of implementing a career strategy targeted at a smaller proportion of the workforce.

The *Virgin Atlantic* case study at the end of this chapter illustrates a particular approach to developing talent, which involved a comprehensive development centre for the management population.

Chapter 3: Building the business case

HR practitioners no longer have the luxury of introducing initiatives into a company that they think will add benefit and there is an increasing need to prove the business case. This chapter explores how to go about this process, from how to lay out your case and gain support for it, through to the tools that can be used for analysis. In addition, this chapter draws together some of the research into the benefits of career strategies in order to provide some useful success measures to build a business case.

The case study at the end of this chapter comes from the *Legal Services Commission*, who developed a comprehensive business case to support the implementation of a talent centre to select people to a newly created talent pool.

Chapter 4: Revitalising your succession management

This chapter takes a look at how succession management has changed in recent years, from a more formal post-by-post process, to a more flexible pool-based approach. This chapter explores the practicalities of assessing demand and supply in rapidly changing organisations and looks at the tools that can be used to do this. Issues such as the use of information technology and the involvement of individual preferences are debated.

This chapter ends with a case study which illustrates how the succession process was reworked within one company, with a focus on identifying the business critical roles and the likely vacancy risks for each position.

Chapter 5: The practicalities of career acceleration pools

This chapter builds on the previous chapter and goes into more detail on how to implement a pool-based approach to developing the careers of high potential employees. It looks at issues such as how to segment pools, ensure flexibility of entry and exit, and how to determine an appropriate size for the pool. More importantly, this chapter explores some of the implications of the pool approach, such as how to deal with derailment and diversity issues.

The *Rolls-Royce* case study at the end of this chapter is a good illustration of a company at the forefront of developing an acceleration pool strategy. The case study outlines the different pools the company has in place and the tools and techniques they use to ensure the process is well managed.

Chapter 6: Developing the key roles

Any strategy requires a clear set of roles and accountabilities, and career strategies are no different. This chapter sets out some of the key roles and explore some of the challenges that are presented by each. The role of line managers, HR professionals, career coaches and mentors are all explored in some detail. Line managers for example, have many tensions in their role that can prevent some of the intentions behind career strategies from being effectively implemented. This chapter explores these tensions and makes recommendations as to how to deal with these issues.

The case study from *LogicaCMG* at the end of this chapter provides an illustration of how to implement an effective career coaching culture. The company has taken steps to accredit managers internally as coaches and this has had a beneficial impact on their career strategy.

Chapter 7: Fostering opportunities for growing careers

Many of the talent management occurring in organisations focuses strongly on the identification of talent and establishment of pools of people with potential. Often, however, it is not clear what the company plans to do with these newly identified groups and how individuals should grow their careers. This chapter seeks to examine the different types of opportunities open to companies and looks at some of the implications for people managing those experiences. This chapter contrasts growth opportunities which stem from role changes, such as secondments and overseas assignments, with opportunities which run alongside the job, such as projects or action learning.

The case study at the end of this chapter is a personal reflection from a high potential manager within *Volvo*, and provides an illustration of the wider impact of assignments.

Chapter 8: Developing career self-reliance amongst your talent

In the current uncertain world, many companies are keen to encourage their employees to take control of their own careers and take responsibility for seeking out opportunities to grow and develop for the future. This chapter looks at how you can encourage this self-reliance on careers in companies and what sort of tools you might need to make available to support this approach. The range of self-help tools and resources are explored, as well as how theories on individual career development, such as career life stages, contribute to people's own understanding of their careers.

This chapter is supported by two case studies. The first case study, from *Lexmark*, describes a career workshop which was put in place to encourage career thinking amongst their high potential manager group. The second case study is from *Nationwide*, and illustrates a technology-based approach to delivering self-help career tools.

Chapter 9: Final reflections

This chapter draws together the themes which emerged in the research for this book and highlights what I see as the main issues and challenges facing companies today. This chapter also makes some tentative predictions as to where career strategy may be heading in the future.

Acknowledgements

It is always difficult to know who to thank, as so many people have contributed to this book in some way. Without sounding as if I am receiving an award at the Oscars, I am particularly grateful to the people who gave up their time within busy jobs to talk to me about the work they are doing on talent and career management. These conversations resulted in some really practical case studies, which are great examples of best practice and are an invaluable addition to the book. I would like to thank the key contributors:

Ann-Marie Murphy from *First Choice*
Andy Cross from *Virgin Atlantic*
Jenny Richardson from the *Legal Services Commission*
Brigid Briggs from *Rolls-Royce*
Emma Roberts and Mark Waight from *LogicaCMG*
David Thomas from *Volvo*
Lynn Goy from *Lexmark*
Steve Lassman from *Nationwide*

I also owe a great deal to Wendy Hirsh, who has stimulated my own thinking on careers since I started work in this field 15 years ago. She continues to be a great inspiration to me, as well as a friend, and once again she gave up some of her time to discuss and debate some of the issues within this book and help my own thinking. In addition to Wendy, I would also like to acknowledge the many other authors whose work I have drawn on to bring you this book and their generosity in allowing me to use some of their work here. Special thanks must also go to the Learning Resource Centre staff at Roffey Park Institute for their help in searching out books and articles to support my research.

Finally, I would like to thank my husband Phil and son, Chris, for their patience and understanding as I worked on this book. With their support and encouragement, my own career has been able to flourish, whilst enjoying a work–life balance that would be the envy of anyone!

List of Figures

List of Tables

1

An Overview of Career Strategy

Career strategies have evolved considerably over time, partly in response to the changing working environment and partly due to the increased sophistication of companies aiming to attract and retain high quality employees. This chapter aims to provide an overview of the topic and sets a context for the remainder of this book. Reading this chapter will enable you to understand what is meant by the various terms used in connection with career strategies and will help you to answer questions such as:

- What are the workforce trends that impact on careers?
- What is the context for careers in organisations?
- How do career strategies link to the overall business strategy?
- How do you go about developing a career strategy?
- What are the benefits of putting a career strategy in place?
- What types of interventions fall within a career strategy?
- What impact does the culture of the organisation have?

What is a career?

It wouldn't be right to start a book such as this without defining some of the terms being used. The first, and most fundamental of these, is the word *career*.

I would love to define the word career as all encompassing, meaning that it incorporates both work and outside work experiences that shape your path through life. In this definition, your goals are met and you achieve satisfaction with your career by discovering your best fit with the world. Sadly though, my experience tells me that employees, and in particular young high potential employees, consider that to have a career you need to be employed. Whilst there is an acknowledgement that your career may be influenced by circumstances and interests outside of work, the essence of the career is viewed as organisational development and progression, rather than personal growth. Interestingly, for many talented individuals, this view may change over time, and leads to some interesting challenges for organisations in the way they manage the careers of their talent group, a topic we will return to later in this book.

So for the purposes of this book, the definition of a career put forward by Arthur et al. (1989), *the evolving sequence of a person's work experience over time,* still holds true, in that it incorporates the possibility of different types of employment, from self-employment through to temporary roles, as well as the sense of a sequence of roles, not necessarily involving promotion. This last point is critical, in that careers often take unusual routes, including sideways and even downward steps in hierarchies and across organisational boundaries.

Career management

What then is career management? Obviously, it is about how careers are managed, and if it is effective it should enable an organisation to attract and retain high quality staff, as well as add to the skill base of the company to help ensure long-term survival and growth. However, the purpose and responsibility for career management has changed considerably over time.

In the 1960s, career management was viewed as a way of helping *individual employees* realise their goals, through interventions such as career planning workshops and counselling. By the 1980s, the business environment had changed and career management was seen as a tool for addressing *business* needs, through improved succession planning and high-flyer programmes for key groups of staff. Individuals marked career progress by looking at the stage they had reached against their age and grade and progressing up a career ladder. Since the 1990s, the focus has changed once again, and career management is now more often seen as requiring an alignment between *both individual and business* requirements, as age-grade progression opportunities are no longer realistic for organisations, but maximising individual potential is still viewed as crucial to business success.

Much has been written in recent years about the nature of this partnership in career management and throughout this book we will be exploring the balance needed for successful career strategies, particularly when they are focused on pools of talent.

Career development or career management?

What then is the difference between a career development strategy and a career management strategy? To an extent, the difference is semantics and either term would suffice if you define your terms clearly within your strategy to ensure you have the meaning you require.

However, with the pace of change in organisations and unpredictability of the future of many companies, the concept of managing careers, even if this is a shared responsibility between employees and employer, is often seen as a rather unrealistic aim. Career management suggests a planned series of steps with an end goal. Such plans are likely to become quickly out of date in the current environment, and lead to frustration from unfulfilled expectations. Career planning, which from an organisational perspective often means succession planning, still exists, but approaches are changing and replacement succession planning is no longer seen as the answer to all problems. Later in this book, we will be looking at how some organisations are now starting to deal with the issue of succession and are moving towards developing generic pools of talent.

Career development however, implies opportunities for growth and enhanced skills, which will open up the possibilities of progression. It implies more of a role for the individual and moves the focus away from jobs, to progression within roles. Consequently, career development is about individuals taking responsibility for developing and progressing their career with support from the organisation. Some of the key requirements for organisations currently are speed and agility of response; adaptability to customers; the ability to deal with ambiguity and I could go on. All of these things require a more flexible and fluid career strategy, where risks are able to be taken. Career development then is more about the means by which people achieve their career goals.

For me, it is a little like comparing the classic, planned model of change with radical or emergent change (Figure 1.1a,b). Both are about managing change, but each takes a different approach.

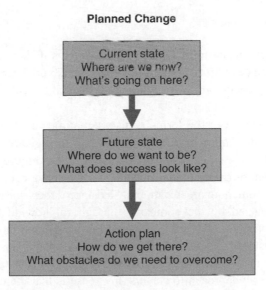

Figure 1.1a Planned change

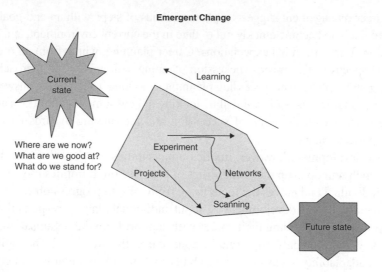

Figure 1.1b Emergent change

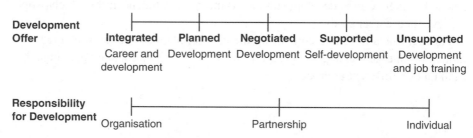

Figure 1.2 The career continuum

Career management assumes a more planned model of change, where the company can grow and develop employees towards a predicted future. Whereas career development involves growth in a slightly more haphazard way, with the end goal more uncertain.

The difference between the terms is also sometimes explained by where the responsibility for development lies. Hirsh and Jackson (1996) have drawn a useful continuum of career strategies, which is replicated in Figure 1.2.

This continuum illustrates some of the shifts that have occurred over time in career strategies, from more organisationally led approaches, where there is planned development managed by the company, through to individual-led approaches, where there is unsupported development and the focus is on the current job. It is interesting to consider where the current trend towards talent management strategies sits on this continuum. Whilst many companies might argue that talent management reflects a partnership approach to careers, my sense is that there is quite a strong shift back towards planned development and more managed careers.

Career management or talent management?

A key theme for this book, and something that I will return to in more detail in the next chapter, is the extent to which career management strategies and talent management differ. Talent management strategies are undergoing a surge in popularity within organisations at present as the pressure to attract and retain high potential staff increases. But is this focus on talent just a new career strategy for the 21st century?

Whilst there are some obvious differences in the types of intervention stemming from talent management, such as the forming of pools of high potential employees, it is questionable whether even this is not just a modern-day approach to high-flyer schemes of old. The more global nature of talent management is often sighted as a differentiator, as this brings with it economies of scale from surplus talent being utilised in other regions, rather than relying solely on a country supply. This global movement also has the added bonus of increasing diversity and knowledge transfer across the business, but yet again could be said to have been in existence with ex-pat strategies.

For the purposes of definitions, I find it hard to make a distinction between the two terms and have a strong sense that talent management is a re-badged and re-packaged career strategy which is more closely aligned to the needs of business today. In writing this book, I considered whether to focus more exclusively on talent management, but for me, this area cannot be viewed in isolation. Whilst talent management encourages a more holistic approach to developing people's careers and is a good approach for companies at present, there is still a need to pay attention to the wider implications of careers and the possible alternative career strategies that might need to come into play.

The external career context

Part of the reason for the shift in emphasis for career management, is the change that has occurred to the economic, social, political and technological environment over this time. Unlike the ample labour supply in the 1960s, the UK along with the rest of Europe, faced a 25 per cent reduction in the supply of school leavers between 1985 and 1995. In the healthy economic climate in the mid-1980s many employers were concerned that this shift was a 'demographic time-bomb' and began to re-focus on new, or under-utilised labour supplies, such as women and racial minority groups.

However, with rising unemployment, and an increase in the number of 25–34-year-olds in the working population as the generation of the baby-boom aged, the declining birth rate was not seen as such a threat in the 1990s. Despite this, concerns over shortages of appropriate skills and qualifications amongst the existing labour market did come into play. The demand for engineers and scientists continued to increase for example, yet the number of students taking science or technical degrees continued to decline.

Currently, the over 50s now make up 26 per cent of the working population and the 25–45-year-old demographics are shrinking. The over 50s have risen by almost half a million over the last 3 years and is a trend that is set to continue for both this age group and the over 40s. Today, 6 out of 10 employees are over 40.

In the last 10 years, downsizing has continued in many companies and there has been a wealth of mergers and acquisitions. Employers have focused on reducing costs as the pressure from competition has increased. Whilst the service sector has boomed and overall living standards have gone up, there has also been a growth in the economies of developing nations which has led to increased demand for knowledge workers.

The last 10–15 years have also seen a dramatic increase in the amount of part-time working. Labour market surveys show an increase of 1.5 million part-time jobs over a 10-year period with a corresponding decrease of 1.9 million full-time jobs. Interestingly, 19 per cent of part-time workers are now men. Predictions for the future estimate a further increase in part-time positions, with a less marked decline in full-time opportunities.

Back in 1995, Hutton stated that only 40 per cent of the working population in the UK were in secure employment, which he defined as being in a job or self-employed for 2 years or more. Of the remaining 60 per cent, half were unemployed or economically inactive and the remaining half were 'newly insecure' and are either on temporary contracts, working part time, or recently self-employed. Some of these individuals are in what Defillippi and Arthur (1994) term a 'boundaryless' career which are 'job opportunities that go beyond the boundaries of single employment settings'. An increasing number also have what Handy (1994) terms 'portfolio careers', which are careers comprised of a number of different and distinct work activities from varying sources – not surprising when approximately 1.5 million jobs in the UK are now classed as temporary and over 20 per cent of British households have no working adult.

As a consequence of this, the 40 per cent of adults currently in secure employment view their careers against a backdrop of insecurity, rising levels of self-employment and increased part-time working. The concept of a job for life is no longer applicable even to this group and many people's attitudes to their job have been re-focused towards survival and development for the short term. As a result, even individuals in secure employment feel dissatisfied, particularly with what they see as reduced opportunities for progression within organisations and a slow down in the speed of movement between jobs due to low labour turnover. Coupled with this, jobs are increasingly being reported as having high stress levels due to the rate of change within businesses. Despite Handy's talk of a leisure generation (Handy, 1985) evidence suggests that the working week for managerial and professional staff is increasing.

Organisational pressures

As a response to increased competition, technological change and the economic climate, many organisations are restructuring their businesses to focus on core activities, with periphery tasks being contracted out to other suppliers – be they other organisations or self-employed individuals. A survey by the Roffey Park Management Institute of 400 UK-based organisations (Holbeche, 1995) showed that 95 per cent had delayered over the period 1992–1995. Holbeche states the primary drivers for the delayering as cost cutting, business re-engineering and increased customer focus. These flattened hierarchies inevitably provide less opportunities for progression, with the survey revealing that 78.6 per cent of staff had fewer promotion prospects despite taking on more work and greater responsibility. Not surprisingly, a study by Inkson (1995) has showed the number of downward moves has also increased.

Not only are the jobs within organisations changing, but also the future of the organisations themselves are becoming less predictable. Markets and operating environments are now subject to rapid change with much shorter product and technology life cycles. Caudron (1994) sums up the situation saying that 'in the rapidly changing global business environment of the 1990s, strategic planning involves 1–3 years at best, making it virtually impossible to plan ahead'. In addition, UK organisations are increasingly under pressure from mergers and acquisitions by overseas organisations.

The UK has seen a massive growth in e-commerce. This increased use of information technology has served not only to reduce jobs, but also to blur the boundaries between jobs, speed up the responsiveness required from organisations and encourage decentralised structures around smaller business units. Often this is accompanied by a decrease in core HR specialists and the responsibility for career management shifting to line managers. Technology advances have particularly affected middle management levels and have increased the demand for knowledge workers. This knowledge-based economy continues to grow and Butler et al. (1997) estimate that knowledge workers have grown in number from 17 per cent in the 1990s to nearer 60 per cent currently. Intangible assets in organisations, such as brands, and intellectual capital are at the heart of this trend.

Boston Consulting Group (2000) argue that a 10-fold increase in memory and processing power will be required by people every 5 years. Products such as mobile phones, emails and blackberries have enabled an increase in home working, 24 hours a day availability and global working, and the chances are that significant changes in these portable skills will continue to be seen over the next 10 years.

As a consequence of the organisational changes, the early 1990s have seen large numbers of redundancies and voluntary early retirement schemes – privatised utilities are an example of this with British Telecom and British Gas reducing dramatically in number. OECD figures suggest that the average length of service for a UK employee with one employer was less than 8 years in 1991, a figure far less than the rest of Europe. CRAC attributes this to a lack of investment in training in the UK.

For many employees, this reduced certainty signalled a change in the psychological contract, which Argyris first defined as 'a set of unwritten reciprocal expectations between the employer and the employee' (Herriot, 1992). The old unwritten deal of loyalty and commitment in return for progression and reward no longer applied. Employees no longer trusted in their future with an employer and yet were being expected to give higher levels of performance in empowered positions. In an effort to provide some pay back for employees, organisations started to move more towards the concept of ensuring employability (Moss Kanter, 1994), by offering greater opportunities for development and continuous learning to keep skills current in the marketplace, in return for high performance and productivity. This is a topic I will return to later in this book.

However, Guest and Mackenzie Davey (1996) in their research into career processes in a number of large UK firms, countered this, by suggesting that whilst the grades have disappeared, many larger organisations have retained a hierarchy, and this still provides perceived progression and a motivation for advancement. They also suggested that contrary to popular belief, middle managers are less likely to have been made redundant than junior managers.

What is clear, is that with organisations becoming more complex, the management and leadership role has also become more challenging. Many small- to medium-size businesses are attracting talent from larger organisations (Ashton and Lambert, 2005) as the excitement and challenge of smaller start-ups coupled with the societal acceptance of people working in different ways make this more attractive.

The recent dot-com years showed that highly marketable, well-qualified people were prepared to give up on secure roles and good packages, to join high risk, potentially high gain companies. They were motivated by the opportunity to influence success and gain a stake in something big and were willing to forgo large company benefits and formal development opportunities to do this. Smart companies have picked up on this, and are adding more experiential development to their more formal offerings.

Political influences

On a political level, the UK government has taken active steps to increase the skills of the working population over the last 10 years. Initiatives such as National Vocational Qualifications (NVQs), Training and Enterprise Councils (TECs) and Investors in People were all examples of Government-led schemes intended to encourage skill development. The Management Charter Initiative and the resulting growth in management qualifications such as MBAs and management competencies were also a strong trend in the 1990s which is still continuing.

Other political influences on careers include initiatives such as Opportunity 2000, which have encouraged organisations to focus on the development of minority groups and the Social Charter, which has implications for both the employment contract and European mobility. The breakdown of European barriers has also led to an increase in international team working and joint ventures across countries, with the consequential need to integrate different cultures, systems and approaches. Legislative changes, such as age discrimination have also had a profound effect on the opportunities open to people.

Changing values

The values of the workforce also appear to be shifting. The new generation want more opportunities for development and meaningful work experiences. Berney (1990) calls the wave of MBA graduates the 'quality generation', because they appear to place more value on balancing personal and professional lives; doing interesting and challenging work; having autonomy and freedom on the job and positively contributing to society, rather than striving for promotion to the top of the organisation. This implies that accommodating these needs is likely to be an increasing priority for career management in the future.

Bridges (1995) talks about what he terms 'job shifting' over history and puts forward the notion that the meaning of work has changed over the centuries from work as a means to earn money to live on, through jobs, which provided a sense of satisfaction, to careers, which allowed progression. Bridges suggests that this notion of careers may now be shifting back to work as being a means to an end rather than the end itself. He refers to the new skill requirements for career-minded individuals as being employability, vendor mindedness and resilience.

Other major societal changes such as the increasing divorce rate, rising crime rates, the increase in homelessness, bankruptcies, rising suicide rates, the trend towards single parent families and the increased number of women in the workforce also have an impact on career decisions.

Interestingly, talented people now have more choice at the disposal than ever before. Traditional approaches, both within and outside of work are being challenged and prosperity and greater mobility has meant that more people are questioning their career purpose. Topics such as work–life balance are increasingly being talked about, potentially enabling talented individuals to negotiate better deals with employers.

There is also a growing propensity for people to switch companies when their expectations are not met. HR Focus (2004) suggests half of US employees will seek new employment in the next 12 months and Mucha (2004) also suggests one in six people are poised to leave their current role. These stark figures are even more extreme when you focus in on younger managers. Michaels et al. (2001) suggest that younger managers are 60 per cent more likely to leave an organisation than older managers. With a decade of lay-offs and increasing outsourcing of key processes, loyalty and trust between employees and employers has decreased and has led to a 'tsunami-like wave of employee defections' (Webber, 2004).

Trends and consequences

So what are the consequences of these changes to the external career environment? Some of the evidence is certainly conflicting. Whilst employees are likely to have feelings of a loss in job security, and perceive a reduction in the number of opportunities for progression, they are also likely to have more say in what they do. Where opportunities do present themselves, there is likely to be increased personal competition for posts and increased demands for more flexible working and the development of new skills. In addition, older workers may perceive greater pressures to perform and provide flexibility.

Outside of work there are contradictions too. Societal influences on employees are likely to make home lives more pressured and stressful. However, the increased wealth and mobility will lead to greater choice and self-exploration of what is important.

Table 1.1 Trends in the external career context

Trend	Explanation
Global careers	Increased mergers and acquisitions, global movement and faster communications indicate that more people will be seeking to develop across country boundaries.
Changing aspirations and values	Employees are becoming more selfish in their demands and will continue to seek out a good 'deal' in line with their life goals. Self-employment will continue to be attractive.
Increased ethnic diversity	The racial and ethnic mix of the workforce will continue to change and we will see more multi-cultural teams at work.
New ways of working	The number of virtual companies, project work and remote working will increase.
Shortage of specific skills	Demand for knowledge workers will continue to outstrip supply. As the baby-boom generation retire, greater skills and experience shortages will appear.
An ageing workforce	The average age of employees will continue to rise and the percentage of over 55s in the workforce will double in the next 10 years.
Increased competition for talent	Graduates in scientific disciplines, finance and technology will be particularly sought after. Smaller startup companies will continue to be an attractive proposition.

What we can conclude is that there are certain trends that can be expected to continue. Table 1.1 highlights some of these key trends.

Why introduce a career strategy?

High performance organisations ascribe very clearly to the belief that the way they manage their intangible assets, such as their culture, values, competence and management style have a direct link to organisational performance. The evidence from research studies back up these approaches and show a clear link between investing in people and paying attention to issues such as career development, and achieving bottom line performance (CIPD, 2003a, b).

This human resource advantage can only come from having the right people in the organisation with the right processes in place to support them and the right support for these processes from the business. Defining and implementing a career strategy which combines and links into other strategies is an integral part of achieving this competitive advantage.

Boxall and Purcell (2003) argue that performance is a function of three elements: ability, motivation and opportunity, described as an equation:

$$\text{Performance} = \text{Ability} + \text{Motivation} + \text{Opportunity}$$

Each of these elements links clearly with all aspects of career management. Effective career management will help to maximise people's abilities, provide motivational experiences and the opportunity to deploy and develop skills and knowledge.

Chapter 3 explores the business case for career strategies in more detail, but it is clear that career development programmes in organisations can add considerable value to the business through enhanced performance, and numerous researchers have also shown that implementing career programmes leads to increased career satisfaction amongst employees which in turn results in greater organisational commitment and ultimately performance.

A range of other potential benefits to an organisation of good career management are identified by Mayo (1991). These include, building organisational capability for the future; fuller use of staff potential; a higher percentage of internal resourcing of vacancies, saving wasted costs in recruitment and retraining; greater flexibility and ability to adapt to changing demands, such as European mobility and redeployment and improved data available for decision making. However, it should not be forgotten that there is also the potential to suffer disbenefits. Garavan (1990) argues that any increases in job satisfaction and productivity arising from career programmes are likely to decline if the employee remains too long in one job, if HR systems become overworked, or if a strain is put on training and development budgets.

The overriding purpose of career strategies are nicely summarised by Hirsh et al. (1995, p. 41) as being 'to clarify the purposes and processes of career management'. The report highlights three key reasons behind having a strategy for careers, namely:

1. To help manage the external and internal contextual changes.
2. To restore the confidence of employees.
3. To achieve coherence in organisational policies.

The literature suggests contextual changes are particularly significant and that successful career management is particularly important to business performance where companies are decentralising and delayering, resulting in greater responsibility being given to line managers. Individuals are often less aware of opportunities and experience difficulties in moving careers across functions (Mayo, 1991; Holbeche, 1995). Whilst there is little evidence of the impact of organisational restructuring, Holbeche's study (1995) of 25 UK organisations showed that delayering can lead to reductions in job satisfaction and organisational commitment, with 78.6 per cent of respondents citing fewer promotion prospects and lower morale as a consequence. Staff flexibility and commitment is therefore seen as essential for business success and career management is thought to be one way of achieving this.

Hirsh's second reason concerning restoring confidence, suggests that organisations may have a more altruistic rationale for introducing a career strategy. This view is supported by Holbeche, who suggests that aside from any quantifiable benefits, some organisations believe they have a moral responsibility in the current job climate to help employees with their career development. Restoring confidence also has a sound business rationale, in that it increases the morale of the workforce, which in turn leads to greater organisational commitment and higher performance.

The third aspect, achieving greater coherence in organisational policies, is particularly relevant to career strategies today. Talent management can only be effective if it integrates the different aspects of selection, performance management, learning and development, business planning and even more peripheral activities such as organisational branding.

Developing a career strategy

Models for developing a career strategy

Strategies for career management in organisations have changed over time, depending primarily, on the economic environment. The balance has largely shifted between organisational and individual control. The emphasis for the future appears to lie not only in achieving a balance between organisational and individual needs, but also in changing people's perceptions to careers and their assumptions about career management within organisations. Individuals and especially high potential groups, need to be encouraged to think in terms of development and growth rather than specific roles. This is likely to mean not just valuing upward progression, but keeping skills updated through continuous development, lateral or even downwards moves.

A number of models for developing career strategies exist and common themes emerge from these about the need to take account of the culture and values of the organisation, its business strategy, the size and maturity of the organisation, and the processes and procedures already in existence. As a consequence, there is no ideal strategy that can be recommended here. Each strategy needs to be tailored to the particular circumstances of the organisation and its employees.

One of the more recent models, Bergeron (2004), suggest a talent strategy should describe the core knowledge, skills and behaviours required by the organisation. She suggests four questions need to be answered by the strategy:

1. What value does your organisation deliver to its customers?
2. What are the core business processes in which your organisation must excel in order to achieve customer value?
3. What key capabilities must we have as an organisation to deliver this value to customers?
4. What value does your organisation offer its employees?

Through this analysis Bergeron suggests will get insights into what the company has and needs today and where it needs to be in the future. A plan can then be put in place to address the four key parts of the career management process:

1. *Acquisition*: How you intend to secure the people you need to execute the strategy.
2. *Cultivation*: How you will develop the expertise and skills you may need.
3. *Retention*: How you will recognise, reward and keep hold of key resources.
4. *Organisational*: How processes work, communication messages, etc.

Whilst this questioning approach has value, it does not address how to approach the task. Whilst there is no set way to do this, it is possible to suggest some guidelines on how to go about formulating a career strategy. My own experience suggests a 10-step approach, which is described below:

Step 1: Understand how the external career context impacts your business.
Step 2: Analyse your business strategy and its HR implications for the future.
Step 3: Understand and review the culture.
Step 4: Analyse the structure of the organisation and processes which support career development.
Step 5: Set the objectives for the strategy.
Step 6: Establish success measures and measurable outcomes.
Step 7: Review and improve the organisational processes in existence.

Step 8:   Review and improve the individual development processes in existence.
Step 9:   Ensure individual and organisational expectations are managed.
Step 10: Monitor and review the process against the objectives.

In working through this process, companies will need to debate a number of aspects. In setting objectives, for example, there is a need to consider what the real purpose of the strategy is. Is it about skilling the workforce as a whole, making the company more attractive to ease external recruitment pressures or making better use of untapped potential? Do particular groups of employees, such as generalists or specialists require attention?

When reviewing the culture, there is a need to explore what the true values are within the company and whether these fit with the strategy proposed. Equally, in step 4, does the structure help or hinder progress – What type of career paths does the company have at present? And are people able to make cross-functional or cross-business moves?

Communication is a critical part of the process and it is essential that the objectives of the strategy are clear and any constraints on careers are made explicit. Individual employees and senior managers need to be clear on what they can expect from the strategy. The communication needs to spell out what the career 'deal' is for employees and what the employer proposition is.

It is unlikely however that many organisations will need to start from scratch. Hirsh and Jackson (2004) recommend a useful framework for re-evaluating current career systems, based on a questioning approach to the current career 'fitness' of the organisation. They suggest that companies complete statements such as:

> The broad career paths, or types of career, in the organisation are described to employees in terms of....
>
> Our employees can make a sideways move to another department and can do this by....
>
> Our approach fits our particular business needs, the attitudes and preferences of our employees and our general approach to managing people. It fits us because....

This technique is particularly useful used with a group of senior managers, to help engage them in developing a revitalised career strategy for the company. It can also help to ensure that a career strategy is not seen as the 'final' strategy but something that needs to be constantly revised and updated.

The link to HR and business strategy

It seems obvious to point out that career development strategies should be linked to the HR strategy and that in turn, should be linked to the business strategy. Yet, this is not as obvious as you might think.

HR management can have a tendency to implement policies and procedures without much reference to the needs and opinions of employees. Yet one of the key features of career strategies involves incorporating the needs of employees, particularly the talent you are looking to retain and motivate. In these circumstances, the top-down models of business strategy being cascaded into HR strategy are now too rigid and are likely to be inappropriate.

Integration with business strategy is therefore likely to be somewhat tentative and exploratory. With companies transforming their approach to defining business strategy and taking a more fluid and emergent approach, career strategies need to be proactive in their own right and build in the flexibility required. Psychological contracts (Argyris, 1962; Rousseau, 1995), a topic we will return to in more detail later in this book, and more emergent strategies which are able to change rapidly in response to business needs, are now more often seen as the way forward in implementing successful career strategies.

In practice, however, a whole range of approaches exist for developing career strategies. Rothwell and Kazanas (2003) make an interesting distinction between the different types of approaches companies make towards linking business strategy and the development of talent. Some of the approaches they identify in addition to the top-down approach are:

- *The market-driven approach*: The perceived future learning needs are derived by managers and high potential employees. This is a type of bottom-up strategy which links clearly with the self-development approach to careers.
- *The career planning approach*: Seeking to integrate the needs of individuals with that of the organisation.
- *The performance diagnosis approach*: The development of talent provides information about organisational strengths and weaknesses.
- *The educational approach*: The strategy aims to develop people in certain ways, such as thinking more strategically, or more in line with the company's competencies.

I would add to this list two other approaches: one based on maturity and one on resource pools:

- *The maturity approach*: Many writers are keen to emphasise the different types of strategy that may be required depending on the stage in the life cycle of the company, their product diversity or their strategic orientation. They argue that organisations encourage certain types of career behaviour, depending on the way they operate as a business. For example, companies with low market share and high growth will have a greater need for more flexible employees with a go-ahead style (Clark, 1992).

■ *The resource pool approach*: Having identified a group of people with high potential, the strategy aims to utilise these people in high profile and challenging projects. They provide useful assistance to leaders in the organisation in areas of need
and as such move the organisation forward. Some writers see the competitive
advantage that comes from career strategies, less in terms of the initiatives in place,
as these are easy to replicate, but more in the human capital that such a strategy creates, that is the knowledge, skills and abilities to better suit the business they are in.

It is worth reflecting on this list and examining your own strategic intentions.
Many of these factors are worth taking into account in defining your career strategy,
but these expectations need to be clearly set out for employees.

Cultural influences

The impact of culture on career strategies is not a new concept. Schein (1984) and
Moss Kanter (1984) both showed culture to be both a cause and an effect on
employee moves both within and across organisations. Or, put simply, people's decision to move jobs is impacted by the culture of the company, as well as the company's
decisions about when and how they move people. Their studies also showed a strong
link between people's job performance and the organisational climate and structure.

Understanding and working with the culture is therefore critical to career
strategies. In addition, if the organisation is seeking to move to a situation where
individuals take greater ownership and responsibility for their careers, this will
place career development even further into the realms of cultural change.

There are many definitions of culture and it is questionable whether it is possible
to influence culture by events, depending on whether you believe that culture is something an organisation 'is' or 'has'. Some of the basic assumptions in the culture, such
as the way people, think, feel or perceive events, remain unsaid and are often invis-
ible. As a consequence, they may be difficult to influence and it is important to consider how these might impact on your career strategy. For example:

■ To what extent does the organisation pay lip service to valuing people?
■ Are line managers helping or hindering career progress?
■ Is performance managed effectively?
■ How committed are your workforce to self-development?
■ How much support is there for people developing new skills?
■ Is there a culture of openness and trust?

This last question is one particular cultural issue which is important to address,
whether the culture in the organisation is based on honesty and trust has been
found to have a strong influence on levels of career satisfaction (Herriot et al., 1994;

Yarnall, 1998). These studies found that the perceived equity of career and HR processes led to increased levels of career satisfaction, and it could be argued that by being more open about the opportunities for development available in organisations today, that HR would be seen as more equitable. However, it can also be argued that raising awareness about the changing nature of career development and the reduced opportunities for upward progression could have a negative impact on career satisfaction, particularly if the culture of the organisation is already biased towards a feeling of 'being done to'.

This issue of culture raises some interesting questions for organisations embarking on a new or updated career strategy. Bergeron (2004) argues that however well thought out your career strategy is, it is the *implementation* of that strategy which is significant. This is not a surprise to you I am sure. There are plenty of calls for more top management support, or greater managerial commitment to make strategies work effectively. What it does suggest however, is that your strategy should address some of the cultural barriers to implementation and seek to identify projects where implementation will be more likely to receive backing.

One of the case studies later in this book describes the implementation of a new talent management strategy as a 'cultural change project', indicating the importance of this aspect. The issue of psychological contracting and the need for equity in career processes links in with this and is a topic we will return to in the next chapter. Adopting a strategy based around the psychological contract requires a more open communication culture in organisations, where managers are genuinely committed to two-way discussions and have an honest approach to development. I would hazard a guess that not all organisations will have the right environment for such a strategy to work effectively!

Goals and objectives

Once the overall strategy has been decided upon, the particular objectives and goals need to be formulated. Gutteridge et al. (1993) state that many organisations now view career development as part of an overall organisational change programme and they argue that for such efforts to succeed, organisations need to have a clear vision of how the company will be different as a result of the change.

Establishing the purpose of any career management system is vital if it is to be effective in the longer term (Hirsh et al., 1995). Organisations need to examine for themselves where the emphasis should lie in relation to the needs of the business and the potential benefits of career schemes and should set the objectives of the system to support these. Often there will be a clear stimulus such as a high turnover amongst a particular group of employees, or divisional managers holding onto good staff and blocking development opportunities.

17

Depending on the requirements, possible objectives of a career strategy might be to:

■ Prepare the organisation for the future by developing employee capability to meet long-term business strategy.
■ Ensure flexibility in responding to business needs, by identifying and developing pools of talent.
■ Improve the morale and motivation of all employees to ensure greater commitment.
■ Minimise employee turnover to ensure a good Return on Investment.
■ Develop a culture and processes capable of attracting and retaining high quality employees.

What do career strategies entail?

Career strategies can cover a vast range of activities, some of which are core organisational processes, such as the performance management system, and some of which stand-alone. Figure 1.3 provides an illustration of some of the more commonly used processes for career management. The diagram draws upon a wide range of literature (e.g. see Hirsh, 1984; Hall et al., 1986; Leibowitz et al., 1986; Jackson, 1990; Mayo, 1991; Gutteridge et al., 1993) and illustrates the main tools and techniques and the extent of individual or organisational influence.

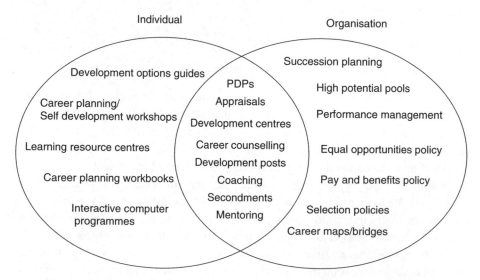

Figure 1.3 Possible career interventions

Organisations are faced with a myriad of choices when contemplating the introduction of career strategies, with little guidance as to the type of initiatives that will work best within their particular culture. The range of possible interventions cover a wide spectrum from the more traditional organisation-led activities to individual-led ones, which underpin many of the self-development approaches.

This model shows career development as having both individually led activities and organisationally led activities. Super and Hall (1978) were one of the first to argue that career development activities need to encompass both perspectives, which enables both the external- and internal-career processes to be incorporated and managed. Both the individual and organisational processes need to be in place and synchronised to maximise the effectiveness of the individual career processes (Stumpf, 1989).

It is not the intention to go into detail on each of the tools highlighted here, as most of these approaches will be discussed later in this book. However, the quality of the techniques and the extent to which they are applied to different employees and grades in the organisations concerned varies immensely. For most initiatives, it is possible to identify companies which have become known as providing examples of best practice in that area. For example, the *BBC* has a number of manned learning resource centres at different sites, and has gained expertise in stocking and siting such centres to best advantage, *3M* is known for its comprehensive information system providing job details through the computer network to all employees, which has increased lateral mobility amongst employees; and *Esso* is famed for its comprehensive career workbooks and development centres.

These best practice approaches, which are often used for benchmarking in other companies, assume that there is an ideal approach to career development. However, given the importance of business culture, structure and strategy, it is unlikely that this is the case and each organisational will need to devise initiatives which are appropriate and tailored to their particular environment.

Case study: *First Choice* case study – Developing a talent management strategy

(Information supplied by Ann-Marie Murphy, HR Business Partner)

First Choice Holidays Plc is a leading international leisure travel company offering leisure travel experiences across more than 17 countries. Their vision is to be the *First Choice* for people wanting to work in leisure travel. Achieving this vision helps drive profitable growth across the group.

The Mainstream Holidays Sector is the largest sector within *First Choice*, in terms of size, profit and employee numbers. In the summer season as many as 7,500 colleagues are part of this sector. The sector takes over

2.5 million customers on holiday every year to around 80 destinations. It also has an airline comprising 32 aircraft – and a distribution network consisting of 264 high street stores, 38 hypermarkets, 2 call centres and an e-commerce site.

In 2005, Talent Management was identified as one of four key HR strategic objectives.

Although aspects of talent management had been in existence before this time, this objective aimed to give talent management a greater focus in the business and bring together and build upon the strands already in existence.

The aim of the project was set out as: 'to source, keep and develop existing and future high performing people'.

Background

The company has been operating a succession planning tool known as the OMR (Organisational Management Review) for the last 5 years. This review is based around the completion of a 9-box grid, with managers being asked to plot their people in conjunction with HR. The review covers all managers and takes place twice a year, with the results being presented to the board.

	New to role	Potential leader	Ready for move/more
High			
	Performance challenge	Good performer	Leading performer
Developable			
	Performance problem	Skilled contributor	Specialist/functional expert
Low			
	Low	Performance Medium	High

Potential (vertical axis label), *Performance* (horizontal axis label)

The top right of the box, potential leaders, leading performers and people ready for a move are all considered to be part of the talent pool for the group.

The tool is seen as beneficial, in that it works as both a performance management tool as well as helping to identify talent.

When the scheme was first introduced, there had been resistance from some managers about the knock-on effects of differentiating people and some initial reservations about pigeon-holing people in boxes. Interestingly, the root cause of some of these concerns, was an initial unwillingness to hold some difficult management conversations and be more open and honest about performance and potential within the teams. Data was skewed abnormally towards more favourable ratings and needed to be challenged by the HR Business Partners.

One of the key messages which have helped to shift this perception is a reassurance that the box for each individual was not static and that there was the ability to move and change where people were positioned.

The tool is now working very effectively and is more embedded in the business, but *First Choice* were keen to ensure that the OMR did not just become a data gathering exercise and wanted to make more use of the data and integrate it into a wider talent management strategy. This strategy aimed to ensure a greater integration with the business and other HR-led processes. In particular there was a desire to create:

- stronger links with recruitment and resourcing plans,
- stronger links with performance management processes,
- stronger links with business planning process.

Developing a new approach to managing talent

The development of the strategy raised some difficult questions about where the focus for talent should lie. *First Choice* wanted to ensure the talent strategy was not seen as elitist as this did not fit well with the culture of the company. However, from an HR perspective, managing the development of talent in the solid performer boxes was fundamentally the responsibility of the line manager, with support from HR if needed. The identified talent group, however, were seen to need more of an organisationally driven approach to development. The strategy was therefore focused on the leaders for tomorrow with an underlying theme that everyone in the company was aiming to work to their full potential.

A core group within the company, led by Ann-Marie Murphy, developed a 5-year plan for managing talent within the business. The initial stages of the plan were focused on data collection and diagnosis. This thorough review of the existing situation and future needs was needed initially to inform the future priorities and plans. Ann-Marie was keen to point out that *Although we have a written plan, it will be tailored to suit our requirements as we move through it. The plan is very flexible and the HR Business Partners will be working with the business to ensure it suits their needs.*

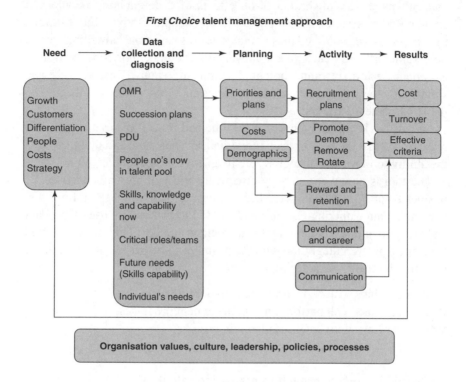

First Choice talent management approach

See 5-year talent plan summary on opposite page.

The plan was presented to the MD and the Board, with a strong case for why the company was focusing on talent and what the business benefits were. Putting in place success measures was a core part of the plan – measures were:

- percentage of the talent pool in relation to the senior management population,
- retention rates and losses from the talent pool,
- percentage of promotions from the talent pool,
- the ratio of external to internal appointments,
- percentage of roles with succession coverage.

Work is also being carried out on defining 'critical' and 'pivotal' roles within the business. Critical roles are defined as those driving the business forward, whereas pivotal roles are jobs which provide a particular development opportunity and are an essential transition through to more senior leadership.

Tour operations 5-year talent plan summary

	Attract: Bring the right mix of skills for the future	Identify: Spotting talent in the organisation	Develop: Developing people to deliver the strategy now and in the future	Deploy: Place people in the right jobs to meet the organisation future needs and individual career aspirations	Engage: Ensuring the right environment for people to do their best
Short term Year 1	Understanding the skills required for the future (Six 5-year plan)	Clear definition of talent and ensuring. We are identifying right people – challenge the teams assessment of talent. (OMR, Board talent reviews, CDC)	Identify development roles (Board talent reviews, CDC)	Agree process to deploy talent proactively (Board talent reviews, CDC)	Understand the factors that engage talent (First Voice, career resumes, line managers, transparency)
Medium term Years 2–3	Clearly defined plans in place (Buy it/grow it) (HR)	Building processes to spot early career talent (Broader OMR, FCA)	Understand and match businesses and individual needs (PDP, OMR, career pathing)	Being clear on the key roles within tour ops, build succession (OMR, board talent reviews)	Embed talent engagement factors into the performance management process (HR)
Long term Years 4–5	Clear employer brand	Have a clear and open plan (Board talent reviews)	Making investment decisions (Top 20 per cent)	Key roles unblocked and succession pools in place. Deployment of talent linked to business cycle (HR, Board talent reviews)	Measuring these factors rigorously (Measure against metrics)

Transparency

Until 2006, the OMR results were not being widely shared with individuals. This approach was seen as inappropriate in the new strategy, as it was important that employees in the talent pool were involved in their own development and were aware of how they are perceived.

The talent pool are now informed of their status and are asked to compete a career resume which is a one-page document covering:

Career resume for xxx					
Job title:		Date of joining:		Photo here	
Grade:		Date of birth:			
OMR rating:		Insights position: (if known)			

Brief description of current role (and key achievements):

Career History (bullet points, dates, companies, roles):

Education/professional qualifications/languages/additional skills:

Career expectations (brief summary of professional goals):

- background both in *First Choice* and prior to joining,
- education,
- career aspirations for the short and medium term.

The line manager discusses the resume with the individual and provides coaching and guidance on their expectations and ambitions. This conversation leads to a career path document, which outlines how to get to their goal and what development needs they have.

This greater level of transparency has led to some difficult conversations within the business. To make the process easier, some business areas have used a bottom-up approach, to expose more junior managers to the OMR process before being told of their own position on it. One of the more difficult aspects has been dealing with peer comparisons and perceptions across the business.

As Ann-Marie pointed out *Implementing talent management is not just about implementing a new strategy and set of processes, it is about influencing a culture change across the business.*

In these early stages of strategy implementation, communicating the message and generating understanding and buy-in to the process is incredibly time consuming and if you are not careful, it can get pushed down the priority list. Unfortunately, HR is still currently in the driving seat and one of our key challenges is to engage greater stakeholder commitment and drive.

Key challenges

Development opportunities

One of the key challenges for *First Choice* is that in a cost focused business, there is little scope to create development opportunities based around projects. People need to be up and running quickly in roles and the business can't afford the luxury of positioning people with a view to development in the role. As a consequence the strategy is less focused on development opportunities and more on role requirements.

However, there are still questions about when the company might need to go to the external market speculatively because they have identified a future gap. Equally, *First Choice* have recognised a need to unblock some key roles to allow progression through key areas, but there is a risk attached to removing skilled specialists who are blocking opportunities for development.

Reconciling this need to position yourself for the future, with optimum current performance is an ongoing tension within the strategy.

Defining future business needs

Despite conversations with senior managers to explore the people implications of their long-term plans, HR is still finding it hard to get managers to

Talent management matrix

	Tools required	Frequency	Individual	Line manager	Management team review	Tour ops board	Mainstream board	CDC
PDU/review against skillsets	PDU form Skillsets Objectives	**Quarterly review** Annual sign off	✓	✓				
OMR review	OMR matrix OMR questions	Quarterly		✓	✓	✓		
Talent review and agreeing plans	Updated OMR Performance results Career resumes	Quarterly				✓	✓ (Bi annually)	✓
Reviewing talent plans	Development plans Talent measures Talent plans	Quarterly			✓	✓	✓ (Bi annually)	✓
Reviewing skills gaps, agreeing plans	Succession plans Talent pool Resource plan	Bi annually			✓	✓	✓ (Bi annually)	✓

articulate their future needs. Ann-Marie suggests that they need to bring these issues to the fore in people's minds and continually ask questions about talent, rather than just focusing on these issues at planning time. Increasing the priority and focus on talent is an important success factor and she would like to see managers asking the questions rather than it being HR led.

To aid this process, a talent management matrix has been developed, which sets out the key processes, tools and role responsibilities. Notably, HR are not present on this matrix!

See Talent management matrix in previous page.

Shifting from organisation led to individual led

The culture within *First Choice* has historically been quite passive with regard to individuals taking responsibility for development. One of the key challenges will be to get people more curious and develop an individual push for career development. Ann-Marie would like to see high potential managers identifying their own opportunities and career paths, rather than being led by the organisation.

Summary

It is a virtually impossible task to condense the topic of career strategy into one chapter and many aspects of career strategies have only been touched on here. However, this chapter has provided an overview of some of the themes that I will return to throughout this book. Four particular themes stand out:

1. The need to take account of the wider career context both within the company and in the external market.
2. The need for consistency in your approach.
3. The need to build flexibility into your career process to be agile for the future.
4. The need to base your strategy on a true partnership between the employee and the employer.

Well-planned career strategies can have a considerable impact on organisational performance and this chapter explored the process of developing a career strategy and some of the interventions that are likely to stem from it. Drawing together the different approaches to developing career strategies that exist, the model in Figure 1.4 has been drawn up to summarise the key themes.

Initially, the organisation needs to examine both the external and internal context and the forces acting on the business. Stemming from this, there needs to be

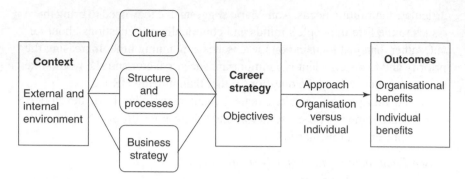

Figure 1.4 A model of career strategy

a comprehensive understanding of the culture, business strategy, and existing structures and procedures, which will then determine the elements of the career strategy and the particular objectives that are set. Successful approaches will focus on achieving an equitable balance between the needs and wants of the organisation and that of the employees, in order to achieve the desired outcomes and benefits for both parties.

There is clearly no one model to suit all organisations and the challenge is to explore each of these aspects to find the solution that is the best fit for your company. The *First Choice* case study at the end of the chapter clearly indicates an approach and aimed at integration across the business and had a clear strategic intent and measures to achieve this.

Checklist

Throughout this book there will be checklists at the end of each chapter, to help provoke thought and encourage the reader to consider some of the implications of the content. Whilst this chapter provided an overview of the topic, some questions are still worth considering:

- Does your company have a clear definition of the terms used for describing careers?
- Are you aware of how the external career trends impact your business?
- What problems are you trying to solve from your career strategy?
- What are cultural barriers to success?
- Is the company structure helping or hindering your strategic objectives?
- Are the long-term needs of the organisation clear?

- What interventions do you already have to support careers and what do you need to put in place?
- How will you ensure flexibility?
- What account will you take of individual needs and objectives?
- Have you thought through the implications of separating out groups of people for accelerated progression?

2

Focusing in on Your Talent: Getting the Balance Right

Organisations are increasingly talking about talent management and according to research, this trend is set to continue. Eighty-six per cent of companies anticipate that the profile of talent management will rise in the next 5 years (Hay Group and Human Resources, 2003) and 70 per cent of CEOs rate retention as one of their top four priorities (Deloitte Consulting, 2003). Talent seems to have become one of the 'in' words on the business agenda, which many attribute to Mckinsey et al.'s research summarised in the book *The war for talent* (Michaels et al., 1998). More recently, the Corporate Leadership Council research (2005) found that talent management directly contributes to increased organisational effectiveness and profitability, leading to as much as a 15.4 per cent advantage in shareholder return.

This chapter aims to explore where talent management fits into the overall career strategy. Is it a sub-set of a wider strategy for developing employee careers? Is it a modern-day career strategy? Or is it something different to that?

One of the tensions that organisations face is where to focus their attention on careers and talent groups are often a high priority. However, this can have implications for the workforce as a whole. Some of the questions this chapter seeks to answer are:

- What is talent?
- How do you identify high potential?
- What can assessment and development centres contribute?
- Should talent groups be singled out?
- How to talent strategies differ from career strategies?
- What are the implications on the psychological contract?
- How do you marry the need for a tailored approach with the need for consistency?
- How do you manage expectations?

Where does talent management fit?

Talent management started off as being a process focused on attracting scarce resources in a competitive labour market. The focus was predominantly on the selection and assessment of new talent. In the 1990s, high performers and MBA graduates were in high demand by organisations and attracting talent was a key issue for organisations. In more recent years companies have come to realise that just focusing on attracting and buying in talent is not enough. The high cost of this approach and high failure rate of external recruits meant that this was a false economy in the long run. Interestingly, the Corporate Leadership Council (2003) found that 40 per cent of external recruits at a senior level are deemed to fail in their first 18 months. The emphasis has therefore shifted to retaining the talent to help maximise their competitive edge. This wider scope for talent management covers all areas of the business including organisational capability, branding, individual and leadership development, performance management and succession planning.

It might seem like a contradiction that in this current world of cost cutting, delayering and restructuring of resources, retaining people should become such an issue. Yet Carrington (2005) argues that the reason retaining talent is essential is due to the slimming down that has occurred in graduate recruitment schemes and leadership programmes, leaving a deficit in high potential staff ready for succession to key posts.

This brings us then to the purpose of talent strategies. McCartney and Garrow (2006) state that the purpose of talent strategies is to target scarce resources to maximise the impact on business performance. They highlight the key drivers for developing talent management strategies as:

- Securing future growth and sustainability
- Reducing turnover and retaining top talent
- Streamlining the business and encouraging movement
- Enabling high performance through a pipeline of succession.

Interestingly, Carrington found that most companies see talent management as a series of interventions:

- 67 per cent about developing people
- 63 per cent recruitment and selection
- 48 per cent succession planning
- 36 per cent maximising the talent already in place.

Both of these descriptions have considerable overlaps with career strategies and talent management could be seen to be more of an evolution and re-branding of strategic career management than a new strategy in itself.

What is talent?

Definitions of talent vary widely, from being focused on particular people, to a set of characteristics, or to statements of need. Companies also vary in terms of whether they view talent as the performance and potential that exists in every employee, or whether it is a more exclusively focused on scarce resources and more senior positions. GE for example, defines talent as people who have the potential to grow into CEOs or top functional leaders (Charan, 2005).

McCartney and Garrow (2006) define this type of talent as 'employees who have a disproportionate impact on the bottom line, or who have the potential to do so'. The identification of talent in this case is driven by capability or skill gaps in the organisation and identifying critical segments of the workforce which are essential to the business.

It is worth highlighting recent research by Corporate Leadership Council (2005), which covered more than 11 000 employees and managers from 59 different organisations. They found that only 19 per cent of high performers were also identified as high potential, and what differentiated talent were three components:

- *Aspiration*: The extent to which the person was seeking prestige and recognition, influence with the organisation, financial reward, work–life balance and overall job satisfaction.
- *Engagement*: A person's emotional and rational commitment to an organisation, the extent of their discretionary effort and intention to stay in the company.
- *Ability*: A person's mental and emotional intelligence as well as learned technical and interpersonal skills.

This suggests that managers have a key role to play in retaining talent and making it work, as they have strong influence over recognition, job satisfaction and commitment to the organisation.

What is clear is that organisations need to define their own terms. Many of the companies researched for this book were very keen to put across a message that everyone has potential and talent and that they will be encouraged to develop that, but equally, sitting alongside this, they often had particular groups of individuals that were singled out as being a 'talent pool' for the more senior positions in the future. This is a topic we shall return to in Chapters 4 and 5.

Identifying high potential

One of the biggest questions is how to identify the people with high potential. Approaches range from a simple question as part of an appraisal process, through to more complex tools such as box models or assessment centres.

Ideally at the start of the process, there needs to be a dialogue between the decision makers to help them decide on and calibrate the selection criteria (McCall, 1998; Michaels et al., 2001; Berger and Berger, 2004). Where many selection tools fall down, is when the criteria are not clear, or they do not reflect the needs of the company in the future.

Box models

Many organisations choose to use some kind of matrix system which maps performance and potential. These box models provide an open framework for discussion with some guidance on what each box means. The approach has the benefit that it opens up a healthy dialogue with a key group of stakeholders on the potential of employees. Often an HR Business Partner will facilitate the discussion and help to minimise bias. One of the most commonly used matrixes is the 9-box model illustrated in Figure 2.1.

The 9 box model can be unreliable, as it depends on the interpretations of the individual assessors, who tend to agree on the relative meaning of the squares as they work through the process. The tool also rarely takes into account particular competencies or characteristics of high potentials, such as their own aspirations or engagement.

Companies often refine the box model approach, with some increasing the categories to 16 boxes (see Figure 2.2) and providing guidance on the likely distributions.

In effect, it is not the model that matters, but the way it is used and one of the difficulties of this approach is helping line managers to differentiate between performance and potential, with clear guidelines as to what is meant by the different terms.

Charan et al. (2001) define three categories of potential, which they describe as turn potential, growth potential and mastery potential. The definitions are:

- Turn potential: The ability to work at the next level in 3–5 years time.
- Growth potential: The ability to do bigger jobs at the same level in the near term.
- Mastery potential: The ability to do the same but better.

High performance			
Medium performance			
Lowperformance			
	Low potential	Medium potential	High potential

Figure 2.1 A 9-box model for identifying talent

Looking at the 9-box model, guidelines will typically suggest that managers focus more on the differentiation between high potential rather than the distinctions between low, medium and high performers. They may also suggest that managers consider what kinds of leadership roles or new opportunities the manager has the capability and aptitude to move into. Some companies also choose to suggest a normal distribution should be reflected in the ratings of departments and suggest actions for people in each box. For example:

- Retention and succession should be focused on high performers with high potential. This group are likely to be eligible for an acceleration pool.
- Development should be focused on groups with high potential and medium performance, as well as high performers with medium potential.
- Under performing high potentials need to be considered for a role change.
- Low performers without potential need performance improvement plans.
- High performers without potential need a focus on retention and continued motivation.

However, even with the most foolproof definitions, leaving the assessment in the hands of the organisation does not take account of the employee perspective,

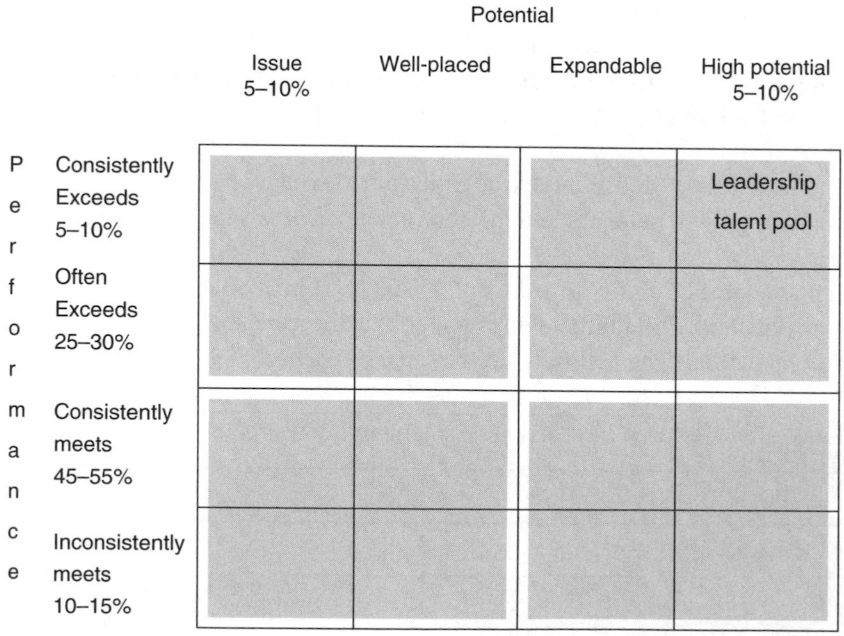

Figure 2.2 A 16-box model

which is so vital in a career strategy. With this in mind however, some companies have usefully identified the needs more from an employee perspective:

- Those with potential to fast track who are interested in doing so.
- Those with potential but not the ambition at the current time.
- Those who are indispensable to the organisation.

Companies also have the choice as to whether they determine their acceleration pools from the matrix alone, or whether to test out potential and performance at a development or assessment centre. The centre approach allows the identification to take account of individual behaviours.

Assessment and development centres

Assessment and development centres are one of the most commonly used tools for accurately pinpointing the gaps between an individual's performance and a set of required standards. Centres are relatively easy to set up and run, although they do have significant resource requirements and need careful positioning in the context of the wider strategy to be effective.

The component parts of an assessment centre or development centre are:

- A set of exercises designed to demonstrate specific behaviours. These may include:
  - Group exercises – with assigned and non-assigned roles
  - One-to-one exercises
  - Written tasks
  - Interviews
  - Psychometrics
  - Simulations
- A high ratio of assessors to participants
- Trained assessors or coaches who work to a common standard
- Observation across a range of exercises
- Feedback is given to participants on their performance.

People are often confused between assessment and development centres and it is worth setting out some of the key differences. Table 2.1 illustrates the main points.

For both types of centre, the starting point is to establish the behaviours, which need to be observed and design a range of exercises to suit this. Ideally, centres would aim to assess each competency in two or three different kinds of exercises, to ensure an accurate measure.

There is some useful research which suggests that learning agility is a strong predictor of promotability (Eichinger and Lonbardo, 2004) and some organisations,

Table 2.1 Comparing assessment centres to development centres

Assessment centres	Development centres
Prime purpose is selection	Prime purpose is personal development
Outcomes are reported	Outcomes are confidential to the individual
Centre analyses and rates best performance	Centre encourages experimentation and learning
Uses trained assessors	Uses trained coaches
Focuses on a few core competencies	Allow a wider range of competencies
Feedback is given after the event	Feedback is given during the event
Scores are standardised by assessors	Development needs are determined rather than scores

such as the *Legal Services Commission* described in Chapter 3, have given additional weighting to these behaviours in their assessment centres.

Typically a matrix would be used to indicate how the two aspects inter-relate. Figure 2.3 is an example of this.

The assessment centre approach is more organisationally focused, with a strong intent to accurately assess performance and identify how participants perform against a set of criteria. To do this, the assessors collect and record data and then take time at the end of the centre to collate and interpret the data and give each participant a score for each competence. Assessors will have a rating scale for each behaviour and they will observe different people in different settings so that results can be standardised. Typically at the end of the centre a wash-up session is held, to discuss the scores of each participant in turn and to plot these on a rating grid. Table 2.2 is an example of a rating scale used at an assessment centre.

The development centre is more individually focused, with the aim being for participants to rate and develop their skills against the competencies during the course of the centre and to end up with a development plan to take them forward into the future. To do this, coaches are often assigned to participants, to both observe and give feedback on performance on the exercises, as well as to provide more in-depth discussions on development needs. Whilst the coaches are trained in assessment methods, they are not asked to score the participants or feedback to the organisation.

Talent centres are likely to draw more on the assessment centre approach, though as can be seen in the case study at the end of this chapter, this is not always the case. Questions companies might want to ask themselves are:

- What is the purpose of the centre?
- How much individual feedback is required?
- How ready are the target population for an assessed approach?
- Are we able to define the behaviours we need from this group in the future?

		Exercises/Activities							
Competency	Behavioural indicators	Visioning meeting	Strategy meeting	Performance management	Stakeholder meeting	Supplier meeting	Communicate the vision	Influencing upwards	Peer feedback exercise
Set direction	Unite people with vision	✓		✓	✓		✓	✓	
	Set challenging standards	✓		✓		✓	✓		✓
	Communicate brand			✓			✓		
Make a personal impact	Show integrity and courage	✓	✓		✓	✓	✓	✓	
	Build effective partnerships	✓	✓	✓	✓		✓	✓	✓
Think strategically	Plan and prioritise			✓		✓			
	Make well-considered decisions	✓	✓			✓			
	Use date to identIfy key issues	✓	✓			✓			
Got the best from people	Observe, assess and feedback			✓			✓	✓	✓
	Champion diversity and team spirit	✓		✓			✓	✓	✓
Learn and improve	Develop self and others			✓				✓	✓
	Enable change and improvement	✓	✓				✓	✓	✓
Deliver results	Deliver against corporate plan	✓	✓	✓			✓		
	Deliver customer service	✓	✓	✓	✓	✓			
	Improve value for money		✓				✓		

Figure 2.3 An exercise versus competency matrix

One of the main success criteria for centres is careful communication to everyone involved – the participants, their line managers, senior stakeholders and the people involved in running the centre. If it is not clear to participants what the purpose of the centre is and how it will be managed, there is likely to be apprehension and

Table 2.2 A rating scale used at assessment centres

Rating	Explanation
1	Performance well below the standard required to meet the criteria.
2	Performance below the standard overall, but meets some aspects of the the criteria.
3	Performance is at the required standard for the criteria to be met.
4	Performance shows potential. The candidate has demonstrated the required standard against all the criteria and exceeds this in two or more areas.
5	Performance shows high potential. The candidate has exceeded the required standard on a significant number of criteria.

suspicion which will get in the way of their performance at the centre. Setting expectations and setting clear boundaries around confidentiality are imperative to a centre's success.

The assessment and development centre approach can experience a number of difficulties. For example, the assessors can be inadequately trained; exercises can become overused; assessment of minority groups may be subject to bias; exercises may not measure the skills required; raw data can be misused and 'good' performance is sometimes not agreed on. Perhaps more importantly, company experience shows that it is difficult to convey the differences between an assessment and development tool and as a result, the company raises expectations of employees and risks breaching confidentiality with their line management (Kerr, 1989; Goodge, 1994).

Despite these difficulties, centres provide a useful assessment, language and framework for employees to develop their careers. Whilst they can be time consuming and costly, assessment centres have the benefit that they can play a strong role in engaging some of the key stakeholders in the talent management process. If senior leaders are involved in assessing, or interviewing on a talent centre, they will get a better feel for the criteria being used and the talent coming through the organisation. Many of the companies involved in the research for this book indicated that participation at this early stage in the process had been pivotal in the success of their talent strategies.

Should talent groups be singled out?

It could be argued that singling out high potential staff and focusing on fast tracking groups of people is not beneficial to the longer-term health of organisations.

Arguably, this approach encourages individualism, elitism, a short-term focus and neglects subordinate development. An excessive focus on work and the working career can also impact family or personal life, leading ultimately to stress, burn out, a lack of focus and derailment.

Interestingly, in Germany and Japan, career development for the whole workforce is a much stronger message than in the UK and America. Although a joint survey by the Hay group and Human Resources (2003) showed that the majority of UK companies also place their emphasis on all employees, see Figure 2.4.

Building individual career resilience and risking a loss of trust from the rest of the workforce may go against singling out talent groups. However, the high potential within the organisation is unlikely to rise to the top on their own without some kind of support and exposure to a wide variety of experiences. A talented individual with a poor line manager for example, may find themselves 'stuck' and unable to take advantage of opportunities to grow and develop.

It could also be argued that talent can be bought in when it is required from the external market. However, apart from being far more expensive, finding the right skills and cultural fit to ensure success is not that easy.

Analysing the success of talent-focused strategies is not straightforward either. Interestingly, Larsen (1997) suggests the success of high potential schemes is often measured by the number of people who end up in more senior positions who were originally identified as high performing. However this does not tell whether an organisation has actually identified and developed the best people or whether it was a self-fulfilling prophecy.

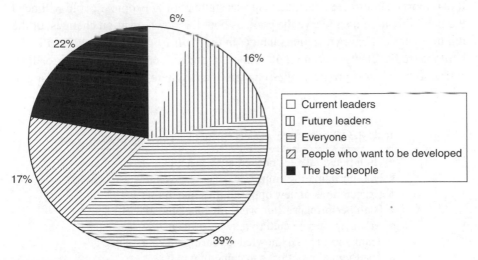

Figure 2.4 What type of talent is managed?

Another factor to consider is that not all companies need to be concerned with future leadership potential. A company may already have a significant cadre of managers and predict a lesser requirement in the future. If this is the case, other types of career strategies, based on motivation of the whole population within existing roles, may be more appropriate. It is worth analysing whether the organisation has experienced problems with long-term vacancies in particular positions, or have suffered from poor quality of leadership in some areas of the business, to help gauge the necessity to focus on specific groups of talent.

However, there are good business reasons why companies choose to focus on core groups of people, which Chapter 3 tackles in more detail. Most companies have limited resources available for training and development and providing opportunities for growth can be costly. Identifying key groups of high potential within the company is likely to provide the greatest added value in terms of this investment, as it is those people who will build the company for the future.

Possible consequences of a focused approach

Interestingly, the findings in Figure 2.4 sit alongside other results which showed that 84 per cent of these same companies identified staff with high potential, typically by means of line manager nominations, performance data or more structured assessment processes. So if companies do decide to focus their approach on key individuals or groups, what are the possible risks and consequences of this? (see Table 2.3).

High potential does not remain constant

It is important not to see a talent group as a static pool of people. People will need the flexibility to join and leave the pool, as both their own position changes, or the requirements of the organisation change. In the *Rolls Royce* case study later in the book, there is a clear illustration of both entry and exit criteria for talent, to allow action to be taken if progress rates change. Unless there is careful monitoring, it

Table 2.3 Possible risks of singling out high potential groups

- High potential does not remain constant
- Non-participating employees may be adversely affected
- Expectations of new opportunities may be set
- High performance can over influence potential ratings
- An inappropriate culture may be cultivated
- Teamworking and knowledge sharing may be reduced
- The Pygmalion effect can come into play

may not be clear who continues to be high potential as shifts in culture and structure will create new requirements for knowledge and skills and interpersonal
relationships may change over time.

Non-participating employees may be adversely affected

The effect on non-participating employees of talent pools varies and appears to be
dependant on how organisations communicate their intentions. If talent management does single out particular groups, how this is communicated to the remainder of the workforce is critical. If this is handled badly, the excluded population
are likely to feel demotivated and devalued and have concerns that their training
and development will be limited. This could ultimately lead to lower performance
and increased turnover, causing the organisation to have a costly recruitment demand
that wasn't anticipated.

Increasingly organisations are becoming more open and managing these messages through line managers and internal media. Worryingly however, a recent
Hay survey also identifies that only 6 per cent of employees were thought to understand the talent management processes very clearly.

There is also an argument to say that non-selected employees could equally rise
to the challenge if they were given a chance and that selecting elite groups limits
potential. Pfeffer (2001) argues that there is a lot of evidence that people can perform above or below their natural abilities depending on the situation and the
leadership and support they receive. He says there is a risk in focusing on small
groups of individuals despite the evidence that high performing organisations do
use a systematic approach to identify and develop high potential.

What is evident is that if the message is not clear, or the process used appears
to be unfair, then there could be significant impact on people's motivation and job
performance and their commitment to the organisation is likely to decline. This
issue of equity is addressed later in this chapter.

Expectations of new opportunities may be set

Having been identified as someone with talent, it is likely that people will have a
higher expectation of the type of opportunities and experiences open to them. One
of the dangers of a focus on high potential groups is that it takes us back to more
traditional career progression models which may not be deliverable in the current
work context. Have organisations got opportunities do go with the raised expectations of planned progression?

Certainly not all organisations have a supply of opportunities at their disposal
and even in larger companies, or where there is less of a cost constraint, not many
assignments give a broad view of an organisation or stretch people outside their

comfort zone. Even if such opportunities do exist, there is a high risk associated with using your talent in this way. Does the company really want people who are inexperienced running critical projects? Organisations need to think through the opportunities on offer and make clear to individuals what will and won't be available to them. Chapter 7 looks at this topic of how to grow your talent in more detail.

Expectations of increased support may also be set. Whilst coaching and mentoring are popular ways of supporting high potential employees, they can also be used to set expectations and orient people more effectively. Beeson (2004) argues that providing proactive support to those in stretch assignments is critical to ensure that people do not 'fail', so organisations need to ensure they can deliver on this.

Whilst these higher expectations may be difficult to manage, it is the lack of such opportunities for growth and appropriate support that often causes high potential employees to leave organisations.

High performance can over influence potential ratings

The words Talent, High Performers and High Potential are often used interchangeably. However, potential indicates a future viability that is not necessarily present in your existing talent. Researchers vary as to whether potential is based to some extent on performance. Rothwell (2001) believes this is the case, whereas McCall (1998) disagrees that it is based on current performance, and argues that potential is the ability to acquire new skills in the face of rapid change. Interestingly, the Corporate Leadership Council research indicated that only about a third of high performers are seen to have high potential in organisations, whereas 93 per cent of high potentials are also high performers.

Many organisations identify their talent and future potential by line managers making judgements. These can often be skewed towards current performance and managers may seek to clone future senior managers from what is currently in place. It is well worth remembering that potential ratings are only as accurate as the knowledge and prediction ability of those making the decisions and may well be prone to be biased towards existing perceptions of good management.

Many organisations are choosing to put in place clear guidelines and briefings on how to rate potential and HR Business Partners will often jointly participate in rating exercises to help ensure these guidelines are followed using the performance and potential matrices explained earlier in this chapter.

The Corporate Leadership Council (2005) has done some interesting research in this area. They identify three key groups of employees, which they term Engaged Dreamers, Unengaged Stars and Misaligned Stars. These groups are all rated as having high performance, but have a particular shortcoming which reduces their potential rating.

The Engaged Dreamer, said to be 5 per cent of the high performers without potential, has both the aspiration and engagement in the company, but lack the skills and ability of the next level. The Unengaged Stars, accounting for 48 per cent of the high performers without potential, have the ability and the aspiration, but are not fully committed to the organisation and are not sure that working for the company longer term is in their best interests. This group are likely to be difficult to spot, as they are unlikely to communicate this openly. The last group, the Misaligned Stars, accounting for 47 per cent, have the commitment and ability, but lack the drive and ambition to move on – something holds them back from pushing themselves. Interestingly, the career anchor work described later in the book, may provide some insights into which group people fall into.

An inappropriate culture may be cultivated

As organisations focus on what they require from their talent in the future and set criteria and behaviours to rate people against, there is a risk that the culture of the company tightens to focus in on these core competencies. Whilst this may be desirable to a certain extent, this narrowing of focus of your key players in the organisation may put the organisation at risk if there has been a poor diagnosis at the start.

There is also mixed research into whether highflier profiles have the skills to empower and develop others. Some studies have shown that subordinates report a lack of interpersonal sensitivity from high potential managers, perhaps due to their drive and individualism. This can however be addressed through techniques such as 360-degree feedback and performance management based on appropriate behaviours. Xerox for example, uses employee motivation – a manager's ability to manage interaction, feelings and emotions, as a key performance measure (Jones et al., 1996).

It is imperative therefore, that organisations take great care when they are establishing their criteria for measuring potential and selecting people into talent pools.

Teamworking and knowledge sharing may be reduced

Segregating pools of talent may encourage more competitive behaviour, both within the group, as they compete for growth opportunities, and also with non-participating employees, who may harbour feelings of jealousy or lack a willingness to cooperate. As a consequence, sharing of knowledge across the company may be reduced as people hold onto information for their own gain. Again, this risk can be minimised by ensuring that the rating of high potential employees and feedback mechanisms focus on teamwork and knowledge sharing as key contributors to success.

The Pygmalion effect can come into play

The Pygmalion effect occurs when one person has expectations of another and behaves towards that person in a manner consistent with those expectations. In addition, differences in self-expectations may result in differences in performance. Livingstones (1969) famed research proved that children performed better if their teachers led them to believe they were excellent performers, whether of not they were. He concluded that people, more often than not, appear to do what they believe they are expected to do.

The implications of the Pygmalion effect are that by telling employees they are in a talent pool, or are rated as high potential, they are more likely to be treated differently by those around them and be expected to perform at a higher level, and the person in turn, will be more likely to fulfil those expectations. Research into the experience of high potentials within Hewitt (Lewis, 2006) found that the employees' behaviour and expectations were impacted by either the direct message or the perception that the person was considered to be high potential. The research emphasised the benefits in making sure that everyone is aware that they have been classified as high potential, something that does not always happen in organisations. By being more open it enables both employees to fulfil expectations and the line manager relationship to be more open and honest, with more effective goal setting.

It could be argued then, that an organisation should set high expectations for all employees. However, the research indicates that people will not be motivated to achieve at a higher level unless they consider their manager to be credible and the expectations are realistic. Also Hurley (1997) found that low self-esteem in the employee or lack of follow-through by the manager in the way they treat the employee will reduce the effect. This indicates that managers have a significant effect on performance, but individual's self-belief and self-esteem can also overcome deficiencies in manager's performance.

Ideally then, there needs to be a clear message to high potential employees that comes from a credible source and carries realistic expectations of the part of both the employee and the organisation. In addition, the employee needs to have the self-belief and self-esteem to rise to the challenge.

The psychological contract

The move towards psychological contracting as a model for successful career strategies has been growing considerably since Herriot and Pemberton's book back in 1996.

The psychological contract model is defined in a number of different ways, many of which describe a mutual expectation, or mutual obligation which is perceived to be in place between the employer and the employee. Whilst the contract is unwritten and implicit in people's heads, it is possible to use the model as a basis for more open and honest communication about expectations and offers.

A person's psychological contract can be influenced by a number of factors, such as:

- comparison with peers,
- views and experiences of other employers,
- expectations created by the employer branding,
- recruitment and induction messages and experiences,
- the way performance is managed,
- promises that are made by managers to employees,
- the way people progress their careers.

Historically, the psychological contract offered employment security and slow promotion up a career ladder in exchange for adequate performance and loyalty. People identified as particularly able were often offered more managed development through a fast track programme. The company managed their careers and offered opportunities when vacancies arose. However, the business environment and contextual factors described in the first chapter of this book have caused this unwritten career deal to change quite dramatically.

Organisations are now offering employability and sometimes greater flexibility in exchange for individuals taking on development and updating their skills. The career ladder has been replaced by a career lattice (Iles, 1997) with multiple career paths and a focus on enriching jobs and opportunities rather than job movement alone.

Herriot and Pemberton conclude that career strategies need to be:

- contextualised,
- cyclical (to allow for changes in context),
- subjective (i.e. do not pre-suppose success criteria for employees),
- interactive between the organisation and its employees.

One of the problems with models dependant on psychological contracting is that they concentrate on negotiation between the organisations needs and wants and that of the individual. Invariably the needs and wants of the manager are likely to be different to those of the individual. If the psychological contract is too difficult to negotiate, employees will only have the choice to leave the organisation. However, the benefit of this approach is that it implies negotiation, which is likely to lead to greater perceptions of equity.

Interestingly, organisations are now making substantial investments in their talent and a recent study by Roffey Park (McCartney and Garrow, 2006) suggest that this might imply a return to the old psychological contract of long tenure and mutual loyalty. Indeed few organisations have done away completely with the more traditional tools of career management such as succession planning and promoting from within.

Recent years have also seen a shift in the balance of power towards high potential employees. If they don't see a fair deal, they may choose to take their intellectual property to another organisation and leave the company with a knowledge gap. This issue of knowledge management is a strong consideration for companies and they are continually grappling with how to embed capability in organisations and processes rather than individuals.

In practice these conversations are difficult to have – a topic which will be discussed in more detail later when we examine the role of the line manager. There is often a fear in employees which prevents them from divulging their true aspirations or career goals due to concerns that it may limit their organisational opportunities or pigeon hole them. Managers too are reluctant to engage, as they may not be able to fulfil expectations that are raised and risk demotivating their key players.

The consequence for organisations is that careers are now more often viewed as boundaryless and portable, with high potential employees gaining a skills set and taking it to the next employer with a better deal. Yahoo (Personnel Today, 2006) faced a challenge in their industry as people tended to move employers frequently and they needed to create a climate with greater loyalty and commitment. They created two new strands within their business to help alleviate this. Firstly they focused on talent acquisition and ensured that the team retained involvement with new entrants for 6 months after joining to help ensure the induction period was successful. Secondly, the talent team ensured that all their senior managers received incentives for good performance management and low attrition rates, to help focus their activity on the issue.

Some organisations have also taken steps to make some generic aspects of the psychological contract explicit, by publishing statements of intent. Figure 2.5 is an illustration of one such statement, which is called an 'Employer proposition' and sets out the expectations on both sides.

The need for equity

One of the core cultural issues which influences the success of a more focused strategy, is whether the culture in the organisation is based on honesty and trust. Herriot et al. (1994) found that the perceived equity of career and HR processes lead to increased levels of career satisfaction and hence organisational commitment. It could be argued that by being more open about the opportunities for

You are a talented individual.

The opportunity exists to apply your special skills and help shape the future of our business.

Through its skills and expertise, the company is recognised as a world leader in its field. It Is our people who are the source of our professionalism, reputation and success.

When you join the company you will work with a great team of colleagues, who have a real sense of achievement and satisfaction in their work and a sense of pride in their contribution to the industry.

We offer a large range of jobs, and we are committed to your training and development. You will have regular opportunities with your managers for discussion about your performance and what we can do to help you apply your skills and knowledge. In support of this you will have performance objectives and personal development plans.

We have a good range of benefits, valued by our people. We will provide you with competitive remuneration, generous annual leave in addition to the public holidays, and a contributory pension scheme.

In return for a rewarding job, we will ask that you apply your particular professionalism and skills and strive for continuous improvement and development In all that you do.

We want you to use your special skills and help us build on the successful relationships with all those you will have contact with, enhancing our reputation further still.

Figure 2.5 An employer proposition

development available in organisations today, that HR would be seen as more equitable. However, it can also be argued that raising awareness about the changing nature of career development and the reduced opportunities for upward progression could have a negative impact on career satisfaction.

Herriot and Pemberton (1996) differentiate between procedural equity which occurs when there is a relational contract, and distributive equity (i.e. equal outcomes to both the organisation and individual), if the contract is transactional. Relational contracts have been found to have stronger emotional reactions in terms of anger, mistrust etc. and lead to a focus by employees on transactional elements if they are perceived as inequitable.

It seems that the perceived fairness of processes and procedures is one of the root causes of success or failure of a career management strategy. Research has shown time and time again, that these perceptions of equity impact on a whole range of measures:

- Career satisfaction
- Organisational commitment
- Absenteeism

- Performance
- Intention to leave the organisation.

And ultimately, the bottom line.

So if procedural equity has a greater effect on career satisfaction and organisational commitment than salary or grade-related outcomes, why is it not given more attention in organisations?

Reason 1: Establishing a culture with a sense of mutual trust, commitment and responsibility is difficult to build.

Reason 2: Organisations often have statements about the need to be consistent across the organisation, but this conflicts with the discretion needed to treat each individual differently.

Achieving the right balance is difficult. For example, how would you address the following situation?

A high potential employee in one part of the organisation seeks sponsorship on an MBA programme. They manage to persuade their manager to support this application and get approval. Some time later, another high potential peer in another part of the organisation also seeks sponsorship and is turned down on the basis that the development budget for their department is being used in other ways.

Given what we know, this lack of perceived equity is likely to have a strong impact on the second individuals' commitment to the organisation, and their performance and may also increase their intention to leave the company. Yet senior managers need to be given discretion as to how to deploy their resources. Whilst guidelines could be put in place for key aspects of the career strategy, such as sponsorship, this will not be possible for all eventualities. So how can organisations minimise the impact of such events?

Honesty appears to be the answer. For the psychological contract model to work effectively, the contract requires a more open communication culture in organisations, where managers are genuinely committed to two-way discussions and have an honest approach to development. When individuals can understand the basis for decisions that are made and have an opportunity to challenge and question, it is far less likely that decisions will be perceived to be inequitable.

However, what this does mean is that instilling the right environment and developing an open and honest culture is imperative for such a strategy to work effectively. This fits with some recent work carried out by Taylor (2004) who lists a number of capabilities that are essential in order to engage and retain employees including:

- Building trust between team members and leaders.
- Building self-esteem in team members.

- Communicating effectively regarding retention and engagement issues.
- Building a climate that is enjoyable and fulfilling.
- Being flexible in recognising, understanding and adapting to the individual needs and views.
- Monitoring these issues so that pre-emptive action can be taken.

As companies operate more globally, this issue becomes even more complex and there is a need to consider equity in terms of cross-cultural fairness of the tools and processes used for managing talent. This may mean for example, ensuring a diverse set of assessors for selection to career acceleration pools.

Case study: *Virgin Atlantic*

Information supplied by Andy Cross, Head of Learning and Development

Background

Virgin Atlantic (VAA) was established in 1984 and has grown at an incredible rate to a point where it now carries approximately 5 million passengers on 26 long haul destinations out of Heathrow, Gatwick and Manchester. It is now Britain's second largest airline, serving the world's major cities, with 36 aircraft and 9,000 staff.

The company has ambitious growth and profitability targets and works in a difficult and unpredictable industry. As a result of this it needs a distinctive leadership style and in 2006 the company set out to develop a new talent management strategy.

The aim of the strategy was to:

- Measurably strengthen the whole Leadership team.
- Build confidence that key roles could be filled quickly.
- Develop a strong leadership bench to lighten the load for Directors.
- Create an 'A' team who could respond quickly to new business/market opportunities.

Approach

The leadership development programme needed to be built around the stated business strategy of increasing profit by 7 per cent. VAA were also keen to ensure that the strategy linked to the manifesto and values of the company, and as a first step in the process the leadership team developed a clear set of leadership principles and behaviours to guide senior managers and underpin development activities. This leadership profile was encapsulated by five principles:

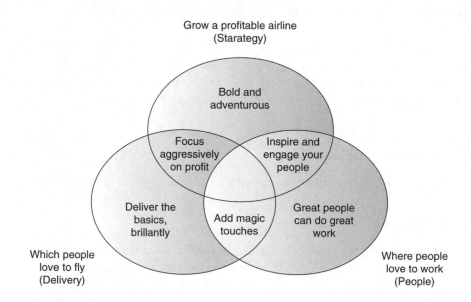

In conjunction with Roffey Park Institute, VAA then designed a developmental approach with three key elements:

- A 360-degree feedback, Hogan Personality Inventory and other self-assessment activities prior to a development centre.
- A 2-day development centre with personal coaching, development activities and feedback.
- On-going peer learning sets to support personal development plans and encourage cross-functional awareness.

The Personal Development Workshop approach

The workshop acted as an opportunity for all the managers in VAA to 'take stock' and gather valuable feedback on how they were doing as leaders – what was behind their success and what would make them even better – an appreciative approach. The workshop aimed to help managers to clarify their personal aspirations, really understand their 360-degree feedback and leadership development needs and plan how to achieve even more in the future. In total approximately 100 managers attended the workshop over a 9 month period.

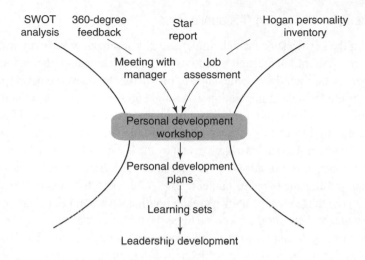

The development workshop included:

- Group exercises to bring out targeted leadership behaviours which were observed by personal coaches.
- 1:1 exercises with actors to practice dealing with poor performance.
- Short input sessions on giving and receiving feedback and taking stock of your career.
- Peer feedback in pairs working alongside a coach.
- Three sessions with a personal coach.
- 1:1 feedback on the Hogan Personality Instrument.
- An introduction to learning sets.
- Personal reflection time to help formulate a Personal Development Plan.

When the workshops were completed, participants produced a personal leadership development plan and then split into two learning sets that met a further six times over the course of 9 months, three of which were facilitated by Roffey Park coaches. These allowed the participants to support and challenge each other while monitoring their own progress against their plans. The groups were also mixed by department to allow cross-function collaboration. This was essential in embedding the learning back into the organisation.

One of the important aspects of the approach developed between VAA and Roffey Park, was the emphasis on an appreciative approach to development. In other words, the workshop was not intended to assess what managers were not doing well, but to look at what worked for them as individuals and to build upon that. Longer term, the strategy aimed to assess and select a high potential pool from within the senior management team, but this was not the aim of the development workshop.

Key decisions in taking this approach

Some of the key decisions which influenced this approach were firstly whether to select a pool of talent (high potentials) from the leadership population first and then assess their development needs, or whether to assess the development needs of the leadership population as a whole and encourage personal development prior to being more selective in streaming development activities.

The decision to carry out development for all – develop and pick – as the first phase was influenced to a large extent by the Virgin culture and the fact that it was important to put across a message that the leadership principles were essential for all leaders not just an elite few. A key objective was to strengthen the whole of the leadership to give greater confidence around future succession from within and encourage everyone to be the best they can be.

Another key decision was to utilise coaching alongside the development activities. Whilst being a more costly approach, this ensured that the development workshop was tailored to the needs of the individuals on the programme and encouraged individuals to progress their thinking whatever their starting point.

Success measures

Virgin assess their success against four criteria and have various measures in place for each aspect:

- *Learning experience*
  - All leaders received personal 360-degree feedback report.
  - Participant feedback on Personal Development Workshops and learning sets.
  - Participant feedback at Executive Lunch and Meet sessions.
  - Observed evidence from learning sets.
- *Leadership performance*
  - Anecdotal evidence from Directors.
  - 360-degree shift in leadership principles.
  - Better balance of internal and external promotions.
- *Leadership team effectiveness*
  - Employee survey 'Love to work' engagement index and leadership drivers.
  - Bench strength index.
- *Business impact*
  - Performance objective profile.
  - Attributed achievements.
  - Executive support and drive for the programme.

Whilst it is early days, the feedback from the development workshops has been very positive and Andy has been delighted with the results so far: 'I have had participants tell me it has changed their lives and increased their effectiveness significantly. One participant was able to use the skills he had learnt to negotiate a £140 000 reduction in a contract thanks to the collaboration in the learning sets'.

'The programme has also had a positive impact on employee turnover. We've increased retention rates at managerial level as well as achieving a stronger balance between internal and external recruitment'.

Next steps

Virgin's strategy is on-going and the current phases being progressed are to:
1. Deliver a schedule of leadership development activities: These will focus on some of the generic needs which arose from the development workshops, such as getting the best from your people and strategic leadership.
2. Extend the talent pool to include 'nominated' managers next level down.
3. Generate a Talent Profile for 120 managers in the Leadership Team: The aim is to develop searchable, current profiles that includes the 'at your fingertips' information which needs visibility. It will include personal development plans and a method for tracking plan achievement as well as manager/self-assessment of potential.
4. Repeat the 360-degree process
5. Develop local talent forums to integrate into the Executive Talent Forum. The purpose of these local forums will be to:
   - Maintain Divisional Talent Profile.
   - Sponsor individuals and challenge them to maintain Talent Profile, plans and undertake development activities.
   - Identify leaders who should/can be moved within next 12 months and facilitate making moves happen.
   - Integrate company-wide leadership development activities into local plans.

Summary

So how do talent strategies differ from career strategies? The answer to this question takes us back to the start of this chapter, as it depends very much on the definition of talent. Is it all encompassing, or a select group of employees? If we are to assume the latter, then talent strategies form a clear sub-set of wider career strategy.

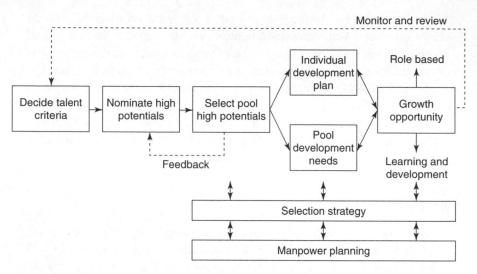

Figure 2.6 The talent process

Typically, what companies talk about when they are discussing managing their talent, is a process which starts at defining criteria and ends with a pool of people to be managed (see Figure 2.6). There are obviously many more steps along the way in this model and the later chapters on succession management and acceleration pools explore this in more detail.

Although in its widest form talent management incorporates aspects such as corporate branding to attract a wider pool of high potential applicants, the core focus is generally on the identification and development of small groups of people. Whilst definitions vary, we are beginning to see increasingly sophisticated box models and assessment centres to determine who should be labelled as 'high potential', providing organisations with a clear focus for learning and development resources.

This chapter has highlighted some of the challenges facing the successful implementation of talent strategies, and three particular themes stand out from this:

- Managing the Implications;
- Generating on-going, high quality, dialogue;
- Managing the interface to other processes.

There is a need to manage the implications of the strategy both for the participants and the non-participants and ensure there is a clear communication strategy to support the roll-out of any new initiatives. To be effective, the strategy needs open and honest discussion throughout, particularly when the message is difficult or expectations are not clear. Finally, the inter-relationships to selection strategies and manpower planning need to be clearly managed.

Checklist

- Have you got agreement on what high potential and talent means?
- Are performance management practices rigorously applied?
- Is there a clear system for identifying potential?
- Does the organisation encourage sufficient dialogue on performance and potential?
- Are employees told the labels they are given?
- Are realistic expectations set about what the organisation can offer?
- Is it clear to people what the consequences are of not reaching particular goals?
- Are the implications for participants and non-participants of career pools thought through?
- How open and honest is the culture?
- How clear are the inter-relationships between the talent process and other HR strategies?
- Do assessment centres have a clear purpose?
- How certain are you that the behaviours measured are those that will be valued in the future?
- Will your high potential employees be open to the experiences on offer?
- How can you be sure you are not missing people with high potential within the organisation?
- How equitable are your processes perceived to be by employees?

3

Building the Business Case

This chapter aims to address the tricky question of how you prove to an organisation that career development is worth investing in, both in terms of time and money?

Business leaders are often conscious of the need to focus on developing careers, particularly for high performing and talented employees. However, their active sponsorship of career strategies is frequently lacking. A strong business case is essential, not only to clearly articulate the strategy but also to put clear measures around the interventions which support it.

This chapter covers:

- The purpose of the business case.
- What measures can you use to support your business case?
- How to structure your business case?
- What is contained within a business case?
- How to gain acceptance and support for your case?
- How to overcome some of the barriers you may come up against?

This chapter also highlights some useful tools for analysing and presenting some of the key information you need within a business case.

The purpose of the business case

Put simply, the business case presents the argument for a particular course of action and highlights the potential impact on the company. Reddington et al. (2005) suggest that it has three key purposes:

1. To get other people to understand the vision.
2. To get approval for funding.
3. To act as a reference point for decisions during implementation.

Building a powerful business case will help you to establish stronger credibility with key decision makers and will greatly enhance your influencing position.

There is often confusion between making a case and writing a business plan. Both are quite different tools, although sometimes a business case may include a business plan. A business plan is usually based on a business case and has a more practical plan for implementation. A business case however, is a tool used for making business decisions on a daily basis. A case is a flexible, dynamic, real-time decision making tool which can be applied to any business decision situation. In other words, if accepted, a business case will provide approval for a particular course of action that further planning can be based on.

Presenting a business case is an opportunity to influence the primary decision makers and a good case will answer questions that they might pose, such as:

- Why is this important?
- Why is it a priority?
- How can this help us achieve our goals?
- What are the business benefits?
- What resources do you need?
- How will we measure our success?
- When can I expect results?
- Why are you the right person to lead on this?
- What period of time are we looking?
- How does this proposal fit with the strategic objectives of the company?
- What are the options and the pros and cons of each?
- What changes will this mean?
- What is the financial cost/benefit of the proposal?
- What are the risks involved?
- What are the critical success factors?
- What skills and competence are required to deliver it?

Within the context of career management, there is likely to be a need to develop a range of different business cases. Aside from approval of an overall strategy, there are likely to be cases made for particular interventions recommended, such as career coaching for line managers or a career development workshop for high potential staff.

What measures can you use?

There has been a lot written in the last few years about the link between a focus on development in organisations and the impact on business performance. Yet even armed with this evidence, it can be hard to focus down on tangible measures of success.

This section aims to draw together some of the key data that you might find useful in compiling a business case. Some parts relate to particular initiatives which might form part of a career strategy, and some aspects relate to strategies as a whole.

So what evidence can you draw on?

Here are just some of the recent findings about the impact of talent strategies on organisations:

The war for talent research (Michaels et al., 2001) showed that 'those companies that scored in the top quintile of our talent management index earned, on average, 22 per cent higher return to shareholders than their industry peers'.

People management practices can give 20 per cent productivity and profit improvement (Beyond World Class, Macmillan, 1998).

Becker and Huselid (1998) carried out research into over 2,800 firms pursuing a talent strategy, which showed that improving HR practices can impact significantly on market value. Integrated and progressive people management practices had a 65 per cent higher market value. It is worth noting however, that it is the implementation of strategy that has the impact rather than the content of the strategy itself.

Studies of good employers, such as The Great Place to work Institute, have shown that the 100 best places to work generated 1,289 per cent shareholder returns over 10 years, compared to 372 per cent by all companies on the Dow Jones. Where these companies differ is that they have high levels of trust, team-working, career development and support for innovation embedded in their culture.

Watson Wyatt's Human Capital Index (2001) showed the 5-year returns to shareholders for companies with a high human capital index was 64 per cent compared to 21 per cent for those with a low score.

CIPD research (2003) found that employees' job performance is a function of their ability, their motivation and the opportunity to deploy their ideas abilities and knowledge effectively.

The Corporate Leadership Council (2006) found that successful execution of talent development programmes directly contributes to increased organisational effectiveness and profitability, leading to as much as a 15.4 per cent advantage in total shareholder returns.

These high level studies are certainly convincing, but some lower level evaluation measures may also be needed to measure your success. A look simple cost-benefit analysis can be a useful starting point.

Costs

Costs are probably the easiest place to start when it comes to preparing your case. There will be certain fixed costs in terms of training, succession planning, resources, etc. There are also likely to be opportunity costs, such as the impact of operating without a skilled manager in a role for a period of time.

Some opportunity costs have been estimated by Sullivan (2000) and Smart (1999):

- The cost of losing a senior talented executive is between $200 000 and $250 000.
- The bottom line impact of a bad hire is $300 000.
- Operating without a key senior executive can cost $7,000 per day.
- The cost of a bad hire is 14 times the person's salary.

Benefits

The Careers Research Forum (Morton, 2004) suggest that the benefits of managing talent include improvement in:

- Competitive advantage
- Business results
- Organisational capabilities
- Strategy execution
- Organisational morale
- Attraction and retention of other key staff.

Yet their research found that the measures that can more easily be put in place are often related to the outputs of the different initiatives rather than linked to organisational performance.

Bottom line benefits are not easy to establish. There are some tangible measures that can, and should, be used, but these in themselves to not tell the whole story. Table 3.1 shows some of the commonly used measures.

Reducing turnover is clearly one of the most obvious financial benefits from a well-managed career strategy and can make very compelling reading in a business case.

As an example: A company pays high potentials in the acceleration pool £55 000 p.a. on average. There are 100 people in the career pool and it takes 6 months to train someone new to fill a position. If 5 people (5 per cent) choose to stay with the company rather than leave in any given year, they will have saved: $5 \times £27 500 = £137 500$ plus any selection costs which will be higher if the company needs to go to the external market.

Calculations can also be made for improved redeployment across the organisation, leading to reduced recruitment volumes, less demand for contractors and fewer redundancy costs.

Table 3.1 Tangible measures

- *Appraisal data*
  - Rate of absenteeism
  - Number of grievances
  - Distribution of performance related pay
- *Changes in manpower data*
  - Turnover rate
  - Job satisfaction
  - Amount of lateral mobility
  - Percentage of successful redeployment
  - Percentage of upward mobility
- *Opinion survey data*
  - Exit interviews
  - Customer retention rates
  - New customer accounts
  - Numbers of high potential employees on developmental assignments

There have been numerous studies that have shown changes in these 'hard' measures, particularly turnover and absenteeism, resulting from career programmes (see e.g. Cotton and Tuttle, 1986; Aryee and Leong, 1991). However, the difficulty with this approach is that many of the measures are open to significant influence from factors other than the career programme being evaluated. The data can therefore often be difficult to interpret and it is hard to attribute the root cause of any changes. This is particularly likely to be the case in organisations where turnover is already low and absenteeism is effectively managed.

The more recent work by the CIPD on understanding the people and performance link (2003) makes useful reading as it shows a significant correlation in all the case study companies studied between career opportunity and organisational commitment, as well as between career opportunity and job satisfaction and motivation. Interestingly, there is also a significant correlation with work–life balance, again emphasising the need for organisations to take account of individual needs and the psychological contract within their career processes.

Later in this chapter we will look in more detail at some of the evaluation measures that have been used in other organisations and research studies to determine the success of career strategies.

Laying out your business case

The development of a business case will typically follow a particular format. Often there will be an initial proposal, which if it is accepted is then developed into a more comprehensive business case. This initial proposal is usually in the form of a short 2–3 pages, outlining the best, worst and most likely case scenarios. These scenarios need to be put in the context of the organisation, and should demonstrate that you understand the organisational priorities and have thought about a wide range of options to deal with the issues.

Having secured approval to put forward a more comprehensive business case, you need to start to gather the information required. Most business cases are around 20 pages in total and typically include:

1. Front page: normally with title, author, contact details, date and version number as well as any confidentiality status that may be required
2. List of contents and appendices
3. Executive summary
4. The main body of the case
5. Appendices: such as a glossary of terms, or more detailed analysis of the points made in the report.

The executive summary

The Executive Summary is arguably the most essential part of the case. Many readers of business cases are pressed for time and the sad reality is that often a business case will only receive a quick scan through. Consequently, the summary pages are your main opportunity to excite and compel the decision makers to take the actions you recommend. The arguments should be clear, influential and most of all interesting to read!

The executive summary should contain:

- A description of current situation and the issues faced
- The proposed strategy
- A summary of the business case
  - links to the overall business strategy
  - a brief analysis of the options
  - costs of the proposal
  - key benefits and success measures
  - key market data
  - any risk associated with the proposal
- The decision required and by whom.

For example, a company seeking to train a core team of managers in career coaching may have an executive summary which reads:

The company has struggled to retain high performing staff in critical areas of the business over the last 2 years, leading to high costs in selection as well as knowledge being lost from the business.

This plan proposes the establishment of a core team of career coaches to work with the identified talent pool, to increase their motivation and commitment to the company and support them in progressing their careers.

Securing a talent pipeline is a key strategic objective. This proposal will actively address this objective by providing a more tailored approach to developing our talent.

A viable alternative approach would be to use external career coaches. However, this is a more costly option and the coaches will be less focused on the needs and culture of our organisation.

The plan calls for £50 000 and the training is scheduled for completion in 4 months. Working with current turnover statistics, the estimated pay-back is 12 months.

A major risk lies in our ability to encourage skilled managers to volunteer to take on this additional role. We intend to address this by using a planned communication strategy.

Approval is required for the additional spend.

The main body of the business case

Cannon (2006) recommend that the main body of a business case should contain:

- An introduction to the topic, with an outline of the current context.
- Terms of reference and scope of the proposal.
- Vision and mission: future picture of what striving for.
- History.
- Situation analysis.
- Strategy options: scenario planning, pros and cons and risks and resource implications of each.
- Proposed strategy: why you have chosen it, why it's the best option, what assumptions you are making, critical success factors in delivering the strategy, expected outcomes.
- Costs and benefits of proposal.
- Implementation plan: resource plan implications, timetables, milestones.
- Risk analysis.
- Key decisions to be taken.

This part of the report is not straightforward and it is not always clear where to start, particularly when dealing with less tangible aspects of the business. Later in this chapter I will be outlining some tools to help wit the analysis as well as some thoughts and experiences from other organisations how to get started.

Gaining support for your business case

Consult widely

Writing a business case should not be done in isolation and a wide range of people should be consulted, such as your peers in other departments as well as more senior collcagues. This means that the case can be widely reviewed and its assumptions discussed and it allows time to persuade the right people about the benefits of your approach. The wider you consult, the wider the ownership of your case.

Stakeholder analysis is a useful technique for ensuring that you have thought through your approach from different people's perspectives.

First identify your stakeholders – who knows about it, who can influence it and who cares about it? Your strategy then needs to try to meet and reconcile the differing expectations of this group.

Mapping your key stakeholders in terms of their interest, commitment and influence can help you to think through your approach (see Figure 3.1). You may choose to survey their views on the proposed project and question them on what they perceive the impact and critical success factors to be. You may even choose to represent their views using a force field analysis, showing what factors arc driving the change and what might prevent the change from working.

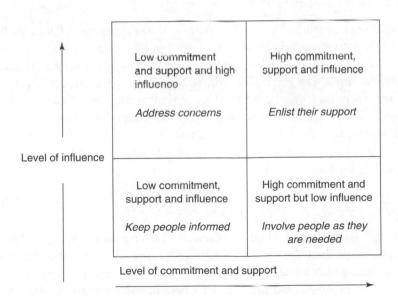

Figure 3.1 Stakeholder mapping

You need to ensure that you are listening particularly carefully to the stakeholders in the top left box, with high levels of influence but low commitment to the proposal. Identifying their sources of resistance and listening and acting on their concerns will be critical in ensuring a business case that meets with their approval. This part of the process can be essential in winning over opinion leaders and addressing potential conflicts before they arise. Before you even present your business case you will need to be influencing and managing your stakeholders in order to establish your credibility and identity and demonstrate your ability to manage the project. This preparation phase cannot be over-emphasised.

Gaining business buy-in is a critical step in making the business case. Selling the vision is often about showing how it is going to have a positive impact on the bottom line. Talking to your stakeholders in their language, making links to customers and the competitive position, as well as using techniques such as the balanced scorecard, will be critical.

Understanding potential barriers

Understanding the barriers you might come up against is a critical part of putting your case forward. Implementing a career strategy is not easy and numerous problems are likely to come your way. Some of the key issues to think though and debate with people at an early stage might be the following.

Opportunities to develop careers may be limited

Organisational structures designed to increase flexibility such as flatter, matrix or decentralised structures have limited the number of job moves that are seen as career development opportunities. For example, slow promotion rates are likely to decrease mobility, as employees will be less willing to move to locations for development purposes where they may be stranded for a number of years. As a consequence, companies need to get more creative in establishing opportunities to develop skills and competence, without necessarily changing roles. Some of the growth opportunities looked at later in the book, such as mentoring, assignments and projects are possibilities here.

It could be perceived as comparatively expensive to run

Where strategies demand a high involvement from managers, it is possible there will be concerns about the best use of manager's time and other costs, such as computer systems which might be developed to support the career strategy. Processes need to be kept simple and flexible and where possible integrated with existing practices so that they don't appear to be an 'extra'.

The company culture goes against risk-taking or long-term investment

Tensions often exist between an organisation's long-term and short-term objectives. For example, a cross functional developmental move is likely to be costly in terms of the initial training and management time required, but will give the organisation longer-term benefits.

Equally, training employees for future needs which are anticipated, such as management skills before they enter a management role can sometimes be hard to justify. Interestingly, union agreements in the public sector aimed at preventing unfair bias also tend to contradict a more strategic approach to development. However, without taking any risks with people's development, the chances are people will take on roles and be ill-prepared for the job, or find little challenge in it to stimulate them and drive their performance.

A belief that equipping individuals abdicates the need for managerial support

If the career strategy aims to encourage employee self-responsibility for career development, the assumption can sometimes be that employees can manage their own careers with little support, guidance or control. However, evidence suggests that self-development systems suffer from a lack of back up and this is essential to success.

Tensions between an approach for all versus an approach for a group

The discussion around whether to focus in on a small pool of talent, or to develop talent in all employees is discussed elsewhere in this book. In developing the business case, you will need to take account of the culture and values of the organisation and present the arguments for and against each approach.

Inter-connected aspects of the strategy are lacking

Successful career strategies rely on other processes in the organisation working effectively, such as appraisals of performance or potential, which are commonly unfair or inconsistent. Conflict can also exist between the organisational and individual needs, with individuals having unrealistic expectations about progression and development opportunities. The strategy needs to ensure that it covers all the inter-related aspects and makes expectations clear to all parties.

A successful system is therefore seen as one that minimises these problems and achieves a balance between the different factors. Part of the buy-in process for developing the career strategy is likely to focus on influencing key stakeholders on these points.

Thinking about your audience

Despite the importance of an advance campaign, your written business case is your main selling document and as such it should aim to persuade the audience and grab their attention. Your style of writing will be critical and you need to ensure a clear structure which is easy to read and well laid out. Allowing space for people to write on the document and ensuring there are no spelling or grammatical mistakes are simple things, but may make all the difference. Timing may also be critical. What other issues are there in the business and can you link to these? How important is your case relative to the other events?

Think about the audience both in terms of content and style (see Table 3.2).

Neurolinguistic programming (NLP) techniques may be helpful to assess the appeal of your document. The most familiar technique is to ensure that the document appeals to all the sensory filters, particularly visual, auditory and kinaesthetic.

Other filters are also worth considering, such as whether there is a strong orientation towards writing in the past, present or future and whether the document is pitched at the right level in terms of 'chunking' (Knight, 1995). Put simplisitically, does your report describe oranges when it needs to be describing a fruit stall?

Using anecdotal evidence as well as statistics can help to sell your argument. Consider these two statements:

Statement one

> *'Research has shown that managers perceived significant improvements in job performance following career workshops'*

or

Statement two

> *This quote is typical of those stemming from career workshops 'I was forced by the course to think about my own career and my career path within the company. I learned that it is me who is in charge of taking the challenge and the responsibility for my career, and that nobody else is sitting in the driver seat.*

Table 3.2 Business case content and style

Content	Style
What is important to them?	Are sensory filters catered for?
What is happening in their world?	Is it pitched at the right level?
How does the business case provides a link?	Does it bring the case to life?
What is in it for them?	

Personally it helped me to open my eyes and focus on my aims and aspects of my performance'.

Which do you prefer? Both statements provide information, but each will appeal to a different kind of reader. Whilst there is a lot of evidence to suggest that people respond well and connect better to stories and anecdotes than figures, understanding the style of your key stakeholders will give you a greater insight into how to shape your case.

Don't be too bound by what has gone before. It is dangerous to assume that the format for other business cases in your organisation are the way to go. It may be that the element of surprise, or a fresh approach may just give you the edge and make your case stand out.

Depending on the level of involvement, a more formal presentation of findings may not be necessary. However, there is likely to be some kind of verbal presentation of the business case, which will also be critical. Staying positive throughout the presentation; developing and maintaining rapport by using appropriate body language and terminology and keeping the supporting material brief and relevant to the listener is essential.

If you have been working in a process or collaborative way with your stakeholders then they are likely to have been involved in the process of data gathering and diagnosis. This will make your position a little easier. However, it is still important to consider what the expectations are and what information they might need at this stage. This may depend on the way in which you work with your stakeholders. Your style if you are presenting yourself in an expert role is likely to me more informative and engaging, whereas a more collaborative process consultant is more likely to present some information and then open up a discussion to encourage views and questions as they go through.

It is not possible to over emphasise the need to prepare yourself for discussions about your business case. Cannon (2006) recommends considering the following questions:

- Do you know what you want to achieve?
- Do you really believe in it yourself?
- Have you got all the facts that support your case?
- What are your strongest arguments?
- What are the benefits to your audience?
- What else is affected by your proposal?
- What are the key arguments against your proposal?
- Is the timing right?
- How will you sum up?
- What would a critic pick up on?

Developing the content

Developing the content for a well-thought-out business case takes time. Ideally, the process should be a collaborative one with the key stakeholders and will continue through a staged process of analysis, similar to that in Figure 3.2

The starting point is likely to be a process for stimulating debate on the topic. This might take place in a workshop, or through a series of interviews. The priorities that emerge from using this help identify the critical aspects to highlight in your business case.

Carrying out a gap analysis can also be a useful exercise in these initial stages, highlighting where you are as a company, where you want to be and what the gaps are. Gathering ideas on what the important links are within your company can also help to generate themes for the business case. At a recent workshop I attended, a team of HR professionals carried out a quick mind map of key considerations for their business case for career coaching. The output from this exercise is shown in Figure 3.3. This illustrates the many and varied issues which need to be considered within a business case for career coaching.

Useful tools

Situation analysis

Cannon (2006) in his book 'making the business case' provides some useful insights into the information needed for business planning. One of these, situation analysis, is particularly helpful in giving a framework for describing the current state of play. The tool suggests you examine each of the following in turn, writing a brief description of each:

■ *History*
  – Why the situation has arisen, trends such as turnover, SWOT (Strengths, Weaknesses, Opportunities and Threats) analysis.

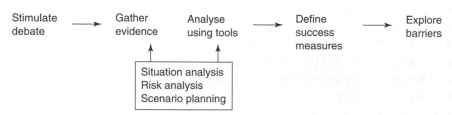

Figure 3.2 Developing the content for your business case

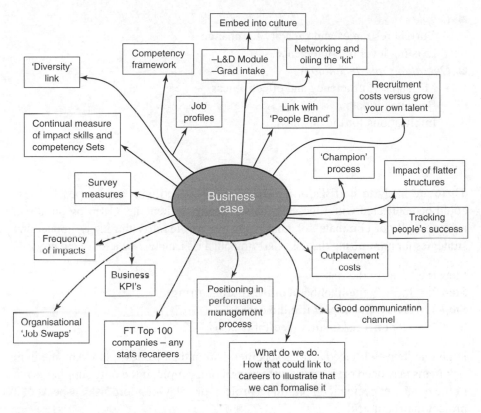

Figure 3.3 Output from a career workshop

- *Issues and challenges*
  - Answers the question as to why this is a concern at this time and what the route causes might be.
  - The explanation may draw on core competencies which give competitive advantage or critical success factors.
- *Stakeholder analysis*
- *Marketplace and competition*
  - What are competitors doing about this?
  - What market pressures and trends are there?
- *Customers*
  - How will this impact on them?
- *Financial information*
  - Current costs
  - Future costs

- *People*
  - Current resources and capacity for change.
  - Existing level of competence.
- *Operations and Technology*
  - Measures of efficiency and effectiveness
  - Benchmark data
  - Implications for the business.

Risk analysis

There are likely to be risks or uncertainties associated with any proposal. These could be connected with timescales, costs, quality or benefits. Carrying out a risk analysis will not eliminate potential risks, but will identify the likely impact and strategies for minimising the risk. Carrying out a risk analysis is a four-step process:

Step 1:   Identify the risks.
Step 2:   Identify the likelihood of the risk occurring.
Step 3:   Assess the impact if it did occur.
Step 4:   Plot on a risk matrix (see Table 3.3).

High risk items will need actions specified within the business plan. Any medium risk items may need preventative measures. For example, if the only supplier is not of the quality expected then piloting a project, or delaying more risky aspects of a project may be useful.

For lower risk items, there may also be a need to put in place monitoring mechanisms.

Scenario planning

Scenario planning is a technique where you create alternative scenarios of how the future could evolve. It requires the ability to think creatively about possible options for the company and fits well with the concept of emerging strategies outlined earlier in the book.

Table 3.3 Risk matrix

	Low impact	*Medium impact*	*High impact*
High (7–9) likelihood	Medium risk	High risk	Unacceptable risk
Medium (4–6) likelihood	Low risk	High risk	Unacceptable risk
Low (1–3) likelihood	Low risk	Medium risk	High risk

Whilst one scenario could be an extrapolation of the current situation, scenarios usually differ from forecasts in that they aim to look at other plausible futures, such as changing market conditions, mergers and acquisitions or cultural change.

Typical scenarios include:

- A do nothing option (i.e. carrying on the same in a changing future)
- The best possible case
- The worst possible case
- Technological or radical breakthroughs in thinking
- Changed market conditions
- Changes to company structure.

As an example, if the company moved from a centralised to a decentralised structure, what would the implications be for the career strategy?

SWOT (Strengths, Weaknesses, Opportunities and Threats) and PESTLE (Political, Economic, Social, Technological, Legal and Environmental) are often used as techniques for exploring the assumptions behind the scenarios and for developing the scenarios themselves.

The consequences of not having a career strategy in place

Beyond the financial measures, a useful selling point for your business case will be to focus on the consequences of not taking action – the 'do nothing' scenario.

Organisations could choose to adopt a policy to pay whatever it takes to get the right person in the right job at the right time. What could happen?

- People are not available at the right time.
- The company lacks people with the right skills.
- There is a lack of specific company knowledge.
- Difficulties are experienced in attracting talent to a company not focused on development.
- Existing talent within the company suffers from inequitable treatment and shows a greater propensity to leave.
- Commitment levels fall and performance suffers as a result.

All of these could be costed as potential consequences.

What evaluation methods are used for career development?

Some of the intended benefits and measures have been discussed earlier in this chapter and the true measure of success of any business case will be whether these benefits are realised. To do this, any business case will require a process for monitoring and evaluating success.

Evaluation of career management systems is critical in every strategy, in order to show the benefits to the business. Normally, the purpose of an evaluation exercise is to:

- Demonstrate the effectiveness of the new activities.
- Convince more sceptical areas of the organisation to increase their take-up of activities.
- Improve the quality of the activities introduced.
- Increase visibility and credibility of HR as a change agent.
- Demonstrate the bottom line impact on the business.

Yet comprehensive evaluation of career management appears is rare. Two of the main reasons why evaluation of development activity is rarely undertaken are the difficulty in quantifying the benefits derived, and the low priority evaluation is often given once a particular initiative is in place.

On first thinking about a process for evaluating career initiatives in organisations, it seemed likely that some useful parallels could be drawn to the evaluation of other HR functions, particularly to training evaluation. Measuring the success of training initiatives has a number of similarities, namely:

- It focuses on employee development.
- It can lead to attitude change.
- It needs line manager support to increase effectiveness.
- The quality of the tool has an impact on the outcome.
- It has a dual role of developing the employee in order to benefit the organisation.

However, those familiar with training evaluation will be aware that despite extensive research and literature in the field, there still appear to be few answers to how to conduct a successful evaluation. The most practiced techniques use either Hamblin's five levels (1974) or Kirkpatrick's (1975) four levels (reaction outcomes, learning outcomes, behavioural outcomes, organisational outcomes).

All but the last of Hamblin's levels focus on validation of the training process rather than evaluation as such. As a consequence, most of the evaluation that does take place is formative (i.e. it is intended to modify or improve the process) and retrospective (i.e. takes place after implementation) rather than assessing whether the benefits outweigh the costs, or the impact on the business. None the less, it is worth exploring these findings in some more detail.

Reaction level measures

The focus here is on evaluating reactions to specific career initiatives and this is by far the most common approach used. Findings from the research studies include:

- 80 per cent rated a career workbook as helpful some years later.
- Increased self-responsibility for career development actions took place following career planning workshops.
- Managers perceived significant improvements in job performance following career workshops.
- 44 per cent of managers in Fortune 500 companies found career development programmes helpful.
- 77 per cent found self-assessment materials helpful and 100 per cent found developmental assessment centres helpful.

(Research drawn from: Kotter et al. (1978); Thornton (1978); Stump (1986); Iles and Mabey (1993)).

Although these studies serve more to validate the quality of the tools than to measure their impact, there are some interesting themes which emerge about which type of initiatives are most helpful for people. Generally speaking more participative approaches, such as career reviews and career workshops are likely to be more popular than more passive techniques, such as the provision of information through resource centres, or career workbooks. This is backed up by a study of participation in career activities amongst 120 part-time MBA students by Iles and Mabey (1993).

Measuring behavioural outcomes

Research focusing more on the learning and behavioural outcomes gives a better indication of the likely benefits to organisations of career programmes. These studies often include well used measures of outcome variables, such as organisational commitment and career satisfaction.

Findings from the studies include:

- Career planning was positively correlated to career effectiveness (i.e. where individuals put plans in place they were more likely to be effective in their careers).
- Staff pursued different career paths and moved away from stereotyped progression following career interventions.
- People perceived a higher level of control over their career actions following career activities.
- Career management led to greater organisational commitment and less turnover.

- Career initiatives led to greater career resilience, insight and identity.
- People gained clarity of career objectives and greater familiarity with career options.
- Organisational commitment increased.
- Self-esteem, growth, motivation and decision making were enhanced.
- Greater achievement of career goals and enhanced job performance.
- The match between individual and organisational career plans influenced career satisfaction and organisational commitment. Participation in career programmes and availability of greater information about careers did not have an influence.
- Employees become more articulate in describing their interests goals and development needs to their managers following involvement in career initiatives.
- Career planning and career proactivity of employees link to career effectiveness (career attitudes and identity) – that is, people who took responsibility for planning and were proactive were more effective and more satisfied.
- Career initiatives led to greater career resilience and insight.
- Career commitment correlated to organisational commitment. Career commitment was enhanced by having a mentor, carrying out further education and lack of role ambiguity.
- Organisational commitment results from a clear vision of an individual's future career.

(Research drawn from Gould (1978); Hanson (1981); Veiga (1983); Burgoyne and Germain (1984); Stump (1986); Granrose & Portwood (1987); Pazy (1988); Colarelli and Bishop (1990); Noe et al. (1990); Arnold and Mackenzie-Davey (1992); London (1993)).

More recent studies include:

The Career Innovation Survey (1999) which analysed 1,000 your high-flyers from 73 countries via the Internet, to help understand their career aspirations and find out about the experience of work. 40 per cent of them said they would leave their present company within 2 years. Making them more employable, by providing a 'development contract' rather than a 'performance contract' was found to significantly impact their intention to remain in the company.

Nathan and Hill (2006) 2-year study of participants in a career development workshop were half as likely to leave the organisation as those who did not participate. The Audit commission justified training a pool of line managers in career counselling techniques by reference to savings in outplacement fees as well as the more intangible cultural shift towards encouraging development and greater commitment to people.

My own longitudinal studies into the impact of self-development focused career strategies found that providing people with a vision of the future and equitable treatment are significantly linked to career satisfaction and organisational commitment (Yarnall, 1998). This vision of the future is also highlighted in the CIPD studies (2003), which states that 'It is the sense of progression and purpose that is important, especially in linking to organisational commitment'.

So what do these studies tell us?

In terms of academic rigour, few of the studies have employed rigorous methodologies with control groups; pre–post designs and long-term follow-up of participants. However, together they certainly make a convincing case for career initiatives, with some key themes emerging:

Career strategies:
- Increase organisational commitment and as a consequence increase bottom line performance.
- Have a strong influence over employee attitudes towards their careers and their future in the organisation.

However, there is limited research to explain *which* aspects of the wide range of career development initiatives available to organisations have the most impact on increasing career satisfaction and hence, organisational commitment. Tentative conclusions from these studies suggest that encouraging career planning and mentoring have a particular impact, and the CIPD research (2003) suggest that it is not the initiatives themselves but *how* they are implemented that makes the difference.

Putting in place success measures

Setting measures for your career strategy and contracting with your stakeholders at the start of the programme will help to focus the business case on key areas of importance. These measures need to be chosen carefully, as they will influence your project.

People management (Simms, 2003) produced some useful metrics of successful talent management systems, which included:

- *Selection*
  - Are at least 72 per cent of vacancies filled internally?
  - So talented recruits make up at least 5 per cent of total recruits?

- *Retention*
  - Is the level of resignation by identified talent less than 3 per cent per year?
  - Do 95 per cent of graduates stay for longer than 3 years?
- *Development*
  - Do employees receive at least 22 hours of training per year?
- *Added Value per employee*
  - Is the organisation in the top decile of comparable companies on a measure of money added per monetary unit cost?

It might be useful to separate out your measures to focus on key stakeholder groups, such as employees, managers and the organisation. The following example builds on work by Liebowitz et al. (1986):

Employees

- Have a process to plan and manage their careers.
- Have enhanced discussions on career development with their managers.
- Can define realistic targets that match organisational needs.
- Establish a plan for their development with activities and timescales.
- Take increased responsibility for their own development.
- Have an accurate understanding of how career development procedures operate.

Managers

- Have a process to plan and manage employees careers, including setting development plans.
- Have the skills to coach staff effectively for development purposes.
- Have the required flexibility in staffing to develop staff.
- Have organisational information to help them assess whether employee goals are appropriate within the context of the organisations needs and requirements.
- Have the organisational support to assist with development needs of their staff.

Organisation

- Increase in career development discussions between managers and staff.
- Planned rather than haphazard career development with quick succession to key roles.
- Enhanced information processes for future staffing decisions, such as talent inventories.
- Increased attractiveness of the organisation to high potential staff.
- Increased satisfaction with jobs leading to increased motivation and productivity.
- Better utilisation of posts/jobs for utilising and increasing potential of staff.
- Reduced losses from key positions.
- Future skill requirements are largely met from internal resources.

Techniques such as benchmarking competitors and using the balanced score-card will also be valuable in this respect.

Case study: Establishing a new talent pool and making the business case in the *Legal Services Commission (LSC)*

Information supplied by Jenny Richardson, HR Consultant

Background

The *LSC*, is the public body responsible for legal aid. Its work is fundamental to social inclusion and access to justice. It employs 1,700 staff across England and Wales and every year helps 2 million people, some of whom are the most vulnerable in society, get the help they need to deal with their legal problems.

In 2005 the *LSC* embarked on a programme to help identify, nurture and retain high potential people within the business. It was keen to ensure that it identified a talent pipeline within the business, as well as enabling employ-ees to fulfil their potential and take responsibility for their career. The aims of the programme were to.

- Increase the range and flexibility of skills in the organisation.
- Create a pool of people capable of driving change programmes and shaping and delivering the *LSC* of the future.
- Improve the ability to promote from within and reduce reliance on the external market.
- Create a more appealing career development structure so that the best people want to stay.
- Create a more open and transparent approach to career development and progression opportunities.

By early 2006, the organisation had completed a comprehensive assessment process and 11 people were selected to be part of the first talent pool. The programme is overseen by a group of six senior directors, known as the *talent panel*.

The assessment process

At the start of the process, briefings were carried out across the organisation to explain the talent programme and what would be involved. Individuals had to gain the support of their line manager in order to put themselves for-ward. In total, 90 people both wanted to apply and secured the required sup-port of their line manager.

Each of the applicants had to complete a competency based application form outlining their key achievements, what they saw as the main issues facing the organisation and why they wanted to be on the talent programme.

Fifty applicants were successful at this stage and attended a launch event. This outlined:

- What to expect at the talent centre?
- What they needed to do to prepare?
- What would happen in the event of selection or non-selection to the talent pool?
- What they could expect from the programme, if successful?

The aim was to get participants thinking more seriously about the process, allowing them to self-select out if the timing and implications of attendance were prohibitive and to get them to consider the risks and plan for different outcomes.

The talent centre was designed and run with Roffey Park Management Institute and the criteria used at the centre drew on Yapp's (2005) model for assessing high performance. Three particular competencies were given particular weighting in the process:

1. emotional agility
2. strategic agility
3. learning agility.

The talent centre was a bespoke 2-day event with group exercises, 1:1 interviews and skill sessions using actors. At the end of the centre, the assessors, who included members of the talent panel, reviewed the performance of each individual and decided on their eligibility for the programme. One of the Directors who sat on the panel commented 'The candidates I saw on the programme were very professional, well prepared, and were a credit to themselves and the *LSC*'.

See LSC *Talent centre: Exercise X competency matrix in next page*

One of the aspects candidates needed to do in preparation was to complete a learning log, which would provide a measure on the centre. This focus on people's commitment to learning was found to be a good stimulus to shifting the culture in the organisation towards self-managed development.

The initial programme put through 50 individuals, with the aim of only taking those who met or exceeded the criteria defined by the talent panel. As part of their planning assumptions, the *LSC* estimated that 20 individuals would be successful. In the event, 11 people were successful. Whilst this was less than it anticipated, the *LSC* was clear that it was not going to compromise.

LSC Talent centre: Exercise x competency matrix

	Test	IV 1	IV 2	Ex 1 Meet chair of SCA	Ex 2 Meet Manager of Unit	Ex 3 Presentation to Head of Directorate	Ex 4 Group Meeting	Ex 5 Strategy Document	Ex 6 Learning log
Set direction				X		X		X	
Think strategically*	X	X				X	X	X	
Learn and improve*			X						X
Lead and F Change		X			X	X			
Deliver results		X		X	X		X		
Working with others				X	X	X	X		
Decision making		X					X	X	
Emotional* intelligence			X	X					

*Competency is given additional weighting

In hindsight, it believes this was the right decision and has contributed to the overall success and high quality of the programme.

Although the main purpose was assessment, at the end of the selection process, all participants, whether successful or unsuccessful, were given comprehensive feedback by one of the assessors at the centre and a written report highlighting their key development areas and performance. Individuals then took responsibility for formulating their personal development plan, in conjunction with their line manager and each had help in planning their personal and career development. One of the unsuccessful candidates commented 'Thank you for allowing me to experience the talent centre. I thoroughly enjoyed it and found it to be very demanding, but also very rewarding. I got a lot out of the whole process and will certainly use the experiences in my career going forward'.

The talent panel

The talent panel are a key component of the process for managing talent. The panel consists of six directors, two of which are from the Executive Team. The members of the panel all have respect, influence and a high profile across the organisation and are enthusiastic about the approach to talent management.

The role of this group is:

- to be advocates for the talent programme,
- to play a key role in the initial selection process,
- to support the on-going development of the talent pool,
- to monitor the talent pool progress.

Whilst Jenny Richardson facilitates the process for HR, she is clear that the programme should be seen as an organisational initiative. 'It is genuinely not owned by HR' she reported 'and while that means there are more stakeholders to manage, the value that comes from top-level ownership is immense and a key part of the success'.

As the programme progresses (another intake is taking place in 2007) the talent panel is to meet quarterly to review whether the programme is meeting the business need as well as the individual needs.

The talent strategy

The strategy in the *LSC* clearly adopts a self-managed approach to development, which is supported by the organisation. Whilst the organisation was keen to retain the message that all staff should and would continue to be trained and developed, those in the pool were given greater access and funding for activities.

Because the organisation is changing rapidly, what are now viewed as critical roles may not exist in the future. Hence, a strategy based on succession to particular roles was not seen as appropriate. The talent pool were asked to aim their development two bands higher than their current role and to focus on generic knowledge, skills and competency at that level.

The process of selection was very transparent, with individuals and their managers fully briefed on the criteria for success.

Having been selected to the pool, individuals were given access to:

■ a coach
■ a mentor
■ an executive sponsor.

The individuals themselves chose who they want for each role and when and how they used them. Each member of the pool also had a comprehensive 1:1 with an executive coach at the start of their development. The purpose of this conversation was to help them focus on what they wanted from the programme and how they could best go about getting their needs met.

The next step in each person' development is tailored to his or her needs and preferences. He or she is given greater access to senior people and opportunities, such as projects, training, work shadowing and secondments, but are expected to initiate these for themselves. Effective networking is therefore a key component of the programme.

Individuals remain on the programme for 2 years, although the talent panel can remove people if they are not seen to be progressing as expected.

The business case

To gain approval for the talent programme, Jenny had to put together a comprehensive case. This focused on the business drivers for the programme, its strategic fit, the objectives of the programme, likely benefits and key risks.

George Lepine, Director of HR at the *LSC*, is clear that producing the business case was critical to the success of the programme, 'Too often, organisations launch talent management programmes because they are "the thing to do". More often than not in these situations, the programme will fail. By establishing at the start why we were doing this, what we hoped to achieve and identifying the main risks, it meant that we could quantify the business benefits and measure the overall success of the programme'.

The key tools used in this case included stakeholder analysis, options appraisal, cost-benefit analysis, risk assessments and benefits realisation. Some extracts from the case are shown here.

Extracts from the Business Case

Business needs and drivers

- Change Programme requires set of people with a range of flexible skills – strong feedback from senior management is we do not have enough people within the organisation who meet this need
- Staff Survey data shows general dissatisfaction with career development (e.g. 67 per cent disagree or are indifferent to the statement 'my career development needs are being met' – 2005)

Key stakeholders

Stakeholder/group	Interest in project
Senior Leadership Group (inc. Exec. Team)	Will be the group with the knowledge of what future opportunities exist and ability to offer these to those on the programme Potential coaches/mentors/sponsors Potential assessors
Line managers	Will be required to complete Talent Audit. Applying for the programme could affect motivation levels and so work performance of those who work for them. Getting onto the programme may ultimately mean their best people moving out of their department
HR Managers	Will need to provide support to those going through the process and to line managers. Potential assessors
Talent Panel	Strategic 'owners' of project

Risk Assessment

Risk	Likelihood	Impact	Actions
Not enough applications	M	H	■ Widespread communications via Intranet, noticeboards, emails and through HR Managers. ■ Direct targeting of people Talent Panel/ Project Manager think should apply.
Lack of buy-in from around the business (esp. line managers)	M	M	■ Widespread communications to publicise benefits of programme. ■ Ongoing communications to highlight progress of project, and of individuals. ■ Communication of what we expect from line managers.
Negative impact on morale for those not selected	M	M	■ Encourage individuals to think about consequences and impact of not getting on the programme. ■ Ensure talent centres are positive experience (through setting of atmosphere). ■ Ensure detailed feedback given to individuals. Encourage those giving feedback to adopt a future focus. ■ Follow-up with individuals six months after talent centres

■ Implementation with Change Programme will inevitably affect motivation levels and retention. We need to create a more appealing career development structure so our very best people want to stay
■ Over-reliance on external market to recruit, especially to senior levels
■ Need for an open and transparent approach to career development and opportunities. A number of secondment/project opportunities, particularly in central departments, are recruited to by targeting a particular individual without selection. This creates issues over equal opportunities and dissatisfaction from around the organisation.

Initial outcomes

Jenny Richardson is 'thrilled' with the progress on talent management. When it was first introduced the concept of picking out a special group of talent filled many managers with horror but it is now an accepted part of the business.

Although the talent pool has only been in place for 6 months, there has already been a notable increase in performance and confidence levels within the group. This has led to more effective dealings across the organisation, particularly at a senior level. As business critical projects arise, there is now a pool of people to select from to lead and participate in them.

The *LSC* has also monitored motivation levels amongst the non-selected groups and there has been no significant difference to the control groups (i.e. those not part of talent management) in place. Many benefited considerably from the feedback they received and enjoyed the process. They are also eligible to re-apply in future years and now have a clear development plan to work from.

On-going challenges

Line manager concerns

Despite briefing line managers throughout the process, one of the key challenges to overcome is a concern by some managers that their talented people will be lost to other parts of the business. To help overcome this, Jenny is planning to involve line managers for the next cohort of talent at the launch event and engage more on a face-to-face basis with managers to ensure their commitment and understanding.

Pressures to make the programme more structured

Due to the high focus on tailored, individual development plans for the talent pool, there is a concern amongst some people in the organisation that the programme is benefiting the individual more than the organisation. Jenny is looking at whether or not there are core elements that could form the basis of the programme and, if so, how to implement these whilst retaining a highly individual focus.

Balancing support with challenge

One of the advantages of being in the talent pool is that the *LSC* provides more active support for development. However, there is also a clear expectation that the individual owns the responsibility for making things happen. This raises some interesting challenges, when the talent panel or HR have been in a position to remove barriers for individuals, but also want the individual to take steps to remove barriers for themselves. This balance between supporting the individual and empowering them is an interesting tension.

Jenny is clear with the talent group that 'they may need to pioneer a new way of working and lead the way in changing the culture'. One example of this was a manager who recognised the need to have closer links with London as the head office but did not want to relocate to do this. It is possible that they may need to pioneer greater home working, or location-sharing roles, to get this need met. The talent programme can provide the resources and support, but expects the individuals to take the lead on making this happen.

Summary

Developing a sound business case is critical to the future success of career strategies. It is not just the document and justification itself that is useful, but the process of developing the business case and engaging key stakeholders is vital to ensure future buy-in. Often this process is over-looked and strategists work in isolation, or with external benchmarks, to develop a sound argument and put measures in place. However, to get active sponsorship for your career strategy and ensure effective implementation, investing time up-front engaging with stakeholders and debating options and approaches is essential.

Evidence from a wide variety of research studies indicates that career strategies clearly lead to productivity and profit improvements for organisations as well as increased shareholder returns. This is generally achieved by improving morale, motivation and commitment to the companies through a culture more focused on career development and maximising potential. My experience suggests that senior managers outside of HR are rarely aware of the extent of bottom line evidence existing and it is well worth educating senior teams on this front.

Gaining acceptance for your business case is not easy. Career development is traditionally seen as a 'soft' practice and as such the business benefits and bottom line impact needs to be spelt out loudly and clearly. Some of the evidence from the research studies outlined in the chapter is useful to help strengthen your case. More importantly though, you need to engage with a wide group of people to both educate them on the benefits and explore different approaches. Mapping your stakeholders and getting a more detailed understanding of their interest and influence can help you here.

Structuring your business case will depend on your organisation and may include tools such as situation analysis, risk analysis and scenario planning as well as financial measures such as cost-benefit analysis. The Executive Summary is a key aspect of your written case as often this is the page that is referred to and read the most. It needs to compel the decision makers to take the actions you recommend and it is well worth investing time developing clear and influential arguments. Expanding on the consequences and costing the 'do nothing' option is also a good way to sell your case.

Thought also needs to be given as to how to evaluate the success of your strategy and what measures you will put in place to monitor progress. The evidence from the numerous evaluation studies which have taken place is that more participative career processes have more impact and measures which look at the impact from different perspectives within the organisation are the most useful.

Checklist

- Do people understand the vision you have for your career strategy?
- How does the strategy link with the goals of the organisation?
- Are the business benefits clear?
- Have you established clear measures of success?
- Have you outlined the possible risks involved?
- Do you have the skills and competence required to deliver the strategy?
- Are senior managers aware of the strong research links between career strategies and bottom line results?
- How compelling is your executive summary?
- Have you mapped your stakeholder's influence, commitment and interest?
- Have you thought through the potential problems stakeholders will present?
- Are you tailoring your style to suit your audience?
- Do you really believe the business case yourself?
- What are your strongest arguments and are you communicating these effectively?
- In reading your business case, what would a critic pick up on?
- Are the consequences of doing nothing clear?
- How are you going to evaluate the success of your strategy?
- Have you got a diverse range of success measures?

4

Revitalising Your Succession Management

Succession management is a key component of an effective career strategy. Not only does it help the organisation to position itself for the future, but it also signals to employees that their careers are taken seriously.

Approaches to succession planning have changed dramatically in recent years. Traditionally, large companies adopted replacement strategies, with 'under the bus lists' to manage succession to key posts and top management positions. Often this process was highly structured, with top down, confidential schemes aimed at replacing forthcoming vacancies with similar sets of skills and experience.

This approach worked quite well in an environment where there were stable systems, with unchanging structures and roles. However, there was a tendency for it to become a form filling exercise once a year. Coca Cola famously discarded their process when they found 250 000 hours a year were spent filling in forms (Simms, 2003). So with flatter structures, fast changing companies and less predictable futures, a more flexible and adaptive approach has come to the fore.

This chapter aims to explore the current trends in succession management. It covers the benefits of such strategies and the practicalities of introducing a more comprehensive approach. In particular it seeks to answer the questions:

- What is succession management?
- What benefits does it bring to a career strategy?
- What are the current trends in succession management?
- How do you measure demand and supply?
- What input should individual's have?
- How can information technology help?
- What are the criteria for success?

What is succession management?

Definitions of succession management vary, with succession planning often used to describe the process of identifying a particular successor for a post, and succession management covering a broader set of activities which ensure a suitable supply of successors for key positions. Rothwell (2001) defines succession management as 'a deliberate and systematic effort by an organisation to ensure leadership continuity in key positions, retain and develop intellectual and knowledge capital for the future, and encourage individual advancement'.

Succession planning can take a number of different forms. Hirsh (2000) identifies four different approaches:

1. *As and when succession planning*: Here vacant posits are dealt with as and when they arise, with very little planning.
2. *One step or job layer succession*: In this approach successors for one job step ahead are identified and the focus is on readiness for promotion to the next level.
3. *Planned development or 'layer and slice' succession*: Here a small group of possible successors are identified as having long-term potential for a targeted layer of jobs. Both post and people plans are taken account of in this approach.
4. *Developing potential*: The focus here is on creating a diverse and high quality pool of employee talent. This is a more person-centred approach.

With the exception of as and when succession, the main activities which form the basis of succession management are illustrated in Figure 4.1. The process is about matching up the likely future demand with the likely supply and taking steps to minimise the gap between the two, both through a focus on developing people for the future and by restructuring role requirements and optimising organisational design.

As mentioned earlier in this book, carrying out some form of succession planning has been found to have a positive impact on a companies Return on Investment

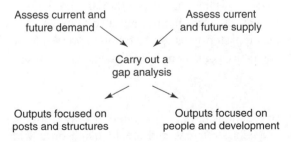

Figure 4.1 Key succession processes

and is a crucial part of the overall career strategy. Often, in a desire to identify high potential employees and focus on their development for the future, the critical demand for particular roles and the degree to which jobs are critical to the future can be overlooked. Many of the companies researched for this book were enthusiastic about the people side of managing talent, but spoke very little about integrating this with the harder role-focused aspects.

Whilst the role-focused elements of succession planning are perhaps more difficult to predict in organisations than the people skills, if organisations are to link the development of their talent with business needs, then it is essential that both sides of the equation are examined.

Succession planning can achieve a number of objectives, including:

- *Improved selection activity*: Succession planning provides a database facility which enables a broader search for candidates when a vacancy arises and enables faster decisions to be made. In addition, having a clear succession system is likely to encourage external applicants as the company is seen to support career development.
- *Ensuring more focused development*: By having a clearer picture of the future organisational requirements, development experiences can be focused appropriately and career paths for high potential employees can ensure exposure to the areas required by the company. This more focused development helps to integrate both the needs of the organisation and that of the individual, aiding long-term retention of talent.
- *Encouraging cultural change*: By spelling out what is required by the company in the future, those behaviours, values and sets of skills and experience receive a greater focus from the workforce. If for example a company establishes a need for innovative thinking in the future that is not in place in the current skill-set of the workforce, there is a greater likelihood that people will begin to develop and focus on those skills.
- *Monitoring progress and diversity goals*: Succession plans allow a company to monitor the progress of talent and accelerate the development of key individuals if required. This constant monitoring also helps to ensure that as people leave the organisation, stop-gaps can be found to prevent losses in productivity. It also enables diversity goals to be monitored and actions taken to address any imbalance.

In recent years organisations have begun to move away from one-step succession planning or replacement strategies and are focusing on a wider population of potential future leaders and linking more closely with other initiatives such as the identification of talent or development strategies. This wider form of succession management is therefore focused on the development of key people and identification of key posts, rather than form filling. Strategies focusing on pools of people and potential are what Byham et al. (2002) refer to as 'acceleration pools'.

Moving from replacement strategies to career acceleration pools

In the more traditional replacement strategies, an individual manager tended to identify and groom a particular replacement for a position. Typically this person would be given greater responsibility and exposure to help position them for the role in the future.

These quite formal succession planning systems were often seen as just a paper exercise which managers paid lip service to, with the successors nominated in the plan ignored when the post became vacant. Often the information in succession plans was based on subjective judgements and could be coloured by personal agendas (Hirsh, 1997). This view is backed up by the survey research which indicated that many prestigious companies had low 'hit rates': that is, few of the nominated successors were placed in the posts as they became vacant.

Even if it is implemented well, this process, apart from having questionable compliance with equal opportunities legislation, can only work where there are relatively static structures and environments. With the rapidly changing nature of organisations and constant emerging requirements, this method of grooming people for a future, which extrapolates from the present day, is becoming less and less relevant.

The acceleration pool approach to succession planning focuses less on particular people or jobs and more on pools of people and generic future needs. Acceleration pools are groups of high potential individuals, who are likely to be suited to a range of possible executive jobs in the future. Typically, this group receive accelerated development through stretching roles and project assignments. These opportunities offer key experience and skills development as well as visibility at a senior level, so that progress can be tracked. Members of the pool often receive more training and are likely to have a mentor or coach. These pools are given various names ranging from 'talent pools' through to 'High Potential (HIPO) groups'.

Where this is different from replacement strategies is that instead of focusing on existing gaps in succession, there is a greater focus on the future needs of the organisation and organisations are focusing more on the skills and competencies needed for the future, in order for the company to position itself competitively in the marketplace.

Boudreau and Ramstad (2005) refer to these groups as 'pivotal talent pools' or groups of people for which small improvement yield large returns. Having identified these pools, different strategic objectives can be applied, be they reward strategies, performance management or career and development opportunities.

It could be argued that this focus on broad groups of people is not new to career strategies. For many years now, many organisations have begun to group their job roles into 'job families', which have common skills and competencies. These job families are often used to help illustrate progression through and across the organisation and as a basis for reward policies. Where acceleration pools differ however, is that they are a sub-set of these larger families, with the potential to move upwards through the organisation at a faster rate.

The practicalities of acceleration pools are discussed in more detail in the next chapter, although it is worth saying here that the size of the pool depends on the number of executive positions, the speed of change and the number of high potential employees. More complex organisations sometimes choose to have a number of pools either hierarchically or functionally based.

The key differences that stand out from more traditional approaches to succession are illustrated more clearly in Table 4.1.

A shift from organisational needs to a more balanced approach

Replacement succession planning was focused predominantly on organisational needs. The system would involve examining likely vacancies due to retirement, resignation or structural change and matching that with the existing capabilities and readiness of the workforce. Acceleration pools, however, work on the principle that individual needs and aspirations will be taken into account in any decisions that are made. The psychological contract described earlier in this book is often made explicit, and options and compromises are more openly discussed. Many of the companies have mechanisms for individuals to input to the process and state preferences and constraints on their development.

Table 4.1 Comparing replacement and pool succession planning

From replacement planning	*To acceleration pools*
Organisational needs predominate	Balance of organisation and individual needs
Focused development	Broader range of development
Focus on jobs	Focus on roles
Hidden/secretive process	Greater transparency
Led by HR	Led by the business
Annual event	On-going, more frequent process
Projections of future needs	Predictions of future needs
All senior positions examined	Lynchpin positions and trends
Inflexible and bureaucratic	Flexible and dynamic

A wider range of developmental approaches

As the focus for a particular acceleration pool is on development for the next broad level, the focus is more on developing a range of skills and competencies rather than specific specialisms. Coupled with this, there is an increasing acceptance that progression can be made by lateral moves and project challenges as well as by upward movement through the hierarchy and if organisations make the purposes of such opportunities clear, then this type of career development will continue to grow in number.

The emphasis with acceleration pools is on changing and developing skills and behaviours vital to the future success of both the individual and the business. The development plans and growth opportunities are therefore likely to continually benefit both parties. With replacement succession planning, the development is more likely to be role based and provide a single route which may or not lead to the intended outcome. As a consequence, the pool approach carries less risk for both the individual and the organisation.

A focus on roles rather than jobs

In the current world of work it is becoming increasingly difficult to predict the specific jobs that will be needed in the future. As a result, the focus has shifted to examining the types of roles that might be required. Will there, for example, be a need for maintenance engineers in the next 5 years, or will there be increased demand for partnership or relationship managers? This broader analysis of requirements can be very helpful in opening up a dialogue about future skill needs.

Greater transparency

As the acceleration pool approach does not raise the question of individuals being in line for a particular job, it is also easier to give the process greater transparency and be open with individuals. Many organisations choose to share with people how their potential is viewed and the types of skills and competencies they need to be developing to put themselves in the best position for future opportunities. Effective and on-going feedback is therefore an essential part of the process.

As mentioned in Chapter 2, communicating high potential status to employees can increase their retention and development efforts. This open contract about performance will encourage participation and commitment rather than the more traditional confidential succession plans. Problems can arise however with the rating of potential and ideally there should be manager guidelines to help support the ratings and conversations with high potentials, to ensure consistency in the communication processes.

More ownership from the business beyond HR

Taking away the emphasis on replacing specific jobs has also made it easier to engage line managers in the process. It is more typical with the acceleration pool approach to see line manager ownership, often led by the CEO, with active facilitation and support from HR. The HR support comes from encouraging managers to think through their future requirements and opportunities more broadly and to identify and take stock of talent progressing through the organisation in an objective way. Many organisations involve senior stakeholders in assessment centres to rate talent for themselves and familiarise them with the criteria for selection.

It is worth bearing in mind Hall's work (1989) which identifies a number of conditions which contribute to the success of succession planning. Many of these related to the culture of the organisation and the style of management such as:

- communication of the succession planning strategy,
- training for managers on the processes,
- rewards for developmental managers,
- inter-unit co-operation.

To gain ownership at the top, the system must be seen as credible and be easily workable.

More frequent discussions

Popoff (1996) suggests that organisations need to create an environment of continuous successions thinking, instead of annual succession planning. Historically people would often block development positions to ensure that the job holder was able to perform to a high standard as soon as they took on the position. With more creative discussions it is possible to ensure that people are moved around to avoid this happening and managers are rewarded for doing so. This would lead to more appropriate levels of turnover in key positions.

The evidence suggests that companies are starting to do this and succession planning conversations are becoming twice yearly, or even quarterly events.

Greater attention to business critical areas

With replacement strategies, the common approach was to plan succession for all of the top two or three tiers of the organisation. Current strategies however are more likely to focus in on key positions which are critical to the business and ensure that there is a pipeline of talent to these core areas. This is an issue we will return to later in this chapter.

Greater flexibility

The framework needs to be flexible enough to enable parts of the process to be adapted in the face of business changes. Although business pressures often have a short-term focus, succession planning requires a longer-term outlook and to be successful people must be allowed to learn and there must be a culture which tolerates failure. As we shall see in the next chapter, ideally acceleration pools need clear entry and exit criteria which will enable people to make transitions in the face of change.

Fast-track thinking

The new approach to succession and a focus on pools of talent raises questions for many organisations about the impact of focusing on an elite group of people. This was a topic that was discussed in more detail in Chapter 2.

Many organisations, such as Siemens, strongly believe that all people have talent and talent strategies should not focus on small groups of people towards the top of the organisation. If the pool approach is taken, care needs to be taken to ensure that employees outside of the pool are also able to access development opportunities and feel they have a fair and equitable system for managing their own careers. Without this, you are likely to demotivate and reduce performance in the workforce.

It is interesting looking at the case studies in this book, that whilst most companies put forward a message about development for all employees, most also had a clear strategy for focusing in on-core groups of employees. What this suggests is that the messages put forward are carefully communicated and understood.

Acceleration pools have a number of potential advantages over traditional replacement strategies. For example:

- Pool members are generally more committed to their development and have a greater understanding of what they need to achieve for the business.
- Individual growth is tailored to individual requirements rather than a future role enabling a number of future options to be viable rather than just one.
- There is less bureaucracy and growth opportunities are more flexible.
- Development is more closely linked to organisational needs.
- Support is generally available to help maximise individual potential.
- Roles and responsibilities are clearer.
- Line management are in the driving seat.

However, the focus on jobs has not disappeared in its entirety. Whilst it is difficult to predict future needs in some organisations, particularly high technology companies, there is still a need to make predictions about future demand in some way.

93

The role of manpower planning

Every organisation needs to improve efficiency and make the best possible use of its resources and a key part of succession management is understanding the future demand and supply of employees. If this is done accurately, the manpower plan will be able to determine future recruitment levels; anticipate redundancies and thus avoid unnecessary dismissals; determine training and developmental needs; control labour costs and also assist with the collective bargaining process.

Many organisations take a short-term view of labour and will react to a labour shortage by carryout out-frenzied recruitment campaigns, increasing overtime or subcontracting tasks. This creates obvious problems in that the quality of the people recruited is likely to be a poor fit to the company and will lead to higher turnover at a later date. Disputes may also arise over pay differentials due to the need to pay higher salaries to entice people to join.

Conversely, when a company is faced with a surplus it will reduce any temporary or contract staff, put a hold on external recruitment and increase wastage through early retirement programmes and costly redundancies. Often, this results in the better staff being lost to other companies and leads to low morale within the organisation.

Manpower planning attempts to minimise these costs by forecasting the future demand, assessing the supply available from both within and outside the company, determining organisational requirements and monitoring the utilisation of people resources.

Assessing the demand

Part of the difficulty of demand planning is that the futures of organisations are increasingly difficult to predict. Some sophisticated technological tools exist within companies for forecasting this information, but the quality of the data will be dependent on the dialogue between business managers and those gathering the data. The long-term business strategy and the likely scenarios that impact this will be the starting point for this conversation. For example, will government policies, emerging markets, economic forecasts or new technology impact the business and the future demand requirements?

To be meaningful, any estimation of future demand will need to be segmented by skills, level, location, by number and by business unit. Table 4.2 details some of the typical quantitative data which is gathered by organisations to help them to assess future demand.

It will also be important to take into account qualitative information such as:

- What are the current skills and competence of the workforce?
- What will be the future skill requirements?

Table 4.2 Quantitative data typically required for a demand forecast

Current data	Future predictions
Employee headcount by location	Will locations change?
Demographics	What demographics are forecasted?
Age	Internal targets
Gender	External population
Ethnicity	
Disability	
Part-time/flexible workers	
Functions	What functional changes are likely?
Numbers and levels	What effect will business strategy have on structures?
Benchmarks and ratios	Are there future targets for ratios and benchmarks?

- What training and development takes place?
- What are the predicted future training and development needs?

Benchmarks and ratios can be useful tools to help aid these future predictions. Benchmarks involve making comparisons with other organisations or processes, whereas ratios compare the relationship between two factors, such as the number of sales staff per sale or the number of HR staff per workforce. For example, if the future strategy predicts an increase in sales, or headcount, then the knock-on effects on sales and HR staff can be determined by applying the same ratio. Many of the traditional forecasting methods, such as time series analysis and ratio trend analysis, have fallen into disuse as companies have less confidence in their predictive ability. Time series analysis uses a set of observed values taken from data of the previous years or months, to ascertain whether there is a connection between the variables studied. For example, the number of computer operators employed in each month in the last 2 years could be graphically represented to show a steadily rising trend which can be projected into the future.

IBM believe that this focus on both where the requirement is and how to develop it has contributed to the company's strong financial performance in recent years and given them a strong reputation for developing leaders, which in turn has helped them attract more talent (Chief Executive, 2002).

Identifying business critical roles

In carrying out the assessment of future demand, it will also be useful to determine which areas of the business are critical and therefore likely to be needed in some form in the future. The case study at the end of this chapter highlights the process used in a large transport company for identifying business critical roles. The starting point for this process is to agree a set of criteria to assess against. In the case study example, the criteria 'knowledge that is specific to the business and does not exist in the open market' was deemed to be one of the important factors.

Conger and Fulmer (2003) suggest that identifying and monitoring the pipeline for linchpin positions is one of the five most critical roles for succession management (the others being a focus on development, transparency, measuring progress and keeping it flexible). They describe these linchpin positions as jobs that are essential to the organisation. These may be difficult to fill positions, have a high impact on the company, or reside in critical business areas. By monitoring these roles, the company can help to ensure an adequate supply of talent to these roles in the future.

IBM has developed a talent process focused on four key leadership areas seen as business critical.

1. General managers
2. Country general managers
3. Technical general managers
4. Business value selling.

The company carried out research to define the experiences, competencies and derailment factors critical to each role. This enabled them to deliver developmental experiences in a more focused way.

Assessing the supply

In order to forecast the supply of manpower, you need to carry out an audit of the existing resources in the company. To be of any use, this analysis of supply of people to the business needs to match the criteria used for assessing demand. Consequently, supply estimates will normally be broken down by skills, level, location, by number and by business unit. Often companies produce skills inventories to show a profile for employees, which contain their skills, abilities, experience and education. Typical information that is contained will be:

- Personal details
- Current post
- Career history
- Qualifications and relevant training
- Performance and potential assessments
- Skills, competencies

- Characteristics: strengths and weaknesses
- Timing for a job move
- Career preferences
- Mobility.

The information needs to be readily available to people and also easily retrievable. Often problems can arise through record systems being inadequate and out of date, or records being held in a number of different departments with no standardisation of how the information is kept.

In addition to making predictions about future requirements, organisations need to factor in turnover rates. To do this accurately, organisations also need to be looking at their vacancy risk (i.e. the likelihood that people in business critical roles will leave the organisation). In the case study at the end of this chapter, the company set some clear criteria to analyse the vacancy risk in key positions, such as how attractive the external market is to the individual. Demand predictions will therefore also gather data on non-statistical information, such as the local amenities and housing availability and the number of competitors moving into or out of the area, in order to assess the attractiveness of the organisation to employees.

As the analysis and predictions of your internal labour market are influenced to a large extent by the external market, you will also need to make some external predictions about your market and sector. The external supply estimates will give an indication of the ease in which organisations can fill posts, particularly in occupational groups with a scarce supply. Environmental scanning is a technique that can help with this.

Environmental scanning

Environmental scanning produces projections based on the labour market. As an example, the current working population of Great Britain is currently about 35 million, of which 52 per cent are men. As mentioned earlier in this book however, this population is ageing and by 2011 the number of people aged over 45 years is predicted to increase by 3.4 million as the baby-boomers mature; the 35–45-year-old population will be relatively unchanged and the 24–25-year-olds will fall by 1.6 million due to the declining birth rate. This data would be factored into any projections about availability.

Scanning relies heavily on statistical data such as the census; population densities within the area; unemployment levels; the pattern of migration; the age structure of the population; etc.

Scanning also focuses on the quality of people available in the labour market. For example, analysing occupational trends will give an indication of the quality of available people. Trends in recent years have been a rise in the number of managerial and professional qualifications, a decline in administrative and secretarial roles and a rise in customer service and sales. Many organisations look to university statistics to assess the number of potentially qualified people coming through into the labour market.

Other statistical techniques for assessing supply include wastage rate calculations, which take the number of people leaving the company over a period divided by the average number employed. The percentage wastage can be analysed to give a wastage curve for different segments of employees, such as the talent group, or people in a particular age band. Survival curves can also be used to show the relationship between turnover and length of service in different groups.

How much input should individuals have?

The move towards psychological contracting for careers suggests that employees should have a much higher level of control and input into the succession planning process. McCartney and Garrow (2006) highlights some key questions that need to be answered:

- Are people nominated, or can they self-nominate to acceleration pools?
- How much information are they given on their potential rating?
- How explicit are the criteria for selection to the talent pool?
- Are they expected to plan their next move or will the organisation do that?
- What impact will it have on their career if they are not a member of the pool?

Whilst organisations have become more open, with increased use of 360-degree feedback, self-assessment tools and personal development planning, the degree to which high potential staff are briefed on the organisational position is still very variable.

The *Legal Services Commission*, who recently introduced a programme to assess potential managers for a new talent pool, chose to be very open about the scheme and encouraged people to explore whether it was right for them and what the implications might be.

Linking succession planning with other processes

In many organisations, this more open, pool-based style of succession planning is very clearly linked to leadership development. Having identified a pool of people for accelerated development, there is often a management training programme or some form of formal learning and development that accompanies participants continued growth. Talent assessment centres themselves are often used to help diagnose generic needs for the high potential population.

Cap Gemini Ernst and Young provide openly available training and development opportunities to all employees. These include lunchtime master-classes in topics such as the latest products in the market. They also have a talent management scheme used to spot Vice Presidents, of which there are 120 in the UK. Management teams pick candidates whom they believe have the potential for future growth. The board inspects the nominees and the successful candidates are assigned a mentor and develop an individual development plan.

However, although management training goes some way to developing future leaders, it does not deliver the range of experience they require for future leadership roles. Succession management also needs to closely align with organisational design activities to be able to deliver more tailored, pro-active career development for its most talented individuals and align this with business needs. Often this essential strategic analysis is missing from succession planning. In smaller organisations in particular, where opportunities to move jobs are limited, re-designing jobs can be a vital tool in sustaining career satisfaction.

Where companies make a more obvious link is with selection processes. Ideally, the information coming from succession plans should be constantly feeding into selection decisions. Some companies do this particularly well and there are examples of companies deliberately bringing in talent with a scarce skill at low levels of the organisation to ensure that there is a sufficient stock for future needs which have been identified.

Use of technology

Technology is increasingly being used to support and aid career processes, particularly around succession and job opportunities. Talent management software can potentially reduce the cost of recruitment, training and administration. A report in HR Zone (21 September 2006) argues that talent software has three key benefits:

1. A reduction in the cost of recruitment, as the company can identify good candidates faster and wastes less time on interviewing.
2. The time taken to identify a vacancy of skills gap should be shorter, thereby improving productivity.
3. Improved quality of selection due to greater clarification of needs.

The report suggests that companies need to weigh up the benefits of bespoke talent software against an integrated suite. If for example an organisation already has a SAP system, then integration will probably more cost effective than a bespoke talent software vendor. Either type of software will usually have reporting tools which allow managers to gain access a person's job function, abilities, training records and contribution towards the wider business goals.

Eli Lilly (in McCartnery & Garrow) have developed a global talent database. Employees are required to fill in a one-page document covering their qualifications, experience, career aspirations and the next two or three likely career moves. The organisation keeps this information, along with their performance management document, 360-degree assessment and development plan on the database. Searches can then be made to find how many people are tracking key positions. They have found that this is an essential aid to succession management and talent spotting.

However, there are implications with storing information for succession systems on computer and data protection legislation means that any information kept on individuals must be made available to them on request. Whilst sensitive data can be coded and the codes kept secure, to help ensure security some of the softer data, such as opinions or assessments are usually held manually.

Case study: Revitalising succession management in a large transport company (anon)

Background

A large transport company introduced a new strategy in 2004, which aimed 'to identify, develop, deploy and retain talent in the company to ensure on-going business success'.

At that time the processes used for succession planning were haphazard and lacked credibility. There were no company wide standards, with different approaches being used in different parts of the business. Whilst there was a replacement planning process used in some areas, where succession planning did occur, the need was usually championed by the HR group and not the business. As a consequence, there was limited commitment or buy-in to the succession process.

The company set up a Talent Management Project Team to help influence and gain support and involvement for the future succession of talent through the business. They established a two-staged project. Firstly, they wanted to understand the specific needs for talent across the business and assess the risk associated with that. The second phase was to determine an approach to be used by looking at questions such as: 'What is meant by talent?', 'Who is talented?' and 'How should these needs be met?'.

Stage one: Understanding the need

As a first step the team analysed the effectiveness of the existing process for the 240 managers in the leadership population. This involved:

- A review of the previous years succession plans and coverage.
- Identifying the percentage of posts with one or more successors.
- Analysing which roles were business critical.
- Carrying out a vacancy risk review.

What soon became clear was that the replacement strategy in place was not appropriate given the rapidly changing nature of the business. It was found to be highly bureaucratic and secretive, with data being produced that was rarely acted on when it came to decision making. More worrying, the review found that about 50 per cent of the management roles did not have successors identified.

Determining which roles were business critical

Whilst all management roles were seen as critical, the project team were keen to ensure that particular roles were identified as business critical. To help this process each area of the business was asked to establish criteria and identify their own business critical roles. These sets of criteria were then shared and amalgamated to provide a final criteria listing for businesses to rank against.

The criteria decided upon were:

- Knowledge that is hard to compete for in the external market.
- Knowledge that is specific to the business that doesn't exist in the open market.
- A point of contact for key external relationships.
- Critical role in a crisis situation.
- Key to business objective or operational effectiveness.

This process led to 25 roles being identified as business critical, and analysis of these roles indicated that existing replacement planning had only a 22 per cent succession coverage in terms of people being identified for the roles in the future.

Carrying out a vacancy risk review

The project team also carried out a vacancy risk review. This review was a rather more subjective process than the role review as it involved making some assumptions about people in the business. The intention was to assess the likelihood of key people (i.e. those in business critical roles) leaving the business. Both line managers and HR Business Partners were involved in the process and used the following criteria to assess the likelihood of vacancies occurring:

- The perceived reward differential to competitors.
- The potential career opportunities.
- Change fatigue.
- The proximity to retirement.
- General health, including stress.

Having carried out the review, it was possible to map this onto the business critical roles using a table similar to the one reproduced here, which showed the percentage in each box.

	Critical role		
Vacancy risk	High	Medium	Low
High			
Medium			
Low			

Matching vacancy risks with business critical roles

This allowed the company to understand and prioritise the potential impact that managers departing the business would have. In other words, they understood who was most likely to leave and what the cost to the business would be.

Stage two: Determining the approach

The project team recommended a two-staged approach:

1. *A short-term replacement strategy*: This aimed to mitigate against the immediate risk for the business critical positions with a high vacancy risk.
2. *A longer-term talent strategy*: This entailed establishing acceleration pools to build the depth and breadth of coverage needed for senior roles.

The talent strategy

Identifying talent for the acceleration pool was a combination of rating leadership potential against a company defined leadership framework as well as looking at past performance. Interestingly, the analysis highlighted the need to have consistent performance management processes in place for recognising good performance.

A phased process was used to help plan long-term development

Phase 1: Nomination to a pool
Annual reviews take place against criteria, these are peer reviewed and nomations are put forward.
Phase 2: Identify development needs for the pool
Each pool has development tailored to the roles in that group.
Phase 3: Establish a range of development solutions
A range of options including assignments, projects, coaching mentoring, etc.
Phase 4: Review and document progress
This is an individual responsibility.
Phase 5: Determine metrics for each pool to show the pool strength

Whilst the resulting strategy has not been in place long enough to review the outcomes, the process has already led to far greater clarity and ownership by the business leaders towards succession management.

One of the main lessons that was learnt by the project team, was the need to involve the business in developing the criteria for assessment. Each business area was able to define its own business critical criteria before pooling these criteria and developing a common approach. This strategy was critical in getting buy-in and support to the assessment against the criteria which followed.

Summary

Whilst the move to managing future succession through acceleration pools has many benefits, the new approaches to succession are not a panacea for success. Whilst traditional manpower planning processes have suffered from a lack of credibility in many companies, attempting to diagnose and anticipate problems with the future demand and supply of employees is still an essential component of successful succession management.

The pool approach to succession brings with it the added benefit of taking into account the complexities of individuals and the unpredictability of future labour markets. However, there are still many difficulties associated with this approach. The on-going dialogue which is required with an ever changing psychological contract is probably the hardest challenge to meet. But the need to increase the diversity of the talent pool, and especially to ensure that the talents of women and ethnic minorities are properly developed also provide tensions.

Succession planning can be time-consuming and take up significant management time at a senior level. Yet the list of benefits is endless. It not only benefits resourcing decisions and training and development activity, but also leads to a higher profile and greater credibility for HR professionals. Done well, it is one of the few activities that aligns both the needs of the individual with that of the organisation and positions the talent in the company to provide optimum benefit for the future.

However, it is always worth remembering that succession planning is only as good as the information used to prepare the plan. For companies starting out on this process, there is a need to agree the key principles, such as:

- What levels will be included.
- Will it be open or closed.
- How it will feed into other systems.
- What system will be used for assessing potential.
- Who holds accountability.
- How the process will be communicated.
- How to create management ownership.
- What account will be taken of individual needs and aspirations.
- How and when the process will link into other business activities.

Most importantly, a company needs to have clarity about what they want to achieve through succession planning and ensure that they have buy-in to the process at the very top. This is often hard to do if there is a diverse operation with strong independent business units. Furthermore, the process needs to carefully balance and integrate the future learning needs as perceived by both the senior leaders and the employees themselves, both within the company and in the external environment. It is the balance between this level of detail and producing something simple and easy to work with that is the key.

Checklist

- How clear are the objectives for your succession management process?
- To what extent do you take account of individual aspirations and needs?
- How transparent are your acceleration pools?
- Are you clear on which roles are business critical in the future?
- Does line management own the process?
- To what extent is the process live and active, rather than a paper exercise?

- What steps are taken not to alienate employees outside of the pools?
- How confident are you in your future demand and supply estimates?
- To what extent do you utilise techniques such as environmental scanning and vacancy risk analysis?
- Are you making best use of IT to support your succession management?
- Is your succession management and leadership development clearly linked?
- Are you considering organisational re-design as a potential solution?
- Does recruitment and selection activity reflect the succession plans?

5

The Practicalities of Career Acceleration Pools

The past chapter examined some of the recent trends in succession planning, including the move towards identifying and growing pools of potential, sometimes described as acceleration pools. Whilst this concept is easy to understand in principle, the practicalities of moving to this approach are much more complex. How, for example, do you select people into the pool? What type of pool are you looking to create? How do you retain flexibility so that people can enter and exit the pool? and How do you deal with the specialists? This chapter aims to answer some of these questions.

In particular this chapter will cover:

- Developing job families
- Segmenting pools
- Pool selection methods
- Entry and exit criteria
- The role of talent reviews
- Dealing with derailment
- Identifying generic needs
- Dealing with specific issues, such as diversity, work–life balance and specialist careers.

Whilst there are no 'right' answers to these topics, the aim is to provide some illustrations of what forward-thinking organisations are doing in this area, with a view to stimulating your own thought processes about your current practices.

In writing this book I have chosen to adopt the term 'acceleration pool' rather than 'talent pool' or 'high potential pool' as the term overcomes some of the difficulties associated with using the words talent and high potential. By using the term acceleration pool, it focuses on what happens with the group, rather than who it contains and implies a speeding up of the careers of a sub-set of the organisation.

Developing job families

As mentioned in the previous chapter, job families have been in existence in many organisations for some time as a way of establishing pay bands and sometimes also for mapping careers. They are a vital first step in understanding the generic requirements of the organisation, and hence where particular acceleration pools may need to be positioned.

Job families cluster together jobs with similar characteristics and group them together by the similarity of their accountabilities rather than their particular function. In *Canon UK* for example (IDS Study, 2006) there are job families for technology and professional services both within business solutions and consumer imaging.

Within each job family, there are generally broad levels, typically described as:

- Entry level
- Team leader/advisor
- Middle manager/operational
- Senior
- Specialist
- Principal/director.

Jobs in different families but at the same level are broadly considered equal, which enables the opportunities for transition to other disciplines across the organisation to be understood and more easily executed. To do this, at each level an organisation would normally set out:

- the accountabilities,
- knowledge and experience requirements,
- core skills and competencies.

Many companies also highlight particular training that is likely within each level, as in the *LogicaCMG* case study in Chapter 6. Many organisations have also established dual career paths, as illustrated in Figure 5.1 (drawn from IDS HR study 814 Job Families). This enables them to retain staff with key skills who are seeking career progression, where they are unsuited to or have no interest in people management. In this case, the job family splits at the higher levels to enable a lead advisor to take either a technical consulting career path or a team and business manager path.

Whilst some companies use job families as the basis for pay structures, they can also be used as a tool for mapping potential career progression of all employees. A clear sense of career families within a company can help establish a framework which sets out clearly the skills and behaviours employees need to progress.

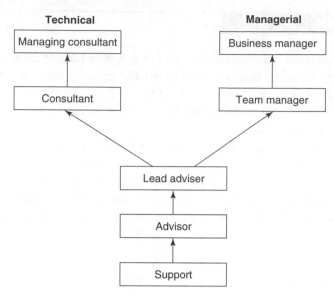

Figure 5.1 Establishing dual career paths

It would be difficult for a company to start identifying acceleration pools, without first identifying the main job families.

Segmenting your pools

The simplest type of acceleration pool is that which focuses on middle managers with high potential progressing to senior management. In this case, in a small organisation the generic needs for both groups can be relatively easily determined. At its simplest level, job analysis can be used to analyse the tasks and account-abilities of groups of jobs and determine the required knowledge, skills, attitudes and experience required.

More sophisticated techniques include reparatory grid analysis or critical incident interviews, which can also help to identify the generic requirements for each group. Reparatory Grid compares the distinctions and similarities between activities or people, in order to draw out the differentiating criteria or one group from another. Care needs to be taken however that the analysis takes account of future needs and is not solely focused on the behaviours and skills of the current population of senior managers. Critical incident interviews involve questioning senior leaders on particular occurrences that impacted their performance and analysing this to find trends in high performance. Again, this technique will not take account of future needs.

In order to take account of future needs, senior leaders need to analyse future demand, as described in the previous chapter, and draw some conclusions about the likely future competence requirements. Questions which can help to stimulate a debate on this include:

- What key capabilities will we need as an organisation to deliver in future markets?
- Where will our added value come from in 5–10 years time?
- What are the trends facing our organisation?
- What are the likely consequences of these trends?
- What competencies will be necessary to deal with these trends?
- What are benchmark companies doing to prepare themselves?

In practice, the behavioural indicators for a particular pool are usually derived using a combination of approaches, including more sophisticated tools and dialogue amongst key stakeholders. A typical process is shown in Figure 5.2. This

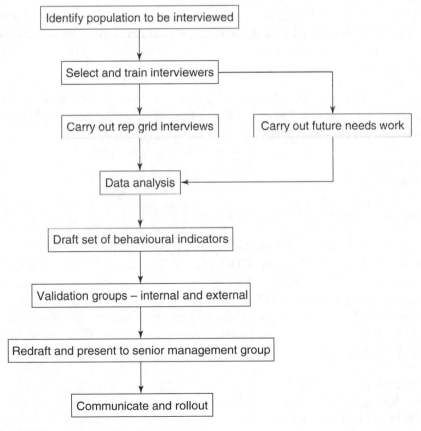

Figure 5.2 Development of pool criteria

shows the need to derive a draft set of indicators which can be validated by carrying out focus groups with members of the population, or external comparators.

In larger organisations, or companies with particular skills shortages in certain areas, it is likely that there will be a need for more than one acceleration pool. Typical segmentation is based on:

- *Structure*: If for example a company has a number of different strategic business units, each is likely to have a pool of its own, with one overriding pool co-ordinated centrally.
- *Level*: With the focus often on management, it is common to see pools based on the management hierarchy, for example, a pool focused on high potential supervisors into middle managers; one for middle to senior management and one for senior to top management.
- *Discipline*: For some organisations certain disciplines suffer from acute shortages of talent, or are core to the companies' success. These disciplines are likely to have their own acceleration pools.
- *Skill requirement*: A company may also identify a shortfall in a particular skill, or set of skills within the business, for example, interpersonal skills, leadership skills or business skills. Pools can be established with a focus on developing a particular skill set.

Lloyds TSB is an example of a company that have looked in detail at the future leadership requirements. They used Ram Charan's work (2001) on the leadership pipeline to segment the capabilities of their managers into:

- managing self,
- managing others,
- managing managers,
- functional directors.

They have put in place a leadership development programme and different talent development schemes across the group. Graduates, for example, are given a £3,000 budget to spend on their development and a career paths scheme operates, which entails a Personal Development Plan (PDP) as well as providing a way of spotting talent.

The *Rolls-Royce* case study at the end of this chapter also illustrates the approach they have taken to segmenting their career pools. Here the segmentations that emerged were:

- leadership,
- graduates,
- business development roles,
- critical pipelines.

Another example is *Shell*, which have three groups of people in their talent pipeline, divided into:

- Top graduate talent
- Experienced people
- Executive and MBA.

Barclays also have three talent pools at different hierarchical levels in the organisation. They aim to build a sustainable pipeline of leadership through all levels of the company. People can self-nominate for one of the three pools and the initial response to the scheme has been shown to help motivate staff. Their pools are defined as:

- Entry level
- Emerging talent
- Top leaders

The entry level is focused on the recruitment of talent into the organisation and aims to build capability for the future. The emerging talent is focused on the identification and development of talent currently in the organisation and is linked to a succession and capability plan and finally the top leader pool is focused on development of the top leadership cadre 'because we should be getting these people right'.

What is clear from looking at the types of pools in place in organisations is that the segmentation is dependent on the business needs. Organisations need to gain clarity through the succession planning process discussed in the previous chapter on where the gaps are in the organisation and what types of people will be needed in the future.

Identifying people for your pool

Chapter 2 looked at some of the commonly used methods for identifying high potential in organisations, ranging from the annual appraisal system, through box matrices of performance against potential, through to assessment centres. Beyond the assessment process, companies have a number of difficult choices to make. For example:

- When is the best time in people's career to select people?
- How big do you need the pool to be?
- Do you ask for volunteers for the pool or tell people they have been selected?

Timing

Usually there will be a particular point in people's career or level in the organisation when people become eligible to enter an acceleration pool. However, the timing can be important. If people have not been with the company long, or are too early in their career then it will be harder to predict their potential. If however, they have established a good track record, they may have limited time left to develop and have less flexibility in their personal life to take on some of the growth opportunities on offer. Byham et al. (2002) recommend 3 or 4 years of diverse experience are needed to make a meaningful assessment of potential for senior management roles. Yet people new into the organisation also need to be eligible.

What is clear is that the pools need to be sufficiently flexible to allow people to enter and exit as the position changes. Some people, for example, develop strengths later in their careers and need an opportunity to enter at a later stage, whereas others may show high potential early on which is not sustained as they progress.

Pool size

The size of the pool depends on the succession planning predictions and the speed of change. As the previous chapter explained, this can be decided from a post perspective, that is, What is the likely future demand for people in the company? or a people perspective, that is, How many people have we already got with the right sort of skills and competence for the future? or ideally, a mix between the two.

Other factors which are likely to be to taken into account are whether the company has the resources to support a particular pool size. Does it have enough people trained as career coaches or mentors? and Are their sufficient growth opportunities to support the pool's development requirements?

If the company is suffering pressure from a particular career group, then this may also sway the balance and number of pool members. For example, if retention is an issue amongst sales staff, the company may choose to increase the number in the pool.

The nomination process

If companies are putting in place acceleration pools, they have the choice between selecting people for the pool without the individual's knowledge, as is often the case with the 9-box methods previously described, or asking people to participate in a further selection exercise such as an assessment centre, or asking the whole population to volunteer for the pool and a further selection process. Again, the culture of the company and the objectives of the process will partly determine which approach works best. However, it is worth pointing out some of the benefits of a more open system.

Active career development cannot be forced on people and the motivation and drive needs to come from the individual themselves. As I've said time and again in this book, to be successful the process needs commitment from both parties and continual dialogue and feedback. If people are told they are in an acceleration pool, they are likely to feel pleased about this and may well rise to the challenge. However, if they actively put themselves forward for a pool, they are likely to have much greater commitment and desire to make the best from the opportunity. In addition, by asking for volunteers, a company is able to tap into hidden talent that may be lurking and overcome some of the potential biases of manager-based assessment.

The *Legal Services Commission (LSC)* case study in Chapter 3 was an example of a voluntary approach. The company explained that they were selecting people for a talent pool and asked for volunteers to participate in an assessment process. In the early part of this process people were given feedback on their application and a proportion of people went on to participate in an assessment centre where the final pool was selected. Whilst this process did mean a great deal of management time was spent providing feedback to people on why they were not being put forward, which could have been avoided if the company had selected the participants for the centre, it did lead to greater feelings of equity in the workforce and enabled other necessary feedback to take place.

Communication issues

We have already highlighted in Chapter 2 the benefits of making people aware of their potential rating, but there are broader communication issues which need to be thought through when embarking on the pool approach. People are likely to have a number of questions such as Are you publishing a list of who is in the pool? How long do people have to wait before being eligible for nomination? What expectations of development are there?

Once again, the more open and honest the company can be with the information available, the more benefits are likely to be derived. Managers in regional areas of the business for example are likely to be more willing to take on someone if they already know they are a member of a pool, and the branding and perception of the company will be improved if people are aware of what is happening.

American Express is a company that took very deliberate steps to improve the communication processes in their career strategy. The company was experiencing senior attrition particularly from newly hired talent and they found this was down to their induction process. In particular:

- A poor explanation of performance expectations
- Excessive pressure on new hires to perform early
- Failure of new hires to form key networks and relationships
- A feeling by joiners that their ideas were rejected.

This led to a 'New Executive Career Launch' which targeted new talent and helped to:

- manage the expectation gap,
- focus on development,
- build key relationships.

The company introduced a series of interventions in the first 12 months and were focused on long-term development, using coaches to support the new recruits. To help build key relationships, people were exposed key stakeholders and given ample network opportunities. The career launch had the advantage that it focused on where intervention was most needed and how to deal with this and has been highly successful. The company turnover is now 13.5 per cent lower than the industry average for newly hired executives.

Briefing plans

People responsible for managing the career strategy and implementing career pools need to have a well thought out communication plan to sit alongside the roll-out. As with any change process, it will be necessary to consider the key stakeholders in the process and develop a communication plan for each of these groups. Figure 5.3 sets out the likely stakeholders in an acceleration pool process.

For each group the communication plan will need to consider:

- What is the message you need to communicate?
- What is the best medium for that communication?
  - Who will deliver the message?
  - Will it be face-to-face or written?

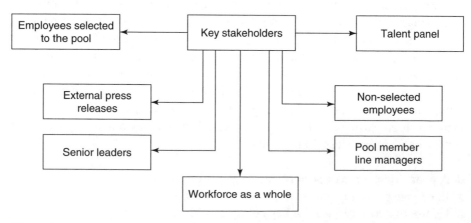

Figure 5.3 Key stakeholders for acceleration pools

- How often is the communication needed?
- How will you gather feedback on the effectiveness of the communication?

For each stakeholder group, the questions they are likely to have are well worth thinking through in advance, as the answers may not be straightforward. For example, employees selected for the pool are likely to have a number of questions such as:

- Who else is in the pool?
- What support will I get?
- What happens next?
- How will I be monitored?
- How does my manager fit in?
- How long will I be in the pool?
- What if I don't want an opportunity that is offered?

If the answers to these questions have not been thought through, the process will start to lack credibility, or worse still, inconsistent messages will start to be given.
The literature suggests that employees need:

- an initial expectation of opportunity and support,
- to understand how success is defined and measured,
- an awareness of career options,
- knowledge of the means by which talent is developed,
- to understand the process by which career success is rewarded.

What that means for organisations is that they need to be proactive in providing certain key information such as a clear performance management process, career path structures, structured learning and development opportunities, and a well-developed succession planning system.

What information do you need for your pool?

Information on people

To help identify the people within your pool and to track their progress, companies need to gather together some key data on each individual, as highlighted in the succession chapter. The type of information commonly held is:

- Personal data – career history, education, training
- Summaries of assessment centre and/or 360-degree feedback
- Feedback on current performance
- Personal development plan

- Career aspirations
- Potential derailers

In *Vodafone*, for example, career development is a managed process for all employees. The company completes a 'talent profile' annually for each employee, based on history, accomplishments, development needs and aspirations and the manager assigns a talent rating based on potential and performance. All those rated 'above band' are encouraged to move jobs within the year to a role above their band and high potentials are proactively managed in terms of career moves and on-going development.

Astra Zeneca focus more on senior posts. The organisation undertakes a 'talent calibration exercise' annually comparing performance and potential ratings for all individuals in the top three layers of the hierarchy, as well as emerging talent further down the organisation. Potential is measured by leadership capability competencies and learning agility. This process results in a global talent pool which is the pipeline for top roles in the future. The company sees management of talent as part of everyone's accountability and train all managers in the use of performance and potential toolkits to assess and develop their employees.

Information on posts

In addition to the personal information, the company also needs to provide information to help individuals and managers understand the different career paths and opportunities in the organisation. Many companies have developed comprehensive career maps of how different job families progress and the requirements for each level. The more sophisticated maps will show how 'career bridges' can be crossed between different groups, for example, What skills and competence do you need to transfer from being a maintenance engineer to a systems engineer? Career bridges are often difficult for the individual to initiate and employees often have to take a move downwards to get across. Baron et al. (1986) showed that within every organisation there are a variety of different career ladders in existence and little cross-ladder movement occurs. If employees are convinced of the longer-term gains then downwards moves are worth initiating, but the skills and competency which will be gained needs to be clear.

Development posts are another useful tool for companies seeking particular opportunities to grow their talent. These posts develop a particular set of expertise or provide exposure to an area of the business which is critical to longer-term progress and movement through the posts is managed by the business as a recognised way of developing future talent.

Career path data and maps are difficult to produce and in the rapidly changing nature of organisations can become quickly out of date. However, managers need to be able to explain likely career paths to employees and tools that can help illustrate a broad sense of the potential routes through the company can be invaluable to people's understanding. This information on career routes should not be underestimated. I was struck recently by a conversation about the career implications for HR professionals of the newly emerging role of business partner. This consultancy style role is a long way from the skills and competencies required for the HR service centre, or more specialist roles and progression up through the HR roles is no longer as clear. It would help HR professionals in larger companies to see more clearly how, and if, they could move between the different roles and what the different skills sets were.

Similar decisions also need to be made about aspects such as job posting. Will all employees have the opportunity to know about and apply for vacancies before they are filled, or Will some posts be restricted to the acceleration pool? and Is there sufficient information available on jobs for people to self-assess whether the opportunity is a good fit for them, in terms of developing the required skills and experience? Without these more mechanistic aspects of the career system being considered, frustration is likely to develop and the acceleration pool will have raised expectations that cannot be filled through the existing structures and procedures.

Dealing with derailment

Not all members of acceleration pools will be successful. There has been considerable research into why some people 'derail', or fail to perform when put under pressure. Much of the evidence suggests that some derailments stem from pool members overusing their main strengths. For example, a beneficial self-confidence being overplayed and becoming an arrogant attitude where other people's views are not listened to.

Development Dimensions International (Byham et al., 2002) recommends using the Hogan personality assessment tool to examine the 'dark side' tendencies of managers. Some of the key traits they highlight are set out in Table 5.1.

Table 5.1 Derailment characteristics

Approval dependent	Seek and need constant feedback and reassurance
Argumentative/defensive	Overly sceptical and protect their own interests
Arrogant	Overly self-assured and confident, poor listeners
Attention seeking	Overly gregarious and charming, melodramatic
Avoidant	Address issues covertly, procrastinators
Eccentric	Creative to the point of being odd
Imperceptive	Lack understanding of the impact of their behaviour
Impulsive	Act before thinking things though impatient
Perfectionist	Micromanage
Risk averse	Indecisive and unwilling to follow untrodden paths
Volatile	Struggle to control emotions, moody

Byham/Smith/Paese, 'Grow your own leaders: how to identify develop and retain leadership talent', 1st edition, 2002, p: 120–121. Adapted by permission of Pearson Education Inc, Upper Saddle River, NJ.

Other possible explanations for derailment are that individuals reach a crisis point in their career, which is not adequately supported by the organisation. Some of the typical crisis points might include:

- *Work–life balance tensions*: Employees in mid-career are likely to be pulled by commitments such as children and parents at the same time as they are engaging in challenging work opportunities. In these cases something often has to give, and for some people the work pressures are too much.
- *Burnout*: Continuous challenge and stretch opportunities may be exciting and stimulating for a time, but if this is not adequately supported, or there are no quieter periods, this type of career can be hard to sustain. People are likely to run low on energy and feel unable to cope, leading to potential feelings of insecurity, stress and failure.
- *Disillusionment with the employer*: Trigger points may occur, such as poor management, insufficient recognition for achievement, or peers progressing at a faster rate, that cause the employee to distrust the company and start to underperform or look elsewhere.

Potential derailment can be limited by the organisation providing on-going feedback to the individual and providing career coaching support which allows concerns on either side to be aired and worked through.

Entry and exit criteria

Acceleration pools need to be able to adapt and change over time in the same way that organisations do. Whilst some pools are likely to have a fixed duration, perhaps whilst a pool of middle managers undertakes some formal development programme, others will be on going. These on-going pools need the flexibility to change their composition to allow emerging potential to join and less successful pool members to leave. This is not an easy process and many companies take steps to define clear entry and exit criteria in order to make this easier.

In the case study illustration at the end of this chapter, *Rolls-Royce* set out very clearly the entry and exit criteria for their talent pools. They outline not only the skill and competency requirements, but also the process to be undertaken if those requirements are, or are not, met.

The role of talent reviews

Talent reviews are the lynchpin of an effective strategy and the members of the review panel need to have a complete sense of ownership of the process

Table 5.2 The aim of talent review meetings

- Review the progress of the pool members
  - What are their developmental goals?
  - What are their career goals?
  - How are they performing currently?
  - What progress have they made towards their goals?
  - What feedback is there from mentors/coaches?
  - Are they in need of a new challenge?
  - Is there a risk of retention?
  - If a new opportunity is recommended, what opportunity will this create?
- Determine new development opportunities
  - Projects
  - Assignments
  - Roles
- Decide which members of the pool are most suited to the opportunities
- Make decisions about entry into and out of the pool
- Make decisions about how to deal with the gaps in either pool supply or growth opportunities
- Review trends within the pool and any group development needs or events
- Agree a communication strategy for the outcomes

to work. Involving the panel from the start in terms of establishing selection criteria, assessing performance and potential in a selection process, etc. can help to achieve this.

Ideally then, the initial meetings of the talent panel will be concerned with setting up activities, to gain their buy-in and ownership of the strategy. The purpose of the initial meetings will be to create a clear vision of the career pool system and how it will operate. Some of the factors highlighted in the business case chapter earlier in this book on gaining support of key stakeholders will be worth re-visiting if you are in an HR role leading this type of change project.

Once the acceleration pools are established, the aim of talent review meetings is likely to follow a similar format to that set out in Table 5.2.

This is quite a comprehensive list of activities, and not all the aspects will be covered within each meeting. However, talent review groups generally meet more regularly than succession planning of old. Historically, succession plans were reviewed annually, but organisations are now reviewing far more frequently. Most of the organisations researched met at least twice a year and often quarterly.

Bristol Myers Squibb Pharmaceuticals, for example, carry out four to six monthly reviews to discuss the progress of people in their talent radar. They discuss business priorities, forthcoming projects and progress of the key talent and aim to move people through and across the organisation more frequently as a result of this.

Lloyds TSB carries out a full review twice yearly, with directors identifying the top talent in each division, assessing development needs and potential development opportunities. This is supplemented by a group talent forum which shares ideas, knowledge and best practice.

One of the main challenges for talent panel members occurs when the member has personal knowledge of a particular individual within the pool, which can often lead to bias. To overcome this, being disciplined about using objective rather than subjective data should be part of the groups' contract at the start.

Assessing the implications of the pool approach

As mentioned in the previous chapter, segmenting out pools of potential for accelerated development does not always sit comfortably with organisations. There is a risk that if companies over focus on groups identified as having high potential, the remaining employees may become disempowered, demotivated and performance and maximisation of potential in this group may decline. Many of the case study organisations in this research were wrestling with how to focus their attention and effort more on high potential pools whilst retaining a philosophy of career development for all employees.

Interestingly the *Virgin Atlantic* case study in Chapter 2 illustrates the tension which exists between selecting a pool of talent to focus on versus encouraging development of the cadre of managers as a whole. In this case, the company made a conscious decision to allow all the senior managers to attend a 2-day development workshop, with a personal coach, to help them self-assess and get feedback on their own development needs. This was carried out before carrying out a further selecting process to identify a pool of high potential managers. By approaching it in this way the company sent a clear message that all managers needed to focus on their development and have the opportunity to work towards the companies' goals for the future.

Essentially any acceleration pool needs to be perceived as fair both in terms of the criteria for selection, the selection process itself and the opportunities open to the pool members.

Diversity

A possible implication of separating out high potential staff into acceleration pools is that they are likely to have an advantage over other employees when it comes to selection for promotion. If your pools are not representative of the workforce as a whole then this could lead to claims of discrimination if your process cannot be justified. Organisations need to ensure that they can defend their criteria for invitation, nomination and selection to the pool as well as ensuring their procedures are fair and equitable.

Many of the organisations surveyed for this book were concerned about the make-up of their acceleration pools and were taking steps to monitor their composition. In the LSC case study, for example, where a comprehensive assessment process into the pool took place, the organisation found they had a higher proportion of women in the pool, but were not representative of other minority groups. This was not surprising however, as the LSC as a whole has an under-represented workforce and is an issue which is being actively worked on as part of their selection strategy. Other larger organisations such as *Rolls-Royce* are actively involving diversity specialists at all stages of the design and implementation of their career strategy, to ensure the widest possible coverage.

Work–life balance

The balance between home and work–life has gained increasing attention in recent years. The pressures on managers to be available 24 hours a day by mobile and laptop have increased and the boundaries of the working week are being blurred. Yet, a survey of managers in the UK recently indicated that nearly half of those surveyed would accept lower pay in return for a reduction in hours (Rice, 2001), so this pressure is unlikely to be sustainable.

Generation X, those aged 35 and younger, are said to hold very different value with regard to work. Influenced by technology, economic instability and AIDS, they are keen to develop careers on their own terms and in particular have aspirations to balance their lives between work and outside work.

Whilst many organisations have taken steps to encourage family-friendly policies, such as parental leave, part-time working and job sharing, this needs to be supported by the career messages coming from the organisations. If none of the talent pool work part-time, or recognise their out-of-work commitments in their approach to development, this will send a strong message to the rest of the population. If people believe that in order to progress in their careers they have to give a commitment in terms of hours and accessibility rather than outputs and achievements, then this will reinforce these messages.

The impact of an imbalance has been said to have three main effects (Sturges, 2004):

- Job and life satisfaction
- Organisational commitment and intention to leave
- Psychological factors and illness.

These effects are hugely significant for organisations as they are the levers of organisational performance. Worryingly, in the research for this book, many companies recognised the pressures that were being put on members of their career acceleration pools. High expectations were being set for individuals in terms of their commitment to and progress of their PDPs, and these plans often had activities peripheral and additional to the person's core role.

To some extent, the attitude from organisations seems to be that if individuals want 'it' enough they will put in the extra effort and will be prepared to suffer the consequences. Whilst this may be true, and I have certainly spoken to many high potentials who do recognise the need for a short-term sacrifice of home life for a potential longer-term gain, these types of statement worry me. Firstly, I wonder if the 'it' that is provided by being in an acceleration pool is clear enough to people and takes account of the many and varying career orientations that people in the talent pool may have. I also wonder whether these consequences really are necessary or how short term they are in reality. Are participants in career acceleration pools able to achieve work–life balance and not be penalised? I would be curious to see the effects of career pools with a strong culture of work–life balance as I believe it would not only attract greater interest from talent within the organisation, but also lead to more sustainable performance increases in the organisation.

In my view, this issue can only be addressed by changing the mindset of what careers mean in organisations, to the more life-encompassing view put forward in the introduction to this text. In other words, a person's life ambitions and constraints need to be intertwined with their progression and personal development within the organisation.

Specialist versus generalist careers

Increasingly over the last decade the emphasis has been on growing top managers with a breadth of experience. Ideally, these managers will have experienced working overseas, dealing with major change such as mergers and acquisitions or partnerships, delivering major projects, working strategically and managing teams of people across functions. Yet interestingly, many more managers work as specialist functional leaders rather than as generalists.

The trend towards career acceleration pools is, in many organisations, strengthening the concept of generalist careers. High potential staff are encouraged to broaden their experiences and develop rounded skills and competencies. Whilst it could be argued that specialist managers also require a diverse range of experience to be effective, there is also a need for such managers to acquire a depth of knowledge that may not come from this approach.

Some organisations have taken deliberate steps to establish specialist career paths in addition to those leading to more general management. *BP* is one example of a company doing just that. They have established a dual career process as illustrated in Figure 5.4.

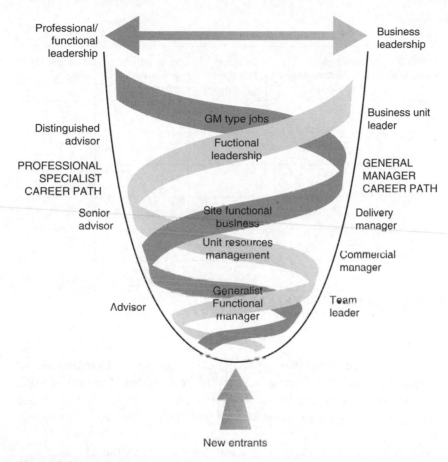

Figure 5.4 Dual career paths in BP

Hirsh (2004) outlines the process used in BP which includes an advisor pro gramme to encourage and recognise functional excellence. Career development workshops are also offered at mid-levels in the organisation to help individuals think about their future direction and which path is best suited to them.

Addressing generic pool needs

Whilst career development opportunities are typically individually focused, it is also common for organisations to look for trends and common development needs within a career acceleration pool.

In order to determine the generic needs of the pool companies will often draw together information on people's PDPs. A simple PDP is illustrated in Figure 5.5.

Name: Date:
Dept:

Development need/objective	Activities planned/solutions identified	Support required (who/what)	How will achievements be measured?	Completion date/s

Individual's signature: Manager's signature:

Figure 5.5 A sample PDP

At particular career transition points, such as the move from middle to senior manager, leadership training is likely to be provided. The aim of such training is to convey a greater sense of what is required at the next level and equip managers with some of the skills and knowledge required to operate at that level.

Common requirements in the transition into general management include:

■ Leadership styles
■ Budgeting and planning processes
■ Coaching skills
■ Project planning
■ Performance management
 – Appraisal, feedback, dealing with discipline and grievance, motivation
■ Decision making tools and processes
■ Influencing
■ Political skills
■ Managing change
■ Time management and delegation

Often these courses are derived from the core competencies required at the next level. The benefit of putting in place generic training programmes are that they not only save costs through economies of scale, but also bring together peers in a safe environment. The benefits of networking across the organisation and allowing people to informally benchmark themselves against their peers is a useful development experience in itself.

Many companies tie in projects to such programmes, getting the managers to work in small peer groups on a particular question facing the business. Often Senior Executives will be involved in sponsoring progress on these projects and will hear presentations and recommendations from the group. Such events are a useful opportunity to raise people's career profiles and are normally held off-site to allow some informal time with senior leaders, whilst utilising varied training methods such as business games, case studies, discussions and input. We will return to this topic of developing your pool in Chapter 7.

Case study: *Rolls-Royce* case study: revitalising your talent strategy

Information supplied by Brigid Briggs, Career Development Manager, Global Talent Management

Background

Rolls-Royce is a technology leader, employing around 36,000 people in offices, manufacturing and service facilities in 50 countries. The company has a broad customer base comprising 600 airlines, 4,000 corporate and utility aircraft and helicopter operators, 160 armed forces and more than 2,000 marine customers in 120 countries. Annual sales total £6.6 billion, of which 54 per cent are services revenues.

Whilst *Rolls-Royce* has long been at the forefront of employee development activities, the company is currently in the process of re-examining its approach to managing talent. The organisation uses a process known as Development Cells to help support their career strategy. Development cells in *Rolls-Royce* plc are long established as a formal meeting where individuals are discussed by a group of managers who can make a judgement on their past, current and future performance and potential.

The business is split into four main areas – Civil, Marine, Energy and Defence – all of which work fairly autonomously. Historically graduate and leadership development had been managed locally within the business units, apart from a regional approach in the UK, and had not been co-ordinated on a global scale. Consequently, in 2005 a major talent management review was carried out, leading to the introduction of talent management on a global scale.

The review process

The review looked at issues such as:

- Where are we today?
- How healthy are our existing succession plans?
- What are the global and internal demographics?
- What metrics should we be using?
- What leadership do we need for the future?
- What graduates do we need for the future?
- What are the real indicators of high potential?
- What additional management development programmes do we need to support us?
- What are other companies doing?

Some key changes arose from this review:

A new stream of graduates known as 'leadership graduates' was identified

Historically, leaders came to the fore from within the specialist graduate streams such as engineering. The need to focus earlier on in graduate careers was identified and an accelerated pool of graduate leaders has been established.

Four high potential pools have been established

Succession planning within the business had historically been based within specialisms such as Finance, or across key groups such as Managing Directors. The company decided to move to a system of succession based on high potential pools to help engender moves across boundaries.

The four key pools: Early Career, Leadership, Specialist and Senior Executives, all feed into the Group Executive succession plan.

See high potential pools in next page

Every member of the succession pools is required to have an Individual Development Plan as a basic requirement.

Clear entry and exit criteria

The company has benchmarked itself against other organisations and set targets for the size of each pool with clear entry and exit criteria. For each pool there is a set of statements outlining:

Entry criteria: Assessment process for approval and endorsement
Entry signals: Review of progress against development

High potential pools

Graduate leadership programme → Early career high potential → Specialist high potential or leadership high potential → Senior executive pool → Group executive succession plan

Graduate leadership programme
Potential to fast track into a leadership role within 3 to 5 years

Early career high potential
Those with high potential to undertake senior management roles, too early to determine how far or career route of progression specialist or leadership

Specialist high potential or leadership high potential
Specialist: Those with potential to develop a depth or expertise and be recognised as a 'World Class' expert in their field

Leadership: Those with high potential to grow into the top 200 senior leadership roles through accelerated development

Senior executive pool
Managing director succession plan incumbents and successors key business director succession plan incumbents and successors

Group executive succession plan
List of names identifying those who have the potential to succeed into a group executive role

Rolls-Royce

Exit criteria and process
Exit signals
Some examples of the type of criteria included is shown here

Entry and exit criteria

Early career high potential – extracts

Entry phase entry criteria
Individual demonstrates the high potential indicators
Individual consistently demonstrates the *Rolls-Royce* values and behaviours as well as
    performing at a high level and with a good track record

Entry signals
Progress should be reviewed and discussed as part of the performance and development
    review process with their line manager
Attendance at a career development workshop
Individual development plan should be completed and tracked
Planned job moves to support the individual's individual development plan

Review phase
Progress against development
An annual review should take place to decide whether or not the individual is making
    progress as expected and therefore should remain in the High Potential Pool or not

Exit phase
An individual can exit the pool if they are not performing in line with the expectations of
    someone in this pool
An individual can exit the pool in order to enter either the leadership high potential or
    specialist high potential pool
Feedback should be given to the individual

Exit signals
An individual development plan should be completed to support the career progression
    of the individual

The criteria has clear requirements about supporting people when they enter
and exit a particular pool and the company is keen to see that transitions in
and out of the pools is handled effectively. The high potential indicators were
developed in conjunction with the Group Executive to ensure user-friendly
terminology and they have gained global acceptance.

Clear guidelines

The company is currently revising the role and expectations of line managers
in the process. Helping managers differentiate between performance and
potential was seen as part of the leadership capability that needed to be built to
make the strategy a success and an extract from the guidelines are shown here.

Extract From manager guidelines

What is potential?
There are many different definitions of potential, but in the business context the clearest and simplest definition is probably this:
Potential is the ability to do or to achieve more: for example, to work at a more senior level, to work in different functions, regions, countries, businesses, to move to a different job and to acquire new knowledge and skills.
All of us have potential to some extent: the ability to do, learn, achieve more.

What is the difference between performance and potential?
Performance is about delivery in the current job and the current objectives and it is, of course, absolutely vital to the success of this business. Excellent performance at one level, however, does not necessarily mean that someone will do well at the next level up. That is why it is essential that we understand clearly – and use – the particular indicators that indicate high potential in *Rolls-Royce*.

Can the high potential indicators to be used to evaluate anyone's potential or are they just for people with potential for the executive team?
They can be used for any of us. Assessment of an individual is always in the context in which he or she operates – so Breadth for the CEO of a business might encompass international dealings and a 30-year time horizon – whereas breadth for someone in a different role might encompass some cross-functional working and a one-year time horizon. But all of the high potential indicators are applicable to the jobs we all do.

Revitalised development opportunities

Many of the development and leadership programmes are being revitalised. A programme for the early career population, for example, has a clear focus on international business awareness. The company publishes a range of development opportunities, including assignments, projects, external opportunities and training programmes, which are open to all employees. People within the talent pools are given priority on some of these programmes, but are not the exclusive participants.

Supported self-development

Again *Rolls-Royce* had developed a strong practice in supporting individual career development and is keen not to lose this focus in the new strategy. There is a global performance development review which examines people's aspirations and expectations and there are numerous tools to support their careers. For example, there are 'how to' guides on career aspirations and career workshops available for employees at all levels. The Intranet also provides various diagnostic tools and information to assist individual career planning.

Challenges

Data management

One of the key challenges has been the management of the data. Within *Rolls-Royce* there was no global HR system and many different processes in place. As an example, due to the level of acquisitions as many as 97 types of appraisal system were running alongside one another at one time. Aligning this data and establishing common processes with the flexibility to meet local business needs has been a particular challenge.

Creating a global focus

Historically *Rolls-Royce* has developed people well on a functional basis and there is now a need to transfer that knowledge across the whole business. This means that all the key stakeholders need to be involved and communicating effectively with one another. Whilst *Rolls-Royce* has a strategy which is driven and supported right from the top of the organisation, this information flow and the processes for communication provide a particular challenge.

Aligning to resourcing

The majority of all posts within *Rolls-Royce* are advertised currently. However, it is recognised that if development cells work effectively not all posts may need or want to be advertised and there will be a need to align closely with Resourcing strategies. The focus is on incorporating resourcing in with talent management to move this process forward. This will support the need to encourage diversity and balance the individual's versus corporate ownership of development.

Revitalising the talent strategy

Within *Rolls-Royce* there is a constant review of understanding about where the organisation is going and they are continually driving all of the talent management processes to ensure they develop the leadership of the future. This takes into account the strengths of the succession plans, the global and internal demographics and continuous benchmarking.

Summary

Establishing career acceleration pools is not a straightforward process. To be effective, a great deal of work needs to be carried out upfront to ensure that the pool approach is adequately supported, not only by the key stakeholders, but also by the required processes and information needs. Implementing this type of career intervention as part of your strategy needs to be managed like any other change initiative. It will require thorough project planning and a strong communication plan to support it.

Before deciding on a pool, companies need to carefully examine their existing career families and career paths and ensure that the focus on the pool is correctly positioned. Larger companies may also want to segment their pools, to ensure a flow of talent through the critical areas of the business.

Once again, the culture of the company will be critical in determining key aspects of the process such as whether to invite people to self-nominate for the pools, or whether to manage the process in a more covert way. The size of pools, the flexibility for people to move in and out of the pool as changes occur, the diversity of the pool and the ability to meet pool needs are all vital considerations.

Whilst this chapter has not provided any foolproof answers, by raising the questions it is hoped that companies will be reminded of some of the essential issues that need to be ironed out before embarking on the acceleration pool approach.

Checklist

- Have you established the main job families in your company and how they interlink?
- What is the best way to segment your career pools?
- How comprehensive and valid are your criteria for each pool?
- To what extent did your criteria take account of future requirements?
- How open are your pools to employees who think they have the potential?
- What size of pool is most appropriate for your business needs?
- Is there a clear communication plan for all the stakeholders in the process?
- How are you collecting and storing the personal information required?
- How clear are the career paths, career bridges and development posts?
- Do the job movement processes support the pool strategy?
- Are there processes in place to deal with derailment?
- How will entry and exit from the pool be managed?
- Is the purpose of your talent review meetings clear?
- Have the diversity implications been considered?
- How will you address the issue of work–life balance?
- What opportunities will there be for specialist development?
- Do you have a process for identifying and addressing generic pool needs?

6

Developing the Key Roles

In order for career strategies to succeed, the roles and responsibilities of the various stakeholders in the organisation need to be clear. Key stakeholder groups to consider will be:

- Line managers
- Senior Managers
- Human Resource professionals
- Specialists such as career coaches, mentors and talent panel members
- Individual employees.

Whilst the particular aspects of the role will vary depending on the culture and strategy of the organisation, it is worth drawing out some general themes to help strategists consider the implications of different approaches. This chapter aims to explore some of the key stakeholder groups and draw out the key activities they need to undertake to make career strategies a success.

If you think about the range of potential roles involved in career strategies within organisations from an individual perspective the possibilities are vast (see Figure 6.1).

Different organisations often give these roles different titles and responsibilities, so generalising is difficult. However, the role of the line manager and HR team are particularly critical and will be explored in some detail, along with the role of mentors and coaches. Individuals too play a key role, and that is explored in greater detail in the later chapter on developing career self-reliance amongst your talent.

However, gaining clarity on intentions for each role is one thing, but getting the implementation to work is quite another! One of the biggest gaps in career processes is a lack of honest discussion with most individuals about their perceived potential and the realistic options open to them. As a consequence, this chapter also highlights some of the difficulties and contradictions within each of the roles and makes some suggestions as to how to overcome these.

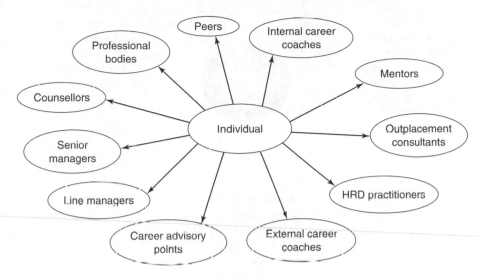

Figure 6.1 People involved in the career process

The manager role

In many organisations the role that the line manager is expected to play in the career development strategy is very unclear. Some organisations have taken steps to set out a clear statement of what they expect from line managers in their strategy and defined what the organisation sees as their key responsibilities. *Nationwide Building Society* for example, clearly sets out the managers role in facilitating career discussions and provides support for managers to ensure they are able to do this effectively

However, even this positive step does not deal with the underlying conflicts and differing priorities that manager's face in trying to undertake what is asked of them. My experience suggests that for every manager willing and able to embrace their role in career strategies there are two or three other managers who place it near the bottom of their list, or file it in the 'too difficult' box. Yet the role is crucial to the success of career strategies. CIPD's research (2003b) showed that career management is far more likely to be effective if line managers take it seriously and senior managers are actively involved.

If you create a map of all the possible activities open to a manager focused on career development, the possibilities are almost endless. There are activities linked specifically to individuals in their team; activities linked to their team as a whole; and yet more activities which have more of an organisational driver. Figure 6.2 illustrates just some of the range of tasks that a line manager could possibly take

Team

- Creating climate for development
- Sharing knowledge and experience
- Providing company information
- Inspire talent
- Role model behaviour

Potential Management Role

Individual

- Performance appraisal
- Career coaching
- Counselling
- Support for PDPs
- Continual feedback
- On-the-job training
- Enabling training and development

Organisation

- Identifying talent
- Succession planning
- Reviews of potential
- Championing interests
- Project groups
- Challenging blockages

Figure 6.2 The potential management role for career development

on to further career development and I'm sure it wouldn't be difficult to add more to this list.

However, if you unpick what is behind this range of activities, three core areas do stand out:

- Spending time individually with people on their career development issues;
- Promoting and communicating aspects of career development;
- Taking action to further the development of individuals and teams.

Spending time individually with people

It almost goes without saying that managers should be providing feedback on individual performance, setting realistic expectations and helping individuals in their team to learn and develop. Yet, done well, these tasks provide the backbone to effective strategies. Companies that ignore the performance management link to career strategies are missing the trick.

The performance appraisal is often the process used as a basis for this essential dialogue. Unfortunately, in many organisations there is evidence to show that this process is not particularly effective. This may stem from a number of reasons:

- lack of training by managers on how to conduct a good appraisal,
- lack of understanding of how the process links to development,

- an inability or discomfort in giving constructive feedback,
- time pressures or differing priorities leading to a superficial appraisal which lacks sufficient depth to be meaningful,
- lack of knowledge on how to develop the different learning needs they identify,
- lack of honesty about potential and future expectations,
- basing their approach on their own experience and values rather than that of the organisation.

Not surprisingly, research from NICEC/CRAC (Kidd et al., 2004), showed that talking to your line manager during an appraisal was one of the least favoured ways for individuals to discuss their careers. The research looked at who individuals in organisations turn to for effective career discussions. Interestingly, as Figure 6.3 shows, the research illustrates that on-going and one-off conversations with the boss and other managers did account for 47 per cent, or almost half of the career conversations held, so the ability of managers to take on this role and carry it out effectively is crucial. What this does mean however, is that managers need to be available to give careers and developmental feedback and advice at times when it is appropriate rather than focusing in on structured processes or sessions.

In an effective career strategy though, the line manager role will go further than this. They are likely to be assisting the individual by providing information on future opportunities in the organisation and ideas as to where the strategy and direction of the company may lead to demand for new or differing skills and competencies. They could also be acting as a sounding board, listening and supporting individuals as

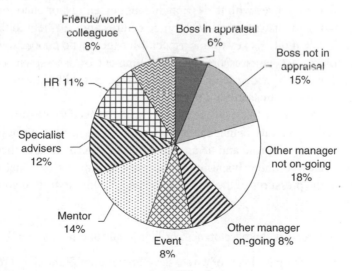

Figure 6.3 Who carries out career conversations in reality?

they examine their own goals and plans and helping them to align these goals with those of the organisation.

Some organisations will provide managers with tools and training to help them in this process. In *Nationwide Building Society* for example, the careers of the potential senior managers are actively managed by the organisation and line managers are given a 'career planner' as a framework for holding discussions about careers. This is separate from the performance review process, although links are made. Managers are also expected to guide their teams towards a range of career facilities on the Intranet, including self-help career planning tools, information on career options and job and role search engines.

Interestingly the NICEC/CRAC research also found that both one-off and on-going relationships with managers other than the line manager featured as effective. With on-going meaning several conversations in the context of an on-going relationship over a period of time. Consequently, managers who are not the boss are often useful to individuals for their career development and nurturing these opportunities may also be valuable for organisations.

Promoting and communicating aspects of career development

Managers also have a potential role to play in helping their team to understand the importance of career development and what it means in their organisation. They should be seen as a promoter of the benefits, rather than a manager that holds onto talent for their own benefit at the expense of the organisation.

This entails creating a climate within the team where development is rewarded and encouraged. Examples of this might be providing opportunities for staff to share learning experiences with their peers in team meetings, or encouraging and openly discussing the use of learning resource centres and self-help tools.

Acting as a role model is key to this aspect. Managers who choose to take time from their role to act as assessors on a development or assessment centre for example, will not only widen their own perspective, but will convey a belief in career development to those around them.

Robertson and Abbey (2003) go even further with the need to role model behaviour and argue that to really manage talent effectively you need to go beyond your conventional managerial role and be an individual in your own right that inspires others. They describe being inspiring as meaning leading by personal example, standing up to the pressures of the organisation and remaining true to yourself and your values.

Taking action to further the development of individuals and teams

One of the interesting paradoxes of career development highlighted in a recent talk by Wendy Hirsh, is that whilst the career is individually owned and controlled, the employer largely controls both the work and the workplace learning opportunities. As a consequence, actively supporting individuals in the organisation and your team who want to progress their career also needs to be part of the manager's role.

This may involve championing people's interests, by promoting their work across organisational boundaries; re-designing jobs to create more challenging opportunities for people; or opening up access to learning and development opportunities. Often, managers will also have a role feeding information into central processes such as succession planning data or potential assessments – a topic we will return to later in this chapter.

Conflicts in the role

In some organisations, even some of the more straightforward tasks outlined here are viewed as a big shift from the predominant culture. Historically, careers were often managed from a central function within the organisation, often in HR. If individuals had questions or concerns about their career development, they would often be referred to HR for a discussion rather than raising it with their line manager. The reasoning behind this approach was that line managers were not best placed to hold the conversation as they often did not have the organisations overview and there was also an inherent conflict of interest between the manager acting as judge and helper.

However, the belief that HR professionals had a wider view of the organisation was often unfounded and indeed, managers were often in a better position to predict the future trends and demands of the business. The openness and trust required to have an honest and constructive conversation is only likely to happen when the relationship between the individual and the person providing the information and feedback is strong. It is more likely that employees will have a stronger relationship with managers close to them, than an HR professional which whom they have less frequent contact. For some individuals however, there may still be a lack of willingness to discuss career issues openly with their manager. They may not have a good relationship, they may work remotely from their manager, or they may just be fearful of repercussions. For this reason, many companies have put in additional or specialist posts held my managers, to act as a confidential port of call. These posts will be looked at later in this chapter.

Some managers also have a desire to hold on to their high performing staff as long as possible as they can benefit from the status and rewards they get from their team achieving good results. Whilst mangers may rationally understand the need for people to move on to progress their careers and take on new challenges, it can be very hard at an emotional level to let go of their best people.

This links with the conflict managers constantly face in balancing between short-term goals and long-term strategies. At a basic level, this could mean a choice between prioritising a thorough appraisal for all of their team against the need to deliver on operational targets at the end of a quarter. At a more sophisticated level, this could mean the choice between taking on a new recruit who meets all of the criteria as opposed to one with potential but not the experience. In this case, it will benefit the organisation in the long run to develop the individual in the role, but in the short term they will require time coaching and training and will not reach peak performance on the job as quickly.

CIPD's research (2003b) showed that line managers tend to focus on short-term goals in career conversations, exploring project roles and immediate opportunities for promotion rather than longer-term aspirations. They were also found to be relatively traditional in their thinking and rarely explored issues such as career breaks or role changes.

The culture of the organisation and the expectations placed on managers by their own managers will influence these decisions. Leibowitz et al. (1986) state that the role needs to 'grow out of their everyday interaction with employees' and should not be seen as an extra responsibility on top of their operational role.

Some of the tensions faced by managers and possible ways to limit these tensions are illustrated in Table 6.1.

Table 6.1 Tensions in the line manager role

Tension	*Ways to limit the tensions*
Wanting to keep hold of high performers	Culture which rewards development of staff
Short-term goals versus long-term strategy	Role models from Senior Management
Acting as both judge and helper	Clear processes to distinguish activities Specialist Managers with a wider career role
Negative attitudes due to own career development	Developing a coaching culture
Role of managers seen as just 1:1	Communicate the wider aspects of the role
Low priority for career activities	Recognise and reward manager contribution ensure the added value is made clear
Lack of skills and confidence to deal with career issues	Establish a programme of support and information; be realistic about role choices

The manager skill set

Managing the tensions within the line manager role and fulfilling their part in a career development strategy requires quite a complex set of skills, as Figure 6.4 illustrates.

CIPD research (2003b) has shown that it is not just the HR policies themselves that are a source of competitive advantage, but more critically the way in which these policies are implemented. They argue that however hard HR try, no amount of guidelines will specify how things should be done, or how much discretion managers have. The values and culture of the organisations are critical in determining appropriate manager behaviour.

Some of these roles, such as *coach* and *mentor* are described in more detail later in this chapter. The performance management aspects of *Appraisal and Feedback* have also been discussed previously. Monitoring the quality of work, controlling absenteeism and poor performance and setting standards are fundamental to successful strategies. Yet interestingly, McKinsey research (Michaels et al., 1998) suggests that half of line managers are unwilling to categorise their people into top average and under-performing, so they are not skills which should be taken for granted.

The *role model* skills may seem obvious, but managers have the choice between doing things grudgingly or with conviction and enthusiasm. Being a role model and displaying this commitment to career development is vital in ensuring the on-going motivation of high potential staff, particularly if managers are having to deal with cases of derailment from programmes. Good *communication skills* are critical in order to keep people up to date with changes, give opportunities to comment, listen, respond to suggestions and deal with problems that arise.

The *Advocate* role is about managers being active in seeking out development opportunities and putting career initiatives into operation. They also need to be able to spot potential talent and promote those people to the organisation. *Broker* skills

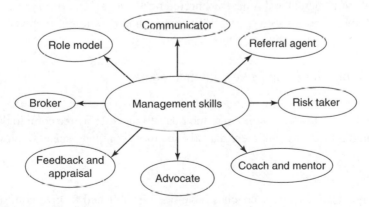

Figure 6.4 The line manager skills set for career development

are concerned with managers seeing talent as a corporate and not a local resource and being prepared to negotiate with others over people resources. This may mean that they need to be a *Risk Taker* and take on people who are not fully developed into a vacant role, or they may need to act as a *Referral Agent* for their own staff who are ready and willing to move on to more challenging opportunities.

Developing this skills set is not easy, and some line managers are likely to have more of a disposition towards people skills such as these than others. Organisations need to educate managers as to the importance and values of carrying out these tasks as well as developing their range of skills as part of their own development.

Senior managers

It is possible to make a distinction between the role of the line manager and that of the senior management group in an organisation. Some elements of the role described previously are likely to be stronger – particularly the focus on promoting and communicating aspects of career development and acting as a role model. The active support and commitment of top management can make or break career strategies and their importance cannot be overstated. A recent talent management survey by Hay Group (2004) showed that 40 per cent of HR professionals need a substantial amount of support to manage talent and commitment from the top that is followed through with actions, rather than just words, is essential if strategies are to be successful.

Yet in many companies, gaining strong support for career strategies can be difficult and it is imperative that HR work with the top team to develop a compelling business case. Their support is not only required on a financial basis, but as role models for behaviour – perhaps acting as mentors or developing their own coaching skills for example.

Senior managers are also likely to be more actively engaged in succession planning, talent management and future resourcing needs. *Royal Sun Alliance* have talent management sponsors on their UK executive board, who get involved in the assessment and identification of talent on a quarterly basis.

Additional roles taken on by key line managers

Within most career development strategies, there are also likely to be some key roles that are held by managers in addition to their day-to-day role. Three commonly held roles are highlighted here, but there may also be more company-specific roles.

Career coaches

In some organisations career coaches have been established to give confidential 1:1 career guidance to employees, or key groups of employees such as the talent pool. Often these coaches will be a mix of HR and line managers who volunteer to receive specialist training and make themselves available to people.

Lloyds TSB is an example of a company taking this approach. They have managers who respond to a few requests each month for telephone or face-to-face conversations about careers. The managers carry out the role as an addition to their operational duties and are trained to a level recognised by the institute of Career Guidance. The scheme is very popular and there has not been any difficulty getting managers to train as career coaches.

The role of career coaches is discussed in more detail later in this chapter.

Career contact points

Career contact points are people within an organisation who take on responsibility for providing career information about a particular function, specialism, job family or location within an organisation. If for example, a manager one business area was interested in opportunities in another part of the business, they would be able to get in touch with the career contact there to talk about what types of jobs and roles existed and what skills, knowledge and capabilities may be required. As with the career coaches, line managers will volunteer to provide information on careers in their part of the business, or their job family, such as opportunities in Finance.

The NICEC/CRAC research highlighted earlier in this chapter found that particular line managers with a natural ability to talk to people about careers are vital in aiding a career strategy. A strong Uncle or Aunt relationship to a group of employees, or the head of particular profession or function, are particularly useful career contact points.

Members of groups of forums

Many managers are also members of specialist groups or decision making forums within their organisation with responsibility for an aspect of the career development strategy. An example of this is *Barclays Bank*, where Key managers are members of a 'Central Talent Team'. This team meet to discuss high potential individuals and ensure that action is initiated to allow the talent that is identified to access key developmental activities and experiences. The role of these talent groups is covered in more detail in Chapter 5.

The human resource role

Research shows that only 5 per cent of companies have a dedicated department for career or talent management (Hay Group, 2004). So for the majority of companies, despite the fact that line managers hold the key to success, career management is likely to fall under the remit of the HR department.

As I am writing this book, many HR functions are in transition towards a 'Business Partner' approach. In reality the role of the Business Partner means different things in different organisations, ranging from an HR Generalist working with a more consultative approach, through to change agents, working on strategic projects in partnership with Senior Departmental or Functional Managers. My own research into this area (Kenton and Yarnall, 2005) shows a range of different structural models, each of which have advantages and disadvantages and are appropriate in different cultures and industries. Career development is likely to sit in different places depending on the over-riding structure in place.

In most larger organisations three key HR roles have emerged – HR professionals working alongside line managers on more strategic issues, with the aim of developing the business for the longer term; HR professionals focused more on the day-to-day transactional HR issues, sometimes in service centres or out-sourced functions and more specialist HR roles, such as resourcing or learning and development. Each of these roles is likely to encompass some aspects of a career strategy.

Interestingly, where the career specialisms sit in the organisational structure has a profound affect on the emphasis of the career strategy. In *Nationwide* for example, career development is linked with leadership development which fits with their career strategy ethos based around on-going growth and development. In contrast, *Rolls-Royce* career professionals sit alongside Resourcing, which fits with their career ethos of positioning people to take on specific roles.

In larger organisations, there is likely to be scope for individuals to take on a specialist role in the career strategy. In addition to the more obvious specialisms focused on leadership training and development and manpower planning, new roles are emerging, such as talent managers and career coaches.

A recent advert in the press for a talent manager, outlines the following responsibilities:

- to attract experienced applicants to the business;
- design and deliver assessment centres to assess applicants skills and abilities;
- constantly review and refine the recruitment process;
- manage the development of new starters;
- continually support team managers to ensure development to the highest standard;
- develop and deliver additional training and coaching as required;
- work with the HR Business Partners to ensure performance improvement is effective;
- identify clear career paths within the company for individuals to develop talent;

- conduct a talent review in conjunction with the senior managers;
- design and develop an appropriate selection process for development opportunities.

This is quite a tall order for one person!

In Table 6.2 some of the key activities associated with career strategies have been mapped onto Ulrich's HR framework (1997, 2006). This framework separates out activities into those that are concerned more with process or people issues on

Table 6.2 The range of HR Career activities

Future/process focused	*Future/people focused*
Developing and designing the career strategy and key processes	Working with Business Leaders to design the key aspects of the strategy
Building the business case	Communicating the key messages to all employees
Benchmarking other organisations	
Managing global transitions	Project managing change within specific populations
Designing and running the Talent management process and ensuring it is fair	Providing the broader organisational view
	Coaching the Career Coach
Ensuring the Talent Management process runs smoothly and is consistent across the company	Facilitating talent forums
	Brokering innovative career moves
	Ensuring fair assessment and monitoring of potential
Population monitoring	Overseeing the career development of high potential groups
Defining career directions and structures	
Defining key populations and strategies for them	Helping the organisation become an 'employer of choice'
Integrating processes	Holding regular dialogue with business stakeholders about careers

Operational/process focused	*Operational/people focused*
Managing succession planning data	Providing career advice on specific issues (e.g. redeployment)
Manpower planning and people flow analysis	Providing self-help resources and psychometrics for individuals
Job redesigns	
Providing information on jobs and careers	Organising secondments, job swaps, projects and other growth opportunities
Monitoring opinion survey feedback	Providing innovative learning and development opportunities
	Advising line managers on their role in delivering the career strategy

one axis and day-to-day operational activities through to more strategic longer-term change issues on the other axis. Whilst all of these roles need to act in partnership with the business, those with a future strategic focus are more likely to be in Business Partner roles.

What is interesting about this list of activities is that the bulk of the tasks are about providing support or influencing others to take action and that a great deal of the role in career strategies is about raising awareness and encouraging responsibility from the key stakeholders. This is very evident in talking to the providers of the case studies for this book. Emma Roberts at *LogicaCMG* for example, described her role as 'driving the career strategy but being careful not to own it' and Jenny Richardson from the *Legal Services Commission* has worked hard to ensure that the process they introduced was 'genuinely not owned by HR'.

Challenges for the HR role

Many of the challenges facing HR concerning careers and talent management are similar to those faced by HR for any strategic issue. To succeed the strategy needs strong support from the top of the organisation and the culture and infrastructure to support it.

In the research for my previous book on HR Business Partners, the need for managers to be both capable of taking on the HR issues and ready and motivated to do so was found to be critical in making the transition a success. The implementation of career strategies is no different. Managers need to feel equipped and confident of their role in the career strategy and fully understand what is required of them. However, they also need to want to take on the role and feel that they get recognition for doing so.

These two aspects of readiness and capability are at the heart of Beckhard and Harris's model (1987) for assessing a client's readiness and capability for change. Readiness is defined as the attitudes of key stakeholders towards the change and their willingness, motives and aims. Whereas capability is about the power sources, influence and authority issues and the skills and information required in order to carry out the change. The key to making a change is described as an equation:

$$\text{Ability to change} = \text{Readiness} + \text{Capability}$$

Many of the organisations which took part in this research, spoke about the discomfort some managers had around dealing with career issues and a fear that they would be asked for answers they couldn't give. The natural response to this seems to be to develop the skills of the managers, and many companies are putting in place clear strategies to deal with the capability issues. These range from training programmes to skill managers in dealing more effectively with issues such as performance management, career coaching or potential rating, through to Intranet and guidance materials to support key processes. However, very few organisations were focusing on the issue of readiness – *were these managers willing and motivated to make the change?* In some cases, the issue of readiness even extended to the HR department itself – with some of the HR team unclear themselves on how they were adding value.

Concerns about line manager capability and willingness are best answered by focusing on your key stakeholders in the business. You will need to:

- gain a detailed understanding of where your stakeholders are positioned;
- get feedback on and examine current perceptions on the different roles;
- be clear on how each role adds value and how this links to the overall strategy;
- consider the process of developing capability and willingness as a change project in itself;
- set clear goals and measure your success.

One of the other key challenges within the HR role stems from the need to act as a broker for career moves across the organisation and yet not having the positional power, or sometimes a sufficient overview of the organisation to fulfil this role. Whilst HR may not be in the ideal position to fulfil this role, they do have the ability to shape their position to achieve this. In larger organisations, the HR Business Partners need to ensure that they come together to share and exchange knowledge on a regular basis.

Career coaches

Coaching is on the increase. Findings in a recent CIPD guide to coaching and buying coaching services (2004) indicated that 79 per cent of survey respondents were using coaching in their organisations and 77 per cent reported an increase in the last 3 years. Parsloe and Wray (2000) suggest that coaching and mentoring have now become the third most frequently used approaches to corporate learning, after on-the-job training and traditional courses.

The CIPD research also found that most coaching is carried out by line managers. Yet worryingly, research by the Work Foundation (Whiteley, 2003) indicates that two thirds of organisations that offer coaching spend less than £500 on developing the coaching skills in line managers.

Definition

My favourite definition of coaching comes from James Flacharty (1998) who says that it is 'understanding people in their wholeness, followed by a conversation and actions consistent with that understanding'. He uses the analogy of a bumpy carpet – if you imagine a person who needs coaching is a bumpy carpet, you can

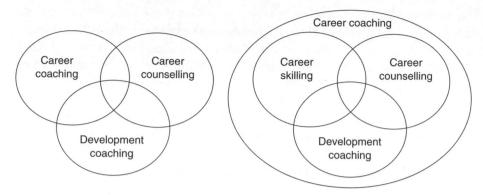

Figure 6.5 Career coaching: overlapping circles, or all emcompassing?

address the lump they present, but it will just pop up again somewhere else. What you need to do is address the carpet as whole.

For me, career coaching fits very well with this approach.

Anyone who has done any coaching training will know that there are a whole spectrum of approaches to coaching, from the more directive 'Tell them what to do' through to the non-directive 'Draw it out of them through questions and support'. As careers are by there nature an individually owned concern, a more non-directive approach needs to be taken, which allows for the coach to guide and make suggestions to aid thinking.

Nathan and Hill (2006) see career coaching as overlapping with career counselling and development coaching. Development coaching is about enhancing the individual's current role and hence their career within their current context. Career counselling deals more with emotional issues within a career, such as outside work issues which are impacting on the career, or organisational change which is creating concerns. Career coaching is seen to deal more with the practical element of helping individuals achieve their career goals (Figure 6.5).

Whilst it is helpful to keep these distinctions in mind, in practice career conversations are likely to span all three areas. Consequently, if Nathan and Hill's third aspect of career coaching is renamed career skilling then all three come under the umbrella of what I shall from now on refer to as career coaching. From my own practice this seems particularly pertinent, as many career conversations digress from the goal which is initially presented by the employee and can easily move into a more developmental, or educational discussion.

The coaching process

Career coaching can have profound benefits on individual's commitment, motivation and hence performance in the organisation. Kidd et al. (2004) researched the benefits individual's reported from effective career conversations and found that the main benefits were a greater sense of future direction (60 per cent), self-insight (60 per cent), values information (55 per cent), a feel good factor (50 per cent), job moves (37 per cent), career skills (22 per cent) and retention (12 per cent).

Career coaching is underpinned by various models and theories. The main benefits of coaching are seen as:

- Increased levels of understanding by recipients
- Opening up the Johari window to raise awareness of blind spots
- Aiding the learning cycle and helping people progress through the stage of reflective observation
- Overcoming negative beliefs.

Typically, a career coaching discussion will move through a number of stages, illustrated in Table 6.3.

Table 6.3 Key stages of a career coaching process

Stage 1: Contracting

Clarifying expectations of the process
Building rapport and building openness and trust
Establishing a contract, including confidentiality, timings, style
Agreeing on any preparatory exercises such as psychometric tests and questionnaires

Stage 2: Developing understanding: clarifying and exploring

Facilitating the individual's thinking and feelings associated with their career working though a staged process, such as:

- Who am I?
- Where am I now?
- What do I want?
- Where do I want to be?
- What's stopping me?

Discussing self-assessment exercises and psychometrics
Drawing out themes to help aid self-understanding

Stage 3: Action

Facilitating idea generation and evaluation of options
Exploring support and barriers to success
Agreeing actions and establishing monitoring mechanisms

Some of the common questions which can be helped by career coaching are:

- I don't know what I want to do next
- I'm in a rut and need to move jobs
- I'm too old to change
- I think I know what I want, but don't know how to achieve it
- I'm not sure whether I should move jobs or not
- I like my current role, but don't seem to be valued for it
- I'm not sure what skills I need to progress
- How should I go about getting what I want?

It can be helpful to utilise career coaches at particular times in a person's career. Nathan and Hill (2006) highlight some of the particular times as:

- Life stages
- Life events effecting values, such as children, illness or divorce
- Work–life balance
- Problems making a career decision making
- Problems implementing a career decision
- Problems brought about by organisational change
- Performance related problems
- Relationship problems at work
- Expression and repression of creativity: style conflicts
- Following attendance at a development or assessment centre
- Re-integration after a secondment or overseas assignment

Some of the tools used in career coaching are explored in the later chapter on developing career self-reliance. For those interested in how they can further develop their questioning ability and facilitation skills in career coaching, Nathan and Hill's book provides an invaluable guide, and has a wealth of practical examples of how to help people through particular career issues.

They also highlight a number of the dilemmas faced by career coaches working in organisations. Not least of which is the tension between the organisation and individual needs. For example, are you working to help the individual fulfil their interests or are you looking to ensure there is a clear benefit to the organisation? And can you reconcile these two needs and make that explicit in your contracting discussion?

Executive coaching

Many organisations make use of external career coaches, sometimes called executive coaches as they have a wider developmental remit than just careers.

The three main uses of an executive coach are:

1. Feedback coaching
2. In-depth development
3. Content/knowledge transfer.

Feedback coaching takes place in particular circumstances, for example on receiving 360 degree feedback or coaching following non-selection for an executive position.

In-depth development may involve shadowing in the workplace and getting feedback from other sources. This type of coaching may also be used following derailment, or unsuccessful career experiences within the high potential pool.

Content coaching provides expertise in certain disciplines, such as marketing or finance and helps convey expertise.

The benefits of executive coaching are that they are focused on specific coaching results and as such have been found to result in increased levels of satisfaction with work and falling stress levels. The external nature of most executive coaches means that people can talk in complete confidence and will often speak the unspeakable.

Choosing appropriate coaches is essential however, as difficulties arise when there is no buy-in to the process or person and where there is no clear link to other development activities or the organisation.

Who is the 'best' person to be a career coach?

There are numerous options for organisations looking to introduce career coaching. The main choices are:

- Line managers
- Trained pool of specialists (often line managers)
- Learning and Development specialists
- HR professionals as part of talent management
- Mentors
- Occupational psychologists
- External career counsellors
- Executive career coaches
- Outplacement services.

The more an organisation moves away from the model of line managers as career coaches, the more it is tending towards creating expert coaches. This has a number of benefits in that experts are likely to be better trained and therefore more skilled at facilitating career discussions and encouraging employees to navigate their own careers. *The Metropolitan police* for example, use occupational psychologists as coaches.

However, the consequence of this approach is that they could be see as a luxury to the organisation if the business case is not made clear and external coaches in particular may not have the organisational knowledge to help individuals manage the internal processes and explore the options effectively.

Establishing expert career coaches may also discourage line managers from holding career conversations – the very thing that is likely to be at the heart of an effective strategy. The decision on who is the best person to be a career coach therefore needs to be treated with caution. In the *Logica* case study at the end of this chapter, the approach taken was to accredit internal coaches to given them more recognition and credibility within the business, as well as support the shift towards a more coaching culture. This approach to use a trained pool of internal specialists is an approach which is also used at the *Audit Commission* with great success when they trained a pool of line managers across the organisation during a time of significant change.

Another way forward is to establish a portfolio of options, such as external coaches, line managers, mentors, HR professionals and allow the individual to choose. Guidelines and parameters can also be set. Linking career coaching with particular projects or initiatives so that the roles are clear is a common approach. Many organisations choose to link career coaching with assessment or development centre activities, as in the *Virgin Atlantic* case study.

Mentors

What is mentoring?

Mentoring stems from Greek mythology and was originally a concept whereby an older more experienced person passes on their knowledge and experience. Whilst this is still largely true, the definition of mentoring has broadened and is now seen to encapsulate not just the advisory role and source of knowledge, but also a more facilitative and supportive role which encourages learning and development.

They might be someone who:

- acts a sounding board,
- is a catalyst for thinking and progress,
- provides expert advice,
- problem solves,
- provides organisational knowledge,

- opens doors,
- coaches,
- acts as a role model,
- motivates and energises,
- gives honest feedback,
- provides insights into organisational politics,
- provides support and encouragement,
- sets goals.

The extent to which the relationship is directive or non-directive and focused on emotional or intellectual needs of the individual will vary, depending on the relationship established. Typically a mentoring relationship will stay in place from 1 to 3 years, but may lead to informal mentoring throughout life! As such, mentoring differs from career coaching, where the approach is much less directive, focuses solely on career issues and tends to have a much shorter life-span.

Mentoring schemes are a commonly used approach to develop careers in organisations, particularly for high potential groups. Companies like *British Aerospace* for example, use mentoring for the first year of graduate careers and mentors are often used in other companies to help with particular career transitions, such as overseas assignments.

Mentoring continues to evolve in organisations and external mentors, peer mentoring and even E-mentoring, which allows mentors to consider their response to individuals by email, are trends which are rapidly emerging.

The business case for mentoring

Mentoring has been found to have a significant and positive impact on recruitment and retention (Clutterbuck, 2004), as well as positive effects on succession planning, dealing with major change and productivity.

As mentoring can be a flexible and broad approach it is able to focus on the individual and have practical work outcomes. The evidence shows that the organisation, the mentor and the individual all gain from the relationship, with mentors citing their own learning and personal satisfaction as particular outcomes.

For the person being mentored the impact on their career can be significant and could include aspects such as:

- wider exposure to key stakeholders in their career,
- advice on how to grow their career network,
- building self-confidence to take the next step in their career,
- developing tactics to help facilitate their progress and performance,
- new challenges to thinking and feedback which may impact career choices,

- ideas on different opportunities for development,
- faster and more effective induction into new areas,
- enhanced relationships to build on.

Setting up a mentoring programme

It is not my intention to go into the different styles, approaches and qualities in any depth here. Those looking to establish a mentoring scheme would be advised to read some of the many useful books on the topic. However, it is worth highlighting some of the key decisions which need to be made when considering a mentoring scheme to support your career strategy, such as:

- Should it be a formal or informal process?
- How do you select and train mentors?
- How do you ensure a good 'match' between the mentor and the individual?

Formal or informal?

Both formal and informal schemes have advantages and disadvantages (see Table 6.4) and the decision will need to take account of the culture and values of the company. If an organisation can create a mentoring and coaching culture, the necessity to put formal processes around the scheme will reduce. However in some cases, formality is needed to help engender a culture of learning and support.

An organisation needs to consider what existing conditions favour establishing a formal programme, such as the management philosophy and style; levels of turnover amongst possible mentors; the type of HR issues prevalent; the degree of short term focus in the business; and the extent to which development is rewarded.

There is also a need to be clear on the purpose and objectives of the scheme. Is the purpose to develop high potential employees? Or to improve career satisfaction and motivation levels? Or to increase performance? Or to engage senior managers in developing talent? Clarity of purpose will enable the success of the programme, whether formal or informal, to be more accurately demonstrated.

Selecting and training mentors

The evidence suggests that allowing mentors to self-select and encouraging the right sort of people to put themselves forward is a better strategy than forcing a role onto managers who are not suited to it, or willing to take the time to make it work. People who have a genuine interest in developing others, have good interpersonal skills and are well positioned in the organisation are likely to make strong mentors.

Table 6.4 Formal or informal mentoring?

Formal schemes

Advantages

- Mentors are likely to be selected, well briefed and trained
- Schemes are well resourced
- They have a clear purpose
- They have a clear structure
- They ensure opportunities to receive mentoring for all involved

Disadvantages

- Corporate interests may override individual interests
- Those selected to mentor may feel obliged to take part rather than being truly committed
- Those selected may not have the skills
- Recipients may not be able to choose their mentor and the relationship may not work

Informal schemes

Advantages

- Mentors will be chosen for their individual qualities and may have better communication and coaching skills
- Individuals will ensure a good relationship fit
- The deeper trust and commitment leads to a longer term and more productive relationship

Disadvantages

- Mentors may not be clear on their role
- Mentors may not be trained
- The purpose will be more individually focused
- Mentors may receive little reward or recognition for their role
- Mentors may have less influence over business outcomes

There have been some interesting things written about the qualities of good mentors. Gareth Lewis (1996) suggests some of these qualities are:

- general Management perspective,
- organisational know-how,
- credibility,
- accessibility,
- strong interpersonal skills,
- empowering orientation,
- developmental orientation,
- inventiveness.

Clutterbuck (2004) also lists a set of mentoring competencies, including self-awareness and commitment to their own learning. However, allowing mentors to work with individuals in the way that suits their style and time constraints is critical. Encouraging the two parties to share expectations and offer feedback to each other throughout the process also good practice to help keep problems at bay.

To be effective mentors need to be aware of different aspects of the mentoring scheme and also be trained in the key skills. Typically, the training will cover:

- the objectives of the scheme,
- benefits and business case,
- the role of the mentor,
- the key skills and qualities of good mentors,
- the process: stages and phases of the relationship,
- possible problems,
- specific mentoring situations if applicable.

Some companies choose to train mentors and participants in the scheme together, so that they are receiving the same message and also have an opportunity to get to know each other in a less formal setting prior to the matching process.

The matching process

As with the selection of mentors, the more people are given the choice in the mentoring the relationship the more likely it is that the partnership will work well. Imposing a mentor on an individual (or vice versa) is unlikely to be a good start to building the rapport and trust needed to make the process work effectively.

Many organisations develop a set of guidelines to help people make an informed decision. These are likely to include considerations such as:

- range of experience,
- location,
- function or technical specialism,
- gender,
- business unit,
- differential level in the hierarchy,
- personality.

Key questions will need to be thought through up front, such as how long the relationships are intended to last, how the relationships are intended to end and when and how either the mentor or employee can choose to end it. As well as how progress and development can best be monitored given the confidential nature of the discussions.

Some of the obvious things that can go wrong stem from a lack of training, or inappropriate selection and matching processes. Other typical difficulties schemes run into are a lack of support from the organisation, politics with line manager reporting relationship, no measurement of success and too little or too much formality.

The line manager role can cause particular problems if the boundaries between the roles are not made clear. Mentors can for example, task their protégé with work which then needs to be prioritised and not in conflict with that given by the line manager. Many companies choose to involve line managers in the mentor training to help clarify these boundary issues.

To be successful, mentoring schemes need to ensure they have visible top management support and careful selection and training of mentors. A project manager who monitors and evaluates progress is also useful.

Case study: *LogicaCMG:* developing a coaching culture to support career development

Information supplied by Emma Roberts, HR Manager and Mark Waight, Corporate Management Development

Background

LogicaCMG is a global company with around 6,000 employees in the UK and over 40,000 people across 41 countries. *LogicaCMG* provides business consulting, systems integration and IT and business process outsourcing across diverse markets, including telecoms, financial services, energy and utilities, space and defence, industry, distribution and transport and the public sector.

LogicaCMG consultants deliver solutions which enable organisations to become more productive and to grow. Core capabilities include:

- business consultancy,
- IT and value-added business process outsourcing,
- systems integration,
- telecoms products and solutions.

LogicaCMG has a career strategy based on career development for all employees and has established career levels and pathways to help employees navigate through the organisation.

From the induction process onwards, it is made clear to employees that they drive their own career and that they need to seek out opportunities and gather feedback on their career progress. Every employee has a personal development plan, which includes a section on their career aspirations.

Each business unit is free to develop its own practices and ways of working and best practice is shared internally across the organisation. In response to feedback from employee opinion surveys, *LogicaCMG* is currently in the process of developing a career framework to ensure it integrates the existing processes and is more focused on the development of high potential. Coaching and Mentoring are seen as a key lever in this transition.

Whilst many of the key aspects of a career strategy are in place, Emma sees the career strategy as an evolutionary process. She commented that 'HR need to drive it, but ensure they don't own it. The challenge is to pull all the existing strands together.' Part of this progression is concerned with equipping managers to advise and coordinate career development more effectively. Whilst the company is lucky to have many opportunities for development and progression, the tendency is still for employees to think of careers in terms of 'steps up' rather than as expanding the breadth of their experience.

Career framework

A number of different pathways exist for careers with *LogicaCMG*. The main pathways are:

- technical,
- project delivery,
- service delivery,
- business consulting,
- sales & marketing,
- functional areas, such as HR and Finance.

Within each pathway there are 6 career levels, from level 1 (entry level), which are typically graduates with a technical background, through to director level. Each level has clear descriptions of the competencies required and is broad enough to house a range of different and varied job opportunities. It is possible to move between pathways, particularly in the early career stages, up to about level 3. After this point, people are generally specialists in a particular area and movement across pathways is more difficult.

LogicaCMG is currently mapping key training activities onto the different career levels. Some of the courses will be compulsory, such as commercial awareness and diversity and some will be optional. The company is also

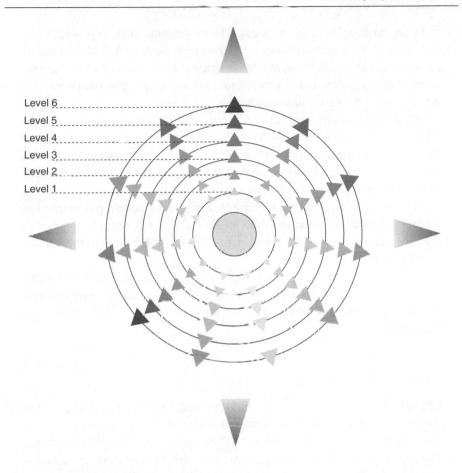

Level 6
Level 5
Level 4
Level 3
Level 2
Level 1

looking to raise awareness amongst managers of the range of development opportunities beyond training.

Nurturing talent

The performance management system is well established and is used to identify the high performers in the organisation. Initiatives are in place, or being piloted, to develop talent at all career levels.

At the lower career levels there is a self-nominated career initiative called 'Grow a Star'. People who are interested apply to join the programme, and are encouraged to find good project opportunities, network across the organisation and use their influence to further their career. Although it is self-managed, the company supports the individuals by giving them a coach and mentor and they are able to shadow senior managers to help raise their profile and give them greater insights in the business. The programme lasts for 1 year, at the end of which the participant is likely to have some form of follow on development, such as studying for an MBA. Participation on the programme does not come with any guarantees of progression, but does inevitably put people in a better position for career opportunities as they arise.

One of the consequences of the 'Grow a Star' programme is that it has raised expectations amongst staff and equipped them with a greater range of skills and knowledge which they can take to the external market. Monitoring attrition and retention has been identified as important measures of success, as the scheme may also act to attract talent.

At a senior level, there are also well-established leadership development programmes, which nominated individuals are invited to attend. Participants are allocated an external coach and an internal mentor to support their career development.

At middle management level, talent management is focused more on succession pools, with each business unit analysing their pools of potential successors, the immediate and longer-term gaps and taking steps to bridge any gaps identified.

Coaching and mentoring

LogicaCMG makes a clear distinction between Mentors, which are seen to transfer knowledge and experience, and Coaches, who aim to raise awareness of opportunities from within the individual using a non-directive approach. The leadership development programme and other management development programmes like it, often utilise both approaches to support the learning and development.

LogicaCMG is aiming to significantly change the culture if the organisation to embrace coaching. As a first step in this process, the company has appointed a senior person to a new position as 'Group Coaching Director' to help signify their vision of coaching for everyone in the organisation.

In addition to a comprehensive coaching strategy, *LogicaCMG* has developed three levels of training to support the development of internal coaches:

- *Level 1*: Introduction to Coaching
  This is aimed at raising awareness of coaching and gives any employee an opportunity to experience what coaching feels like.
- *Level 2*: A 2-day Coaching Skills Programme
  This covers coaching approaches and models and gives managers more in-depth skills practice.

- *Level 3*: An Accredited coaching programme which takes place over 9 months.

  This programme is accredited by the International Coaching Federation (ICF) and consists of a series of workshops and group tele-conferences on specific topics spread over a 9-month period. The participants coach at least 3 people during this time and are required to write up case studies of their experience and learning. Each participant has a mentor assigned to support and guide them in their learning.

Mark Waight explained that 'the decision to accredit the training of internal coaches was felt to be important in order to give them recognition for the role.' The company will be launching its fourth accredited programme this year and partici p ants can also go on to get externally accredited by the ICF.

The coaching strategy has three key strands to it:

1. Leadership development programmes
   - exposing senior managers to coaching,
   - aiding Succession planning and development of future leaders.
2. Organisational Change
   - helping to facilitate organisational change,
     integrating new staff following mergers and acquisitions.
3. Demonstrating bottom line improvements
   - tailoring solutions to ensure measurable impact from coaching.

The impact of the coaching approach is already showing significant benefits As an example, the management development team worked with the Financial Director in the UK to design a programme for Operations Directors to help improve profit margins. The programme had clear measures around both profit targets and succession ability to larger roles. A set of capabilities

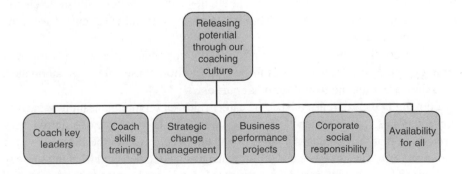

was determined and 360 degree feedback was gathered on each participant, prior to attendance on some business focused modules. Each participant was given both a mentor and a coach to help them achieve their goals on the programme and their achievements over the period were presented to the UK Board at the end of the programme.

Summary

Establishing clear roles and responsibilities to support your career strategy is vital to its success, but is not without its problems. The trend in organisations is to task line managers with an increasingly comprehensive role to support career strategies – not only coaching and nurturing talent and helping employees with their careers, but also dealing with derailment when opportunities do not work out and the implications on their own resourcing plans. Yet the evidence would suggest that this intention is not always realistic.

There are numerous tensions within the line manager role, which are likely to make even the most skilled and willing line manager shy away from placing a high priority on people development. The short term, bottom line focus of many organisations for example is likely to mean that HR need to be highly influential to demonstrate the added value that comes from focusing on career strategies and talent management over operational priorities.

Ideally, HR need to be intertwining their strategy and involvement with the operation in such a way that enables the activities to drive the business rather than be an add-on. Cultural change programmes aimed at introducing coaching cultures, as in the *LogicaCMG* case study, are good examples of this. In this case career development and profit are both measures of the same activity, using coaching as a key tool for implementation. Where the Career activities sit within the HR structure can also have a profound effect on the emphasis that is given, from a more resource-based approach to a more developmental one. Driving the strategy from the top of the organisation is also vital and the case studies within this book illustrate clearly that HR need to ensure that they have this commitment and engagement from the start of the process.

Career coaches and mentors are often vital components of a successful career strategy, but again, thought needs to be given to how these roles are established, who they are available to and for what purpose.

Looking at the examples of specific career roles set up in organisations – such as contact points, career coaches, mentors, talent panels – what came across very strongly is that the essential factor is to engage people around the business in the career strategy. The more line and senior managers who understand what the strategy is about and why it matters and the more people who have been on the receiving end of a positive career experience in the organisation, the more likely it is that the strategy will come to life and demonstrate the benefits intended. Developing an internal as opposed to an external resource for coaching and mentoring can benefit this.

Checklist

- Does your strategy clarify the manager role?
- How well equipped are line managers to take on the role?
- Is support available to managers when issues arise?
- To what extent do managers in your organisation:
  - Know who their talented people are?
  - Share their capabilities widely?
  - Allow their talent to move on?
  - Actively develop their talent?
  - Offer quality feedback to their talent?
  - Spend time individually with their talent?
  - Promote and communicate career development?
  - Deal effectively with the inherent conflicts in the role?
  - Understand the wider career options, such as secondment and career changes?
  - Give a priority to career issues?
- How clear are the HR team on their role in supporting the career strategy?
- How influential are HR in demonstrating the added value of career strategies?
- Is your strategy being driven by HR or the Line?
- Is it clear to individuals where they should go for career support?
- Are sufficient people trained in career coaching?
- Can you articulate the added value that comes from coaching and mentoring?
- Are decisions about internal or external resourcing taking account of the culture?
- Are you clear on whether mentoring should be a formal or informal process?
- How good is the 'match' between the mentor and the individual?
- Are the roles properly integrated with the strategy as a whole?

7

Fostering Opportunities for Growing Careers

If you ask successful people what they learnt from most in their career, the chances are that they will talk about being exposed to a range of different and challenging experiences. Often these growth opportunities are not concerned with a change in job, they are experiences that people are exposed to or find themselves taking part in. For people managing career growth, the ability to create and maximise these opportunities is essential.

A wide spectrum of opportunities from formal training programmes and job moves through to self-managed learning exist to aid development. The aim of this chapter is to focus on the growth opportunities in the middle of this band, which can be either employer or employee led.

This chapter seeks to answer such questions as:

- What are the range of growth opportunities?
- How can you differentiate projects?
- What types of projects are most useful?
- What are the benefits of overseas development?
- How do you go about seconding employees?
- What are the benefits to individuals of different types of opportunities?
- What are the important considerations in managing development opportunities?

Should opportunities be organisation or individual led?

In the organisations researched for this book the emphasis varied considerably between the organisation managing the development of talent and purposely finding and sourcing opportunities for growth, through to strategies which expected individuals in the talent pool to find and influence their way onto key activities and projects. Whilst there is no right answer to this, what is clear in both approaches is that there needs to provide clarity about where the responsibilities lie.

With either approach, however, the opportunities for the different types of experiences need to exist within the organisation for it to work. In my discussions with smaller organisations, and organisations focused on cost reduction this was often a challenge, as there was less scope for project work and assignments outside of the core roles.

If the opportunities to grow your talent in a particular way are not available inside the organisation, then the company will need to recruit externally for these skills, or look to second managers outside the organisation. Take for example a public sector company wanting its managers to gain more commercial experience. The opportunities to do this within the company are likely to be minimal, so cross-company mentors, or short-term assignments are likely to have immense value.

Talent managers need to be creative in their search for development opportunities and think widely about possibilities. For example, Could customers and suppliers be a source of opportunity for a developmental assignment? Companies need to consider:

- What projects experiences do we have a demand for from our talent pool?
- Where in the organisation can we source these experiences?
- Where are the gaps between the opportunities we can provide and the experiences needed?

Projects

Projects are a powerful developmental experience and have a number of benefits to the organisation as well as the individual. Projects are defined as a temporary endeavour aimed at achieving a specific objective in a set time period. The key features and benefits of projects as a developmental experience are that:

- they can be of any duration,
- they can be managed to minimise risk,
- performance is more transparent and easily monitored,
- they can be targeted at specific skills or knowledge gaps.

Making a clear link between the purpose of the project for the business and the intended gain for the individual is essential. If for example the individual feels they are just being used to fill a gap or current need, they are unlikely to show a great deal of commitment and motivation. However, if it is clear that they will be given the opportunity to gain a new skill or important piece of knowledge, they are likely to

Figure 7.1 Project experiences

view the project as a challenge as well as a stepping stone in their career. Briefing project teams on their role and expectations is a key part of the process. A whole host of different types of projects exist and Figure 7.1 depicts some of the more common purposes.

Initiate and innovate

Projects aimed at initiating new ideas are often carried out alongside current roles. These involve researching a problem or issue and developing a solution or recommendation for dealing with it. This *independent learning* is often seen as a key part of talent development. In this type of project, the line manager usually takes responsibility for coaching and challenging the individual.

Analysis and turnaround

These are projects which are focused on problem areas in the business, with a view to analysing what the causes of the problem are and addressing these to gain a positive outcome. This type of project builds consulting skills, such as asking effective questions and dealing with a range of people.

Task force/implementation

Task forces are usually groups of people brought together to deal with a specific issue or problem and implement a solution to it. Often they are composed of different hierarchical levels and there may be a number of task force groups running concurrently on a larger project. As such, they have the benefit of exposing people to cross-company issues. Task forces can last anything from a few months to a couple of years and are usually full-time assignments.

Exposure to people

Some projects provide an opportunity to meet and gain exposure to people who are in key roles in the organisation. These people are likely to be instrumental in helping the acceleration pool members to achieve their career goals. Not only can such projects provide an opportunity for senior managers to observe high potential staff and see them in action, but they can also help to establish whether the chemistry is right between people. If a strong relationship is formed on a project, then the likelihood is that those people will be willing to work with that person and offer them opportunities for their career in the future.

Exposure to new areas

Increasingly senior managers are valued for their ability to think outside of the confines of their department and bring synergy to the organisation. By exposing talent to different areas of the business through project work, they are more likely to break out of silo thinking and start to integrate their actions across the organisation. Building strong networks with other areas of the business will be likely to enhance problem solving and communication skills.

Managing people/resources

Some projects provide the opportunity to work on particular competencies that the person has no scope to develop in their current role. Managing people, or resources, particularly financial resources, is a common area where project work can provide a temporary exposure to an activity, allowing the person to develop their style and competence. For example, a person working in a specialist product development role may have no requirement for staff, but a project managing a team of people launching a new product will give them the temporary challenge of managing staff. This will allow them to see if the people management role suits them, as well as getting feedback on their management style.

In reality, most project opportunities provide several learning experiences in one go. A project seeking to implement a new process, for example, may well give exposure to senior managers as well as new areas of the business. What is important however is that the intended learning and development is clearly established at the start.

Temporary roles and internal secondments

Temporary roles or internal secondments are similar to projects, with the main difference being that the person is filling a vacant or newly created position which becomes their sole function. Project experiences can often be carried out in addition to, or alongside existing roles, whereas temporary roles provide different reporting lines and a move away from the person's day-to-day activities.

Like projects, the experience can have a number of different purposes for the individual including:

- increased people management responsibility,
- increased financial scope,
- increased decision making scope,
- exposure to a particular specialism or part of the operation,
- exposure to a particular location,
- developing skills in particular situations (e.g. poor performance areas).

For some organisations, gaining approval for temporary roles is an easier process than project-based development, although the business case should be clear for both. When vacancies occur in the business, interim roles can also be a useful temporary opportunity, not only for providing a fresh set of eyes on a role prior to a full-time person taking over, but also for the exposure that person will get.

Internal secondments work on the same principle as temporary roles, but often the types of roles that are suitable are different. Within flat structures with limited opportunities for promotion they can help the employee to gain wider experience and new skills without too much disruption to their planned career. The types of activities often filled by internal secondments include:

- review projects,
- the introduction of a new initiative,
- policy development,
- a specific task of limited duration or with an uncertain future,
- a short-term appointment to start a new work area prior to making a permanent position.

Job rotation or job swaps

Rotating or swapping roles within the talent pool can be a good way to give a short-term exposure to different aspects of the business. The managers are likely to gain insights from the exposure to different activities and people, as well as the sub-culture of different parts of the business. Before implementing a job swap, certain factors need to be considered, such as:

■ What are the intended benefits of the role transfer?
■ What are the possible barriers?
■ What support with the organisation need to give, particularly with induction?
■ What will the knock-on effects be on other people around them?
■ How will the experience be structured?
■ How will the outcomes for the organisation and individual be measured?

Job rotation is most commonly used to enhance graduate learning and development as part of an overall scheme, but can also be applicable to other groups. In the *Civil Aviation Authority* for example, aircraft engineers follow a series of short-term postings in different departments to enable them to gain experience of working in a regional office as well as viewing the process from end to end.

Overseas roles

Many organisations now operate on a global scale and as such the demand for global leaders is growing. In many companies the implication of this is that to develop talent to the top of the organisation, you need to be managing mobility. In *Gillette* for example, 80 per cent of the top management have comprehensive international experience (Novidevic and Harvey, 2001).

It is important not to assume that all overseas roles will be developmental experiences. Just because a role is overseas it does not necessarily make the experience challenging. Many overseas roles are start-ups and as such the country and experience is likely to be developmental. However, moving to an existing office, with low levels of activity may provide little more than a different perspective and lead to the individual feeling under-utilised and frustrated. Organisations need to ensure that they link the development of managers overseas with the broader organisational strategy.

Figure 7.2 illustrates the key skills that are typically gained from overseas assignments.

Despite the fact that overseas roles no longer lead to the automatic assurance of career progression in the way that was previously the case in organisations, they are still valued by managers for the opportunity they bring to enhance skills and experience. Interestingly, however, companies do need to take account of the employee side of the psychological contract in selecting managers for overseas roles. Some will have more willingness and interest in taking on international development than

Managerial skills
- negotiation
- questioning

Decision making skills
- the ability to tolerate ambiguity
- acting with incomplete knowledge

Interpersonal skills
- building rapport and empathy
- working with diversity
- appreciating different perspectives
- clearer communication

Greater self awareness

Market knowledge

Figure 7.2 Overseas learning for the individual

others, and companies need to balance their interest with their capabilities to ensure a good fit. Keeping hold of managers at the end of international assignments is a critical part in the talent strategy and the next move needs to be appealing or you will risk losing them.

Sparrow et al. (2004) highlight some of the trends in expatriate assignments. They note that there have been gradual increases in the number of female expatriates as well as more dual career couples. This can lead to different and often more problematic management issues, such as expatriate commuting for one member of the couple trying to maintain a career in the home country, or dual location requirements. In addition, they highlight a trend towards expatriates undertaking a series of overseas roles rather than one in isolation.

Perhaps for this reason, many organisations are looking at different forms of overseas working. These are outlined in Table 7.1.

Despite the difficulty and expense of relocating people and the disruption to their personal life, the predictions are that all forms of international working are increasing. Not surprisingly though, short-term assignments and 'virtual' assignments, where an employee is a frequent flyer due to a particular project (such as the introduction of new technology overseas), are a definite growth area (Petrovic et al., 2000).

Interestingly international commuting and frequent flyers are hard to identify in organisations as they are not in a different role and as such, the costs are not always evident. Certainly the issues over work–life balance, stress and long hours are often talked about, but there are few examples of companies carrying out a proper cost–benefit analysis of this form of working and the implications for the development of talent. It is suggested (Byham et al., 2002) that frequent flyers get less exposure to the culture of the country as they tend to stay in hotels are escorted to meetings

Table 7.1 Forms of international development

Type of assignment	Key features
Expatriate assignments	Long term, usually over one year Relocation to the country in accommodation of choice Any family relocate
Short-term assignments	Usually less than one year Relocation to the country, with or without choice Family may or may not relocate
International commuting	Weekly or bi-weekly travel to another country Some temporary accommodation Family remains at home
Frequent Flyers	Frequent international trips

Source: Drawn from Sparrow et al. (2004).

and are insulated from the day-to-day pressures. As such, their ability to develop cultural competence is questionable.

Managing the global assignment

Managing global assignments is a challenging task, with potential difficulties arising both before, during and at the end of each assignment. Companies need to maintain an overview of their overseas opportunities and constantly rotate high potentials through the business at a time which suits their needs and brings value to the business.

Companies need to determine appropriate selection criteria for overseas assignments. Interestingly, Harris (1999) found that more women were likely to be selected for international assignments if the process was more formal and less account was taken of informal recommendations and individual networking and reputation. Yet often, people will make themselves known as being interested in working overseas.

The pre-preparation also needs to take account of the family. The rise of dual career families means that there are difficult considerations for the remaining professional. In some companies schemes are in place to help find career opportunities in the new country for the spouse, but some choose to retain a property in the home country to enable long-distance commuting.

As part of the preparation most people receive some kind of cultural orientation, which usually involves at least one visit to the target company with the family. If there are several expatriate families in one location then steps are normally taken to establish informal support networks and local briefings. Settling the family in and helping them to adjust is vitally important and getting this right helps to alleviate stress and ensure that the role can be taken on with minimal distraction.

During the assignment, it is critical that the employee does not lose touch with the career opportunities in the home country. Often they will have a sponsor or mentor in the home country to maintain this link. The issue of re-integration is particularly difficult with overseas assignments. The individual may sense a loss of autonomy from that previously experienced, as well as possibly a higher standard of living, which can lead to feelings of lack of status and commitment to the organisation. Having conversations about re-integration prior to starting the assignment is essential if companies are to retain their best people. On-going conversations with the mentor or HR professional and clear succession planning are also critical. The personal reflections from a manager on international assignment in Russia with *Volvo* cars in the case study at the end of this chapter illustrate that this issue is constantly in focus throughout the posting.

Short-term, one-off experiences

Short-term growth opportunities are often self-led. Some of the key benefits of such activities are that they target development needs very specifically and help to build organisational knowledge. Typical experiences include:

Conferences and events

Most professional bodies and industry groups hold conferences, workshops and networking events. The purpose of funding these activities is normally:

- to update skills and knowledge,
- to benchmark progress,
- to generate new ideas and thinking,
- to broaden networks.

Often the benefits of such events are not realised and it is worth thinking about how the developmental outcomes can be enhanced; for example by:

- asking participants to state their learning objectives upfront and assessing against that on their return,
- getting participants to orally brief others on the key messages on their return,
- writing a report for circulation on the highlights of the event.

Visits and trips

Fact-finding trips are visits to other businesses and are generally looking to benchmark best practice in terms of management practice or methodologies. Done well, these events will result in employees reporting back on ideas and observations and applying their thoughts to current problems or issues. To be effective this requires the manager and employee to plan in advance what they want to gain from the visit or conference and to pose some broad questions to be answered by the experience.

Joining committees and working parties

Joining a committee can have a number of different developmental benefits, such as:

- the opportunity to lead and facilitate,
- exposure to cross-organisational events,
- gaining knowledge of a particular function or activity,
- working with external consultants to gain a wider perspective.

In some organisations status issues, or lack of delegation skills from line managers, prevent these opportunities being utilised as much as they could. However, this is one of the easiest growth opportunities to put in place and should be actively encouraged.

Work in the voluntary sector

A range of experiences are possible within the community and voluntary sector. Larger employers typically release people to work in voluntary organisations for periods of as little as 100 hours, either over a period of time or in a single block, and fund this from a community relations budget. Organisations that co-ordinate such secondment opportunities are listed in the appendix. However, the CIPD warn against companies making too much of their altruistic motives to prevent the whole exercise being regarded simply as a cynical PR move whereby 'helping a charity' is seen as patronising.

The voluntary sector, not for profit agencies and special interest groups may also provide opportunities to work as a part-time board member. Assuming a board role can be a challenging and developmental experience for people's careers. Byham et al. (2002) outline the benefits of such assignments as:

- exposure to alternative business operating models,
- developing strategic focus,
- marketing and fund raising experience,
- networking with a wider set of individuals,
- media and community relations experience,
- possible opportunity to experience a start-up,
- a source of pride.

External secondments

Another effective way to achieve knowledge exchange and broaden skills is by seconding employees to clients or partners, or working on external projects or ventures. An external secondment is a temporary movement to a different organisation. Employees are now seconded into organisations ranging from major commercial concerns through public services and schools to small local groups and charities.

Typically, paid secondments require formal arrangements, are full time and last up to 12 months. Usually, the organisations that supply the secondees continue to pay their salary during the secondment period. For a commercial secondment, however, this cost is then reimbursed by the host organisation.

Secondment is increasingly being recognised as valuable for development. As organisations adopt ever flatter management structures, opportunities for promotion through a succession of line management positions are limited. Secondment offers employees' career development opportunities, and for organisations the chance to develop its skills base.

Although secondment is often regarded as a marginal activity that is supported mainly by large organisations, the increasing flexibility of working patterns means that it may become increasingly important in the future. According to the CIPD's managing employee careers survey (2003), secondment is one of the top 10 most commonly used career management practices and 67 per cent of respondents considered them to be 'effective' or 'very effective'.

By exposing firstly the host organisation and the employee, then subsequently the seconding employer, to different work practices, external secondments can benefit all three parties. However it is essential that all three are clear about their responsibilities in this situation.

Table 7.2 highlights the typical information that is normally provided within a seconding agreement, but there are also likely to be peripheral questions that need to be answered prior to a secondment, such as:

- Is the secondment for a fixed term or for an indefinite period that is subject to notice?
- Although the seconding employer will generally be responsible for basic salary, what are the arrangements for overtime, bonuses, expenses, training, etc.?
- What will happen if long-term absence or persistent short-term absence occurs?
- How will supervisory and disciplinary matters be dealt with?
- If it is long-term, how will performance management and development be managed?
- Does indemnity insurance need to be provided?
- Who will fill the role in the home organisation?
- How will the secondee retain contact with the seconding organisation?

Table 7.2 Typical information in a secondment agreement

1. *Parties' details*
   - *Names and addresses*
     - releasing department/organisation
     - receiving department/organisation
     - secondee.
   - Name and contact details of principal contacts in releasing department and receiving department/organisation.

2. *Employer*: A statement to specify the employer for the period of the secondment. This will normally be the receiving department/organisation.

3. *Period of secondment*
   - Duration (minimum and maximum periods)
   - Commencement and termination dates
   - Notice period for the secondment, by any of the parties
   - A statement specifying that the secondment will end automatically on termination of the job

4. *Secondment role details*
   - Job title
   - Hours of work
   - Location of work
   - Name of line manager
   - Job description and summary of main duties.

5. *Terms and conditions of service*
   - *Pay*. Normally the salary point/scale will be that appropriate to the employer. Special arrangements are sometimes made to match an external releasing department's salary/scale. Payment arrangements to the secondee need to be specified.
   - *Benefits*: Arrangements for superannuation should be stated. Normally employees remain with the previous companies' scheme and continue to contribute to the scheme.
   - *Conditions of service*: This specifies the range of conditions required under a contract of employment, including policies on leave, discipline, grievance, sickness absence, etc. These will normally be those of the employer during the secondment.
     Additional arrangements for consultation between the releasing and receiving organisations in relation to disciplinary/capability procedures to ensure that any action is coordinated.

6. *Funding*: A statement which specifies the funding arrangements between the releasing and receiving organisations, that is, who is bearing the costs for the secondee. Normally these are borne by the receiving organisation, but part or total funding by the departing organisation is sometimes negotiated.

(*Continued*)

Table 7.2 (Continued)

7. *Outcomes of the secondment*: A statement specifying the intended outcomes of the secondment both to the organisation and the individual.

8. *Review process*: A statement outlining how performance will be monitored during the secondment and on completion. Formal review dates are normally specified.

9. *Return to releasing organisation*: Arrangements for return at the end of the secondment including,
   - A programme for re-introduction if the secondment is over 6 months
   - Salary/grade on return
   - Any guarantees of job role.

It is essential that all parties are clear about their obligations, expectations, accountabilities and performance objectives.

The host employer should be careful that it does not treat the secondee as an 'employee'. For instance whilst it will need to know when an employee intends to take holiday it should not assume direct responsibility for either authorising or paying for holidays. Similarly expenses may form part of the 'charge' between the host and seconding employers.

The host employers should not be responsible for disciplining the employee, but will want access to a mechanism, by which it can require the seconding employee to institute such a procedure. Alternatively, the host employer may wish to define an employee's misconduct, as a 'trigger' event, allowing it to terminate the agreement with the seconding employer. 'Trigger events' could also include, for example, long-term sickness of the employee.

Failure by the parties to resolve these matters prior to entering into a secondment arrangement could cause the employers, and particularly the host employer to lose the advantage gained by entering into such an arrangement.

Benefits of secondments

As mentioned previously, secondments can have significant benefits for all the parties involved. Typical gains for the person being seconded (often referred to as the secondee) are:

- the opportunity to gain broader career and personal development,
- exposure to a different company culture and management processes,
- the ability to test and apply specific skills in a different organisational environment,
- acquisition of new skills and experiences in challenging areas.

Whilst the host organisation obviously gains from the assistance they receive on their project and the external knowledge and perspective that come with it, there are also strong gains for the seconding organisation. The secondee's employer is likely to gain by building a stronger relationship with another company. Seconding to a supplier or customer organisation will strengthen the partnership. Even secondment to schools and colleges are likely to expand the influence of the company and bring back new knowledge into the organisation in the future. This wider set of networks and contacts can help build the reputation of the employer and help to develop their brand image to that of an 'employer of choice', able to attract and retain a stronger talent pool.

Ensuring a successful secondment

Secondments are not without their difficulties and problems can occur either during the secondment, if the secondee fails to fit into the new culture, or the role does not turn out to be what was expected – or more likely, at the end of the secondment, when they may have difficulty settling back in their own role. The HR team can take a number of steps to help ensure that these and other problems are minimised. The CIPD suggest that these may include:

- Ensuring that the organisation has an effective secondment procedure that is well publicised to all staff.
- Establishing a clear business need for a secondment and specific outcomes.
- Convincing senior management of the advantages of using secondment as an organisational and staff development tool.
- Advertising secondment positions effectively to the widest possible audience.
- Using local and national networks to make links with the external community.
- Providing a tailored induction and monitoring process for secondees.
- Reviewing how knowledge and experiences gained by secondee have benefited the organisation and encouraging feedback and evaluation from secondees on their return.
- Acting as a contact point to facilitate communication between the home and host organisation.

Managing developmental experiences

All of the types of developmental experiences discussed in this chapter need careful managing. The three key areas to focus on are illustrated in Figure 7.3.

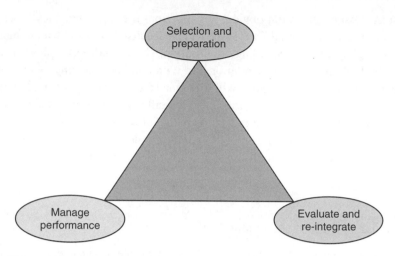

Figure 7.3 Managing assignments

Selection and preparation

Questions that need to be asked at this stage include:

- How clearly defined are your criteria?
- Is the selection open to all?
- Are selectors clear on the measures to be used?
- What influence does the individual needs and wants to have?
- Does it fit with their personal and family needs?

For all developmental roles, be they projects, assignments or secondments, the individual needs to be well prepared for the role. This means setting expectations and clear role boundaries. In the case of international assignments, factors such as family briefing will also be the key. How people are prepared for developmental experiences can dramatically affect the outcome and HR can play a useful role in working with the individual to think through questions they may have and clarify these for them.

One of the key considerations is how long should an experience last? If an assignment is too short, it is likely that the person will not have the opportunity to properly take on the responsibilities of the task and learn from it. People need to be in long enough to make some mistakes and learn from these. Equally, if the assignment is too long, they will become demotivated and their performance is likely to decline. Ideal lengths depend on the skills to be developed, the nature of the task and the speed of learning. Anywhere between 2 months and 2 years is typical, but progress needs to be monitored to ensure the length is appropriate.

The degree of 'stretch' is another consideration within opportunities and is an interesting conundrum. On the one hand, the experience needs to be sufficiently stretching to encourage learning and challenge people to deploy a wider range of skills. Yet, it also needs to enable success and not lead to the individual derailing of their career by not rising to the challenge. The way that stretch is perceived will vary according to the person's background, their motivation and their predicted ability to carry out the task. In deciding what and who is appropriate, predicting these factors can be a useful exercise.

The need for upfront planning was highlighted by Ohlott (2004) who cites organisations such as 3M and Citicorp, who have a planned approach to development, identifying appropriate assignments that will develop competencies. Ohlott states that 'implementing a system that targets key assignments for high potential managers requires significant organisational investment and a commitment to individual development by top leaders, who realise that the policy can yield organisational benefits as well. Involvement at every level of the organisation and tight collaboration between the HR department and top management are critical success factors'. Ohlott suggests that organisational support, pre-assignment goal setting and planning and management communication are critical and need to be established upfront.

Managing performance

Growth opportunities are there for a purpose and one of the key questions to ask is whether or not the experience will develop the competencies required. To ensure this happens, it is essential that the person receives effective feedback on their progress, support and coaching, as well as the opportunity to apply their skills. This latter point is critical. When experiences are particularly stretching and individuals are working outside of their comfort zone, there is an even greater need for support.

Take Joe as an example. He has become recognised as a high performer due to his skills at data analysis and has identified in his development plan a need to develop his negotiation skills. Having identified a suitable project, Joe joined a project team to develop his negotiation skills, but was soon drawn into taking on the role of analysing the data. Whilst he was utilising his strengths and was critical to the team's success, he was not gaining any different skills. In this case, he needed the support of his mentor to appropriately challenge the members of the team when these occasions arose and position himself to take on the intended negotiation role.

Support can come from a number of places, such as peers on a project team, mentors, coaches, the line manager, HR or project sponsor. Problems like Joes however will only be picked up if there is careful monitoring of performance and a clear support structure.

Another aspect of managing performance is providing recognition. Holbeche (2001) states that 'lack of recognition of a major achievement can be disheartening for anyone, but is particularly damaging for a high flyer'. She highlights a need for on-going constructive feedback for high potential employees whilst undertaking assignments, projects and other developmental activities.

Evaluate and re-integrate

In order to maximise the insights from the experience, participants should be encouraged to give comprehensive feedback and review whether or not it met the developmental intentions. If considerable learning has taken place, as is often the case with overseas assignments, then issues of re-integration and the need to re-motivate and provide a new challenge will also be critical.

Other growth opportunities

This chapter has touched on some of the main growth opportunities used by companies to grow their talent base. Some of the more obvious organisation-led activities, such as educational programmes, training and simulations are not addressed here, but will also be part of an individual's development. Leadership development courses in particular, are well established in many companies as a way of providing the core skills and knowledge expected from their management teams.

At the other end of the spectrum, self-led activities, such as reflective learning and experiences outside of work, are also important. 360-degree feedback is often used as a tool to focus individuals on their development needs and is worth more of a mention.

360-degree feedback

360-degree feedback is an assessment of skills, competencies and behaviour by the person's manager, peers, direct reports and key contacts such as customers or suppliers. The process emerged in response to limitations in top-down feedback systems and is of particular relevance to organisations today, where there are fewer hierarchical relationships and wider business relationships which are critical.

360-degree processes in career strategies benefit both the participants and the organisation, with some of the main benefits outlined in Table 7.3.

360-degree feedback is often based around the organisation's competencies at a particular level and can take place alongside other developmental activities such as leadership training. The questionnaire can be quantitative or qualitative, but is normally a mix of both. Often the final questions are an open comment on strengths and development areas.

Ideally, the reported feedback will be coupled with a 1:1 session with a coach, to help the person reflect on the results and provide a more balanced view of the

Table 7.3 The benefits of 360-degree feedback

Benefits for the individual
- Allows them to see how their behaviour is perceived by others
- Provides a better understanding of performance
- Helps identify training and development needs
- Encourages a more open dialogue with people on performance
- Emphasises strengths and areas for development.

Benefits for the organisation
- Improves communication
- Creates a better understanding within and across teams
- Creates a climate of honesty and trust
- Assists cultural change
- Empowers people to act on their development
- Provides more focused development plans.

issues and points emerging. They can also work with the person to help them develop a personal development plan which addresses the needs identified.

If it is being used for the first time, the implementation and approach to the 360-degree process is vital. Best practice would suggest:

- All participants and recipients of questionnaires should be well briefed on the process
- The letter or email that accompanies the questionnaire should cover any concerns
- Sufficient time for recipients to respond should be allowed (3 weeks is typical)
- Issues of confidentiality should be clear
- The need for honesty should be stressed
- The individual should own the results and have the sole copy of the report
- Some guidance on what to look out for and what to avoid in reading the results is beneficial
- Face-to-face feedback of the reports is the most beneficial means of delivery
- Feedback to people completing the questionnaire should be encouraged

360-degree feedback should be avoided in threatening circumstances, such as during a major restructuring or when there is competition for a vacancy.

Unplanned growth opportunities

Not all short-term experiences are likely to be planned. Often opportunities to develop careers come at the most surprising times and from unexpected places. The types of activities that may appear to help to grow careers include:

- Observing or working with a good role model
- Involvement in selection or assessment processes

179

- Inducting people in a new process
- Involvement in outsourcing or company restructure
- Coaching or mentoring people
- Team away-days
- Speaking on behalf of the company
- Benchmarking exercises.

Learning through others

Some people learn best from working with other people and coaching and mentoring are often vital components of a career strategy. The coaching and mentoring approach has been discussed in more detail in the previous chapters. However, it is worth remembering that in addition to being on the receiving end of a coach or mentor, high potentials can also gain a great deal of challenge and satisfaction from taking on the role of coach or mentor for others.

Another approach, which has been found to be valuable in growing talent, is action learning.

Action learning

Action learning is an approach which was pioneered by Professor Reg Regans back in the 1940s (Revans, 1982) and is essentially about learning by doing. Typically, a learning 'set' of about six peer managers meets at regular intervals to carry out a structured process of learning based around the challenges and issues of their current work. Each participant will bring to the set a particular issue and they will be given a set period of 'air time' to explore the issue and decide on actions to be taken before the next meeting. The role of the other participants at that time is to listen and question the individual to help them work through their problems. Normally learning sets have a set facilitator to ensure that the focus remains with the individual and does not degenerate into a general discussion about the topic raised.

The advantage of action learning is that it deals with real problems facing individual's and if a trusting and open atmosphere is established, great insights can be found from sharing and working through experiences. The learning set approach can be highly successful in broadening people's thinking and developing their awareness of other aspects of the business through working with their own and other's issues. It also helps to develop listening and questioning skills and a cross-company network, which are core to effective management. The success of a learning set depends on everyone taking personal responsibility for preparing for it, as well as participating effectively on the day. Many organisations have found it a valuable tool for sustaining a focus on development following a more structured training intervention. The Virgin case study described earlier in this book is an example of this. Here the focus on the learning sets was implementing the development plan the individual's had devised at the development workshop.

Not all action learning sets work well however and those interested in this technique would benefit from reading Tom Bourner's article on some of the possible pitfalls (Bourner and Weinstein, 1996).

Case study: Personal reflections on an international posting

Information supplied by David Thomas, Managing Director, Volvo Cars, Russia

Background

David Thomas is currently MD of *Volvo* Cars, Russia, and is on a 3-year posting with his wife and three children. He has retained his home in England and makes frequent trips back to the UK. This case study illustrates his personal views on the experience of undertaking an international assignment.

What do you see as the main benefits to your career from working internationally?

The main benefit is gaining a broader experience and having to handle a greater diversity of functions than a similar role in the UK. This allows me to both use and develop my breadth of knowledge about the industry and *Volvo* at a faster pace than in my home market.

Coming from a developed market, I don't have the data I would normally have to base decisions on, so the role requires a greater entrepreneurial approach, as many decisions have to be made on 'gut' feel having assessed what limited market data is available.

A fast developing market like Russia, whilst more forgiving of mistakes, will also generate more, we're growing at 80 per cent this year and adding 40 per cent to our staff and dealer network. Consequently, I have to make more decisions and thus will make more mistakes than I would be making in a developed market, which is great experience and learning!

What do you see as the main benefits to the company?

The company gains from the personal development of staff stemming from the opportunities described above. Also, by having people work in diverse markets this means that some of the skills and mindsets from those markets can be applied to either developed markets or the centre, thus challenging some preconceptions and barriers to growth.

It also demonstrates to staff in stable markets that the company does have opportunities for career development and that it's prepared to take some risks in sending people on international assignments.

The company also develops a pool of people willing to move and with a skill set and experience that can be applied to different markets or business areas.

How does your experience differ from your expectation?

Probably that it's been easier than I expected! The industry and business model for *Volvo* in the UK and *Volvo* in Russia is not that different and I found I could apply my knowledge from the UK fairly easily. I've had to accept that the data available for decisions isn't available but at least by knowing what I'd like to have I can make decisions with the best available info in the market.

The scale of the country is a big difference but that's more specific to Russia.

The domestic move has also gone smoothly as *Volvo* already rented a house and school places were available. Some luck has played there and I know plenty of expatriates where that has been a real challenge, so it's really important that companies properly support families in the move.

How did *Volvo* manage your preparation for the assignment and how are they monitoring it?

We had a pre-visit with the whole family and I wasn't allowed to accept the job before that took place. I also retained the acting MD for 6 weeks in Russia to provide some continuity.

Volvo expatriates have a 'mentor' often from their home market who also maintains contact particularly in the early days. Beyond that it was just 'get out there' which carries some risk but is the best way to learn.

In terms of monitoring, there is normal on-going appraisal and contact with the mentor. There's also a lot of support which comes from spending time in Gothenburg to build contacts and in spending some time maintaining contact with the home market. There is a degree of 'if you're quiet you must be OK' but that fits with the organisational culture.

What plans do they have for your re-integration at the end?

It is difficult to plan, as in my case there's probably only one job back in the UK that would be interesting, so it's more likely my next move will be to another market or Sweden.

There's at least a quarterly discussion on the next move even though it's 2 years away. We had the overseas markets HR manager over this week and he described his role as playing global chess, trying to fit people into different markets and then moving others to fill the gap.

Any other thoughts/reflections on the experience – good and bad

Overall it is a very good experience both from the point of view of my career, skills, knowledge and profile within the company. It's also been very good for the children, giving them an international perspective and exposure to a different style of school and learning.

What's the one thing that is critical for organisations to get right for individuals going overseas?

Selection and preparation: the person has to be right and have their family on board. It helped that my boss had a lot of international experience including Russia.

Preparation is more I think domestic based – making sure the accommodation and support services are good – then the expatriates can concentrate on the job rather than finding/moving houses or school places.

Summary

Whilst there are a vast range of possibilities for growing careers in organisations, there is a clear distinction between the opportunities which come from a job move or change (however temporary) and the opportunities which come from learning and development within or peripheral to an existing role. Often, this message is not clear to individuals in organisations and companies could helpfully map out the types of opportunities in both of these camps.

Whilst a particular project assignment may take an individual away from their existing role, for example, others may not and it can be useful for organisations to make a distinction between the different types of projects and assignments on offer.

Table 7.4 highlights some of the methods which have been suggested in this chapter and it is open to debate which type of opportunities provide the greatest learning and career growth. Certainly, in my experience of working with high potentials, greater value is placed on opportunities which involve a change in role and yet these are often the hardest to establish.

Table 7.4 Growth opportunities – changing role or within the role?

Growth opportunities involving changing role	Growth opportunities within or peripheral to the existing role
Internal secondments	Assignments
External secondments	International commuting
International assignments	One-off events – conferences, visits
Job swaps	Working parties, committees
Job rotation	Voluntary sector
Full-time projects/task force	360-degree feedback
Short-term postings	Action learning

Part-time projects and assignments are one of the simplest ways of enhancing the learning and development of high potential employees and talent managers need to be creative in their search for such opportunities. Some of the essential management skills can be developed in this way, such as exposure to board members leading to more enhanced political skills.

For more global companies, international assignments play a key role in their career development strategies and well-managed postings can provide invaluable experience. Increasingly, international commuting is becoming common to save on costs and the upheaval of relocation. However the more protected exposure this provides may well limit the developmental gains and may even have a detrimental impact on work–life balance and wellbeing. It would be good to see companies start to measure the frequency and impact of this style of working on their talent pool.

For all of these types of opportunities, care needs to be taken over the selection process, the on-going management of performance against the intended objectives and the re-integration of the individual at the end of the experience.

This chapter has also highlighted some of the many considerations needed for different types of intervention. Action learning, for example, is in my view an underused way of developing careers, but can easily prove ineffective if it is not properly introduced and facilitated. With each of these methods the more planning which takes place upfront, the more likely problems will be averted.

Checklist

- What experiences do we have a demand for from our talent pool?
- Where in the organisation can we source these experiences?
- Where are the gaps between the opportunities we can provide and the experiences needed?
- Are the purposes of developmental opportunities clear to individuals?

- Are the expected learning outcomes from such opportunities tracked?
- How proactive is your company in seeking opportunities for development in your wider supplier or customer networks?
- Are people aware of how secondments and developmental assignments can be achieved?
- Are managers encouraged to consider a broad spectrum of developmental approaches?
- Is it clear to individuals what opportunities are open to them?
- What are the possible barriers to success for each opportunity?
- What support will the organisation need to give, particularly with induction?
- What will the knock-on effects be on other people around them?
- How will the outcomes for the organisation and individual be measured?
- Is the company tracking unplanned development occurring in the talent pool?

8

Developing Career Self-Reliance amongst Your Talent

One of the questions that need answering when considering a new career or talent strategy is the degree to which you want employees to manage their own careers and utilise self-development strategies. You have the option as a company, to control and manage careers and career opportunities, particularly for your high potential employees. But as fast-track approaches of the past have proved, this is not always the best approach, particularly given the individualistic nature of careers and the changing nature of the psychological contract.

This chapter explores the self-development approach to careers, in order to help understand the extent to which companies can and should include these elements into their career strategy. This chapter answers questions such as:

- What does a self-development approach to careers entail?
- What impact does this kind of approach have?
- How do you encourage a focus on self-development?
- What tools exist to support self-reliance for careers?
- What can careers research contribute to your strategy?

The self-development approach to careers

The self-development approach to careers is based on the premise that individuals take more responsibility for their own career planning and proactively seek out development opportunities. As a consequence, individuals are taking on a significant part of the career management role. This approach is said to lead to savings in both increases in organisational productivity and less personal stress, with people developing a solution which is a better 'fit' all round.

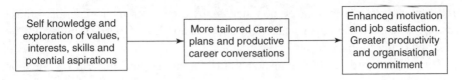

Figure 8.1 The self-development approach

Over the years, trends in career management have undergone various shifts between formal processes (such as succession planning and managed fast-track schemes) and self-development approaches. Self-development is defined by Pedlar et al. (1988, p. 2) as:

an increase in the ability and willingness of the manager to take responsibility for him or herself, particularly for his or her own learning.

The approach is underpinned by research which indicates that by increasing an individuals self-knowledge, they are better able to develop effective career plans and engage in more productive career conversations (see Figure 8.1).

In terms of the range of career interventions available, the self-development approach focuses on individual-led initiatives. This definition of self-development as being self-initiated training or development fits well with the shift in attitudes and approach sought by many organisations that employees should take more personal responsibility for career development.

Implementing a self-development approach requires a cultural change throughout the organisation and is based on the assumption that all individuals are capable and willing to be developed. Because of this, self-development strategies are closely aligned to organisational development strategies aimed at becoming a learning organisation (Senge, 1990; Burgoyne et al., 1994). The learning organisation extends the principles of employees maintaining flexibility, continual growth and employability, suggesting that the employees will transform the organisation as a result of continuous development and learning.

Jackson (1990) argues that self-development approaches are also potentially better than traditional approaches for promoting equal opportunities as it focuses on all employees rather than a selected group. However, there is some evidence to suggest that in practice the self-development approach for lower grades tends to be less supported by organisations than it is for managers who are perceived as having potential (Hirsh and Jackson, 1996).

A vast array of planning and guidance tools were introduced back in the 1990s, ranging from individual workbooks at one end of the spectrum (such as Bolles, 1988, 'What colour is your parachute?' and Hopson and Scally's 'Build your own rainbow', 1991), through to group workshops focusing on raising self-awareness and exploring career options at the other. Many organisations have tailored these resources to suit their own needs and some examples of best practice will be described later in this chapter.

This shift towards employee responsibility for career management was seen by some as an abdication on the part of the organisation and there was a confusion over what the tools meant in practice. Although employees needed tools to help them plan their careers, if the opportunities to develop were not apparent, or the managerial support for their plans were not in evidence, there was little incentive to continue working with them. Individuals were found to need encouragement and support from the organisation to keep them growing. In particular, they needed some key information from the company about opportunities and expectations.

With frequent job changes and downward mobility becoming more commonplace in the work environment, the ideal of self-development and individual's being proactive in furthering their careers appears somewhat inappropriate. It is unlikely that employee's will be willing to invest in themselves unless there is some underlying motive, such as advancement, to prompt action. Without this, self-development is likely to be more geared towards self-fulfilment and arguments of lack of business focus will hold true.

Does the self-development approach work?

It would be expected that any self-development initiatives will benefit the individual concerned, but there is little evidence to suggest that this has subsequent benefits for the organisation, particularly if self-development initiatives are not targeted towards organisational requirements and are a way of focusing on *selfish* development rather than *self-development* (Williams, 1985). Burgoyne and Germain (1984) were one of the first to warn of the dangers of self-indulgent development which focused on personal rather than organisational needs. They designed one of the first programmes in the UK for Esso Chemicals Ltd, which aimed at bring together individual career planning with future organisational needs. They introduced a workbook with a series of issues to work through about career development and the line manager was involved in discussing these issues with each employee.

Personal development processes such as self-development workshops and development centres can help employees gain insights into how they can improve their existing roles to enhance their job satisfaction. However, expectations about career development need to change if career initiatives are to be successful, so that individuals begin to think in terms of continually updating skills rather than of continual upward progression.

Little research has taken place to evaluate the success of facilitating self-development approaches in organisations. Indeed, the evidence would appear to suggest that other factors are more likely to influence career success, such as mentoring, organisational politics and the opportunity for managed development.

The desire to participate in voluntary career activities

Participation in voluntary career initiatives is largely unknown, but indications are that take-up is low. Evidence suggests that where career development programmes are open to all employees, participation generally only takes place at managerial and professional levels and consequently there is a need to identify the factors that are impeding the uptake of career interventions. Barney and Lawrence (1989) also argued that if participation is low, this is likely to be due to the perceived value of the career investments or lack of fit to the individual's career anchor – a topic we will return to later in this chapter.

Giles and West (1995) undertook one of the few studies in this area. They studied the participation levels of 72 employees in an organisation introducing a voluntary personal development planning (PDP) process and showed only 31 per cent had fully participated in the process. They found that employees with a career anchor of security/stability were less likely to be proactive in career planning, whilst those with a general managerial anchor were more likely to fully participate in planning processes. Other correlations indicated that employees with long service in the organisation, or in more junior positions were less likely to participate.

A comprehensive study of 2000 individual's from a variety of industries (Stumpf, 1989) indicates that few individual's had done any sort of systematic career planning or self-assessment and had not formulated a career plan. This indicates perhaps that despite putting the tools in place, take up is low. However, individual's understanding of career processes was found to be an important factor for organisations in achieving career satisfaction.

Another study by Noe (1988) backed up by a study by McEnrue (1989) showed that age and organisational commitment were likely to affect employee's willingness to engage in self-development activity. It was suggested that this may be due to the fact that self-development requires the individual to invest their own time and energy, particularly off the job and that older employees perceive less payback from such an investment in terms of advancement in the organisation.

So what can we glean from this research? Certainly it is likely that self-starting talented people are most likely to seek new and challenging experiences in their career development, particularly where there is a clear link between the learning they gain and their future marketability. Formal education, training and development opportunities are likely to be less relevant than experience-based opportunities such as stretch roles, lateral moves, projects, secondments etc., which may stem from more self-led career planning.

The other key factor is support. With encouragement and the ability to discuss self-led career planning tools, both participation and the value will be likely to increase.

The need for self-reliance

Many of the existing career development strategies, and self-development approaches in particular, aim to re-educate employees as to the changing nature of careers and shift the responsibility for control more towards the individual. But does this approach lead to any greater career satisfaction or organisational commitment?

Whilst it might be expected that employees who feel they have an influence over their career and take responsibility for their own development will have greater career satisfaction levels, it may equally be true that they view this approach as abdication of responsibility by the organisation and are in reality only taking greater responsibility when they are most dissatisfied. Indeed, a survey of Fortune 500 companies in the USA showed that employees were reluctant to assume responsibility for their own development and less than 25 per cent of employees participated in voluntary career initiatives (Russell, 1991). My own anecdotal evidence supports this. Many companies that have set up learning centres and voluntary career development tools report little take up or use by employees, unless there is active encouragement as part of a structured learning experience.

Whilst, from an organisational standpoint, increased self-responsibility and control for careers is seen as beneficial, the position is not so clear for the individual.

There is also evidence to suggest that a changing organisational context reduces the willingness of employees to pursue voluntary self-development initiatives. Herriot (1995) states that a common reaction to changes in the external and internal career environment is to 'get safe' by taking less risks and keeping your head down, particularly if the employee has financial constraints such as investments in good pension schemes. Moss Kanter (1977) also argues that where there are limited opportunities for advancement, employees become frustrated and lower their aspirations and commitment to the organisation, as well as their willingness to accept responsibility. In a blame culture, employees tend to be more risk-averse and when faced with job insecurity are unlikely to take on responsibility for managing their own career (Holbeche, 1995).

High potential individuals are often typified by a desire to maximise their future options and position themselves well for possible opportunities. Some of the key characteristics of talented managers being people's drive and ambition. As a consequence, self-development approaches stand a good chance of being viewed by high potential individuals as an opportunity to improve their chances of promotion. But even where individuals are willing to assume greater responsibility, the extent to which they are able to do so can often be limited.

190

- The future organisational demands are unpredictable.
- The style of their immediate managers are not under their control.
- Lack of understanding of how a self-development approach can lead to progression.
- Constantly changing work environments encourage a shorter-term focus.

Figure 8.2 Factors limiting self-development

A number of factors go against individuals focusing on self-development of their career, as shown in Figure 8.2. One of the most fundamental for me, is that of gaining a greater understanding of yourself, your abilities, interests and values, which is at the heart of many approaches, does not in itself lead to progression. Unless this added value is clear to employees, it is unlikely they will put in the effort.

To get self-development approaches to work, employees need to be given more help in developing an entrepreneurial approach to their careers. Most employees are likely to remain passive due to cultural conditioning at work, unless there is a strong stimulus to do otherwise. Where self-development approaches are introduced, emphasis needs to be placed on providing encouragement and support for employees and ensuring the rationale for the approach is well communicated and understood.

My own longitudinal research (Yarnall, 1998b) into the impact of self-development tools on careers, indicated that one of the clear outputs from participation in voluntary career tools, was the ability to gain support from managers – coming perhaps from using the tools to help guide a more productive career conversation.

The importance of individual characteristics on participation and outcomes

The characteristics of 'successful' employees in flatter structures can be described as being more self-empowered and challenging, risk takers and influencers, who will seek out opportunities for themselves. Bell and Straw (1989) also put forward a model to suggest certain characteristics such as risk seeking, the need for power and having a creativity career anchor, are likely to influence the degree of control employees have over their own work behaviour, outcomes and ability to predict changes in the environment. Successful personal control leads to increased satisfaction with career and greater information exchange with the organisation.

Ironically, the characteristics of employees sought in new organisational structures, are the very same characteristics that may make the employee more likely to exit the company. It is also possible that this lies at the heart of some senior managers reluctance to allow high potential employees to shape and control their own career to any great extent, as they have underlying concerns about it not being in the business's best interests.

The question of the importance of individual characteristics closely mirrors the debate over whether a person influences the situation to suit their career needs, or the situation determines the attitudes and behaviour of the person. Straw and Ross (1985) found that job satisfaction is consistent over time regardless of whether the individual moves jobs. This suggests a person's general disposition remains the same despite changes in the situation. Bell and Straw (1989) also argue convincingly that career attitudes are shaped by the person and not the situation. Consequently, the culture and nature of the organisation will follow from the people in it rather than being an influence on the people themselves. If this is true, then to change to a more open, supportive coaching culture will need a shift in emphasis within the selection strategy.

Interestingly, although there is little research into sex differences, some studies have found women more likely to participate in voluntary career activities. The reason for this is possibly because women have been found to have a more value-driven approach to careers than the more goal-oriented male approach. For women, attachments and relationships play a central role in evaluating life choices and their career decisions are often seen as more complex. Exploring personal values and priorities is therefore a potentially more fruitful exercise for women.

Career resilience

One of the characteristics often sought from high potential employees is 'career resilience' (London, 1983; Waterman et al., 1994). This is described as the ability to adapt quickly in the face of change, coping with negative work situations such as barriers to career goals, and taking ownership for managing ones career in line with the companies vision.

Certainly studies have found that high potentials often have the ability to push hard and have a self-confidence to exercise influence on their situation. Yet this may lead to a high cost to organisations in the longer term. Organisations often pressure high flyers to devote a lot of time and energy to work – part of the psychological contract – and reward them for doing so. Continuous travel, weekend working, 24-hour availability on mobiles, etc., are all seen as signs of commitment and motivation. Yet this is not sustainable in the longer term. Neglect of personal lives can lead to stress, health problems and an unsustainable work–life balance. Ultimately, this may mean losing the very talent you are seeking to keep in the organisation. Self-development approaches may help to combat some of these issues by helping individuals re-focus their lives.

There may also be consequences of encouraging resilience in that encourages 'me plc' (Caulkin, 1995) from the ability that talented employees have to market themselves more effectively. If they don't feel they are getting their needs met they are likely to become more instrumental and lack loyalty in their contract.

How do you encourage aligned self-development?

What companies are seeking from their talent is the ability for people to play their role in shaping their own development. They are particularly looking for individuals to:

- Communicate their needs and ideas.
- Discuss expectations they may have.
- Carry out a self-analysis of skills, competencies, etc.
- Show a willingness to develop.
- Understand how the business needs relate to their own career plans.

In order to get the career development needed, most individuals need to be able to work in a boundaryless, less managed environment, where they take some responsibility for finding opportunities and making things happen. Inkson and Arthur (2001) have called these skills 'career competencies'.

Career competencies

Career competencies have been divided into three areas, shown in Figure 8.3

Knowing how competencies are about finding job-related knowledge, such as what's needed to perform well in a job – the technical expertise and soft skills. Understanding this can help the person focus their development more accurately. *Knowing why* competencies are about understanding your career orientations and the values, meanings and interests a person holds. They are about developing the confidence, motivation, energy and self-assurance needed to progress. Finally, *knowing whom* is about identifying the key players that determine success and gaining proximity to those people that can aid development, such as through more effective networking.

This model can be a useful frame for high potentials trying to understand how to work on their career plans. Typically, organisations will support the development

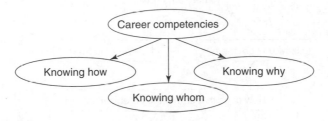

Figure 8.3 Career competencies

of these career competencies by making some of the core tools and techniques available, or by providing training in certain aspects, such as networking and political skills.

A survey by the Careers Research Forum of its members (2001) showed that most companies viewed providing 'self-help' career tools as an important part of supporting their career development strategy.

Tools to achieve career self-reliance

The self-help tools for career development tend to follow the stages people need to go through to think through and work on their career plans effectively. These stages are, firstly, achieve greater self-knowledge, either through workshops, psychometric assessments, workbooks or interactive computer packages used for analysing transferable skills and values. Secondly, explore and find out about jobs and opportunities either by referring to career path guides, interviews or videos about different posts; and thirdly, prepare for the next role by taking appropriate training opportunities and using support networks.

The stages I've used in Figure 8.4 are often replicated on career workshops or during career coaching as a simple frame of reference, although I have chosen to add in the piece on organisational fit, which differentiates it slightly from other models, but is more appropriate for developing careers within an organisational context.

Where am I now?

The tools commonly used to help people assess their current career position are outlined in Table 8.1. Some organisations make these available to all employees in career workbooks, or on Intranet sites. Others may utilise some of the tools as the first stage of a career workshop for core groups of employees. Whilst all the tools can be completed in isolation, it is likely that more value will be gained by working through the output with someone else, such as a peer, career coach or their line manager.

Figure 8.4 A framework for career planning

Table 8.1 Tools to assess the current career position

- Using career metaphors
- Career lifelines
- Understanding your values
- Focusing on core interests
- Assessing your key skills
- Personality diagnostics
- Qualifications and achievements
- Gaining career feedback
- Assessing your career competence
- Career life stages
- Career anchors

The essence of this stage is on reflection and taking stock. Many of the tools, such as qualification and achievements records aim to reposition and categorise existing knowledge the person has about themselves, to help them understand their strengths, interests and transferable skills.

Achievements records for example, list satisfying achievements and then analyse them to identify the underlying skills and qualities of the individual. This can also be a useful way to build self-esteem, if this is low. Transferable skills exercises work in a similar way, often categorising skills to help give a greater understanding. On career workshops, packs of cards can be used to help identify skills based on Hopson and Scally's (1991) classification into Working with Data, Working with Ideas, Working with People and Working with Things. Career values can also work with a card sorting exercise and usefully helps people to identify what is most important to them from a role, for example, is challenge or variety more important?

A useful starting point however, is to create greater understanding of what is meant by a career and to look back over the person's career history. Career metaphors, is your career like a ladder, a roller-coaster or a backpack, etc., can help people to explore some of the patterns. Within more creative cultures, drawing pictures of your career, or web pages, can be another way of capturing key themes. For more structured thinkers however, the life-line exercise is often used. This maps the key aspects of the person's working life on a time line, with highs and lows dictated by the degree of fulfilment felt at any one time. Individual's often derive useful insights from exploring their lifeline, such as highs being categorised by working in a productive team, or early career events which provided fulfilment being lost as they progress their career.

Additional information can also be gleaned from tools such as personality diagnostics, with the Occupational Personality Questionnaire (OPQ), Myers Briggs and the Hogan Development Inventory (HDI) being particularly common. Career anchors and career life stages are also two useful career theories which are discussed in more detail later in this chapter.

Table 8.2 Tools to help explore career direction

- Visioning
- Understanding your preferences, interest inventories
- Understanding your career drivers
- Analysing priorities and constraints
- Exploring work–life balance
- Is organisational life for me?
- Exploring influences and expectations
- Creative career thinking
- Blocks and bridges to progress

Readers are referred to Nathan and Hill's book on career counselling for more detail on how to go about using many of the tools listed in this chapter.

Where do I want to be?

The range of tools to help explore career direction are listed in Table 8.2. The extent to which these types of tools are helpful will depend on the degree of confusion facing the individual. For people without a clear sense of what they want from their career, or what the next steps might be, then tools such as visioning, where people are encouraged to paint a picture of the types of things they would like from a future role, can be helpful. Creative career thinking tools, such as mind maps of interests and dream roles, can also help fill this need.

Career drivers (Francis, 1985) and interest inventories can also be helpful tools if people are unclear on their direction. Career drivers are similar to career anchors and can help to identify your inner feelings which help determine what you want and need from your working life. Interest inventories, such as Holland's questionnaire (1985) map different types of work onto your personality type. The theory works on the basis that people feel most fulfilled in work that suits their personal style and values. Whilst the results of these tests are often not revealing in themselves, they often enable a discussion to take place at a much deeper level.

Sometimes at this stage, people are exploring particular options, such as whether to work independently or as part of an organisation, or whether to devote more time to out of work interests. Questionnaires which look at aspects such as working as an independent consultant, or diagnosing work–life balance may be useful here, to help people work though issues at the back of their mind.

If they do have a particular goal in mind, there may also be reasons why they are not pursuing it. Exercises which look at what is blocking progress and what may provide a bridge to progress can be useful here.

Table 8.3 Tools to explore the organisational perspective

- Researching opportunities internally
- Understanding the psychological contract
- Utilising the appraisal process
- Building a personal business case
- Widening your business contacts
- Mapping out the key stakeholders

How does that fit with the organisation?

Comparing what you might want with the possibilities within the organisation is a key component for most high potential employees. Table 8.3 highlights some of the tools which can be used to help with this process.

In the *Lexmark* case study described later in this chapter, the psychological contract model was a vital component of their career workshop for high potentials. Through discussing and exploring the needs and wants for both themselves and the organisation, the participants were able to gain a better insight into how to position themselves for the benefit of the organisation as well as themselves. Stakeholder mapping, where the key people who have an influence and interest over your career are explored, is another useful tool to help with this.

How do I get there?

The tools to help people at this stage can be divided into those that assist with developing the career plan and more tactical tools, such as how to write a good c.v. or application for a job. Table 8.4 outlines some of the more common approaches for this part of the cycle of career planning.

Most of the tools listed here are self-explanatory and involve input on 'how to…' that is ideally tailored to the organisation. The exercise on mapping satisfiers referred to is explained in more detail in Nathan and Hill's book, and in brief, involves drawing up a grid of potential options against a list of key priorities sought from future roles, in order to help prioritise a person's plans.

Deciding on your method of delivery

As we have mentioned previously in this chapter, the tools which support self-development can be provided in a number of ways. Some of the more commonly used methods are explored here, but for me, supported use of the tools works best, be that with a career coach, peer or as part of a career workshop.

Table 8.4 Tools to assist with career tactics and career planning

Tactical tools
- Writing CVs
- Preparing for an interview
- Learning from the interview process
- Networking
- Building your reputation
- Finding a mentor or career coach
- Maintaining momentum and motivation
- Researching opportunities externally
- Understanding organisational politics
- Developing career resilience

Planning tools
- Mapping out the opportunities
- Choosing options
- Mapping satisfiers
- Goal setting

Intranet and Internet sites

IT solutions, such as the sophisticated tools used in *Nationwide* which are described in the case study at the end of this chapter, are particularly useful for covering a large and disperse workforce. Nestle also have an in-house Intranet site which offers tools for self-assessment and action planning. There is also information on who supports the various career processes and career contact points for information of particular types of job.

Many of the organisational tools which started off as workbooks have now evolved into toolkits for computer use and the web has a wealth of tools which are useful for career planning. One of my favourites, and one of the longer standing, comes from Lifeskills Career Builder, which covers the tools required for each phase of career planning quite comprehensively and can also be adapted for companies, so that they can link in with their own processes and information. *Rolls-Royce* has successfully used this approach.

The web resources can be loosely divided into three different categories:

Category 1: Self-assessment tools and psychometrics

These sites provide on-line testing, for example Honey and Mumford's learning styles can be accessed via the web, as can Strong's Interest Inventory. There are also many varieties of personality diagnostic questionnaires available.

Category 2: Information on jobs, roles and opportunities for development

Whilst organisations are unlikely to be encouraging the wider opportunity searches that can be useful to individual career planning, there are still useful sites which may be of relevance in this category. Professional bodies for example, may provide careers advice and courses and training can also be searched.

Category 3: Tactical tools

Sites abound on how to network effectively, produce a good CV or hold a good interview and there are even on-line interview simulations. Career tactics (www.andrewsmunro.com) is an example of a site in this category. It contains a questionnaire to assess a person's career tactics and whether they are able to effectively address aspects such as building a reputation, or managing complex relationships.

The sites available are constantly changing and companies could help employees by providing clear and up-to-date links to such information and resources, much of which is freely available.

Booklets and books

Some organisations choose to produce folders for all their employees, or just the high potentials, which contain booklets on different aspects of career development, such as self-assessment, personal development plans, career tactics and job maps.

Organisations also make good use of external resources, often within learning resource centres, as there are numerous books to help with career planning and career tactics. Two of the best known self-help books are 'What colour is your parachute?' (Bolles, 1988) and 'Build your own rainbow' (Hopson and Scally, 1991) but there are also some excellent books on specific tasks, such as interviewing skills.

Career workshops

Career workshops are typically 1- or 2-day programmes which bring together groups of employees to work through a facilitated set of interventions aimed at exploring their career. Whilst on the face of it appearing quite indulgent, career workshops can have immense benefits, in both motivating employees and making them feel more valued, but also in helping to develop more tailored career plans which support the organisations needs for the future.

The *Lexmark* case study which follows is a nice illustration of what career workshop might consist of. Typically, a workshop will be held with small groups of people at a similar level in the organisation and will use external facilitation to take the group through a series of exercises. Often a company will choose to use external facilitators, in order to retain the anonymity and confidentiality of the individual's concerned and therefore allow them greater freedom to open up and explore issues. Sometimes however, internal facilitators may be useful, if they are able to add company-specific information to support careers.

Case study: Career development workshop for high potentials, *Lexmark*

Information supplied by Lynn Goy, Lexmark Europe

Background

Lexmark is a leading provider of printing solutions, with a $5.2 billion revenue in 2005. The company operates globally and employs approximately 13 000 people. *Lexmark* sell into 130 countries through 30 sales subsidiaries; 47 per cent of their revenue comes from consumers and the remaining 53 per cent from business customers.

Objectives

Lexmark introduced a programme targeted at its High Potential (HiPo) population, which ran from 2004 to 2006, in partnership with the Roffey Park Institute, the objectives of which were:

- To think about your own career in the changing world of work.
- To understand the importance of taking ownership of your career at *Lexmark*.
- To identify some practical strategies for a healthy career development plan.

Lynn Goy, responsible for Talent Management Programs for *Lexmark* Europe, was keen to provide the HiPo's with some guidance and support on their career development planning in order to enable them to have more in-depth development conversations with their manager. This programme was also a clear signal to the HiPo's that *Lexmark* valued them and wanted to help them in their career development at *Lexmark*. The programme provided the opportunity for participants to take stock of their careers and put across a strong message that development was taken seriously and managers had a key role to play in their own career development.

Confidentiality was a strong consideration for the programme and Roffey Park ensured that an open environment was created, where managers felt safe to disclose their true needs and talk about their careers in the widest sense. If participants wanted to discuss family constraints or more longer-term career ideas, this was encouraged. No information received from the participants was passed back to the organisation.

All individuals that had been identified at HiPo's during the annual succession cycle were eligible for this programme. Groups were put together to provide a maximum mix of nationality, gender and functional responsibility; building an internal network with colleagues from other areas of the business was seen as an additional benefit of the programme. Participants could be at differing stages of their career; some were already people managers, some had recently moved jobs and were to be a people manager for the first time and many were trying to clarify what their next move should be.

The programme content

In preparation for the programme, participants completed a number of tasks. They are asked to complete the Career Orientations Inventory (Schein, 1990); complete a life-line exercise; surf the Internet to find something of interest relating to career development and bring other information about themselves which may be useful, such as personality profiles and 360-degree feedback.

The 2-day programme itself included the following sessions:

- Exploration of what a career means
- Careers in the 21st century
- The psychological contract
- Career anchors
- Skills and interests
- Work–life balance
- Peer coaching
- Developing career purpose
- Raising your profile in the organisation
- Working with a mentor
- Lifelong learning.

The programme was a mix of practical tools, raising self-awareness and providing opportunities to think creatively about what participants really wanted for themselves. The programme delivery allowed for the content to be adapted to suit the needs of the group.

Further 1:1 coaching was offered to all participants by the facilitators in the weeks and months after the workshop, to help them think through issues connected with their career plan. Again, these discussions are confidential.

Outcomes

The programme was perceived as a huge success, not only by the partici-pants, but also by country general management. Participants returned to the workplace with a much clearer picture of what they needed to do in order to more effectively plan their career, and they shared these ideas in discussions with their management.

During the subsequent succession reviews, country management confirmed that attendance on the programme had been very worthwhile and they were keen to nominate additional HiPo's to attend the class as soon as possible.

Feedback on a sample of participants over a year after attendance on the programmes was also sought. This feedback indicated that the programme had made a clear impact on the individual's attitudes towards their career and that of the organisation. Some of the comments made are shown below.

What impact did the programme have on you and your career?

'The programme confirmed that it is better to have a career plan, both short and long term and to communicate this effectively to my manager if I want to progress'.

'The themes developed at the course are a solid reference whenever a deci-sion on my career has to be taken'.

'The course forced me to think about my own career and my career path within *Lexmark*. It also made clear that the only person who is responsible for my career and my career path is me. It is me who is in charge of taking the challenge and the responsibility for my career, and that nobody else is sitting in the driver seat. Personally it helped me to open my eyes, to focus on what my aims are and to reflect on myself'.

'Since attending the course I have re-evaluated my career path, had an open discussion with both my line manager and reporting Director and was pro-moted to a European role after using the elements of understanding my goals within the course'.

'An increased awareness of how to manage my career goals but most impor-tantly the organisation's expectations of me'.

What effect did it have (if any) on your view of careers management within *Lexmark*?

'The fact that *Lexmark* offered me the opportunity to think about my career had a very good effect on me and my involvement within the company has improved'.

'I came away highly motivated from the programme and was more willing to make my written career plan happen, because *Lexmark* had shown respect towards me and acknowledged my ambition by seeing me as a significant part in the Company. For me there was a stronger psychological connection with *Lexmark*'.

What value do you think organisations get from providing workshops like this one?

'Loyalty'

'Involvement'

'Increased motivation of employees'

'More people achieving their personal career goals and getting satisfaction from that'.

What other support do you think high potential managers need from the organisation to develop their career?

'A regular review or follow up between high potential managers and their managers to check that expectations from both sides are in line'.

'Greater support for mentoring and peer coaching schemes. The OK interesting, but let's go back to our business approach is hard to remove from the organisations, I'm afraid'.

'Constant objective monitoring of the abilities of each individual member of staff and a greater openness about progression to other areas of the company'.

Taking account of career theories: how do these contribute?

A wealth of theory exists on individual career development and the way careers typically progress through the course of people's lives. Whilst some of this is useful to organisations in helping shape career strategies, much of it individually focused and more relevant outside of an organisational context. This section aims to highlight some of the more commonly applied theories in the corporate world, which can provide useful insights into how to shape and define your career strategy to suit the culture and makeup of your employees.

Although numerous models and theoretical explanations of adult career development exist, three particular models have gone on to become available in commercial test form and have consequently had a greater impact on practitioners. These are Schein's career anchor questionnaire (1990), Super's career concerns inventory (1988) and Derr's career success map (1986). All three of these models are used as a basis for occupational choice. However, the particular advantage of Schein and Derr's models, are that they create a balance between the individual and organisations, rather than having a purely individual focus.

There are also a number of models which focus on life stages, which are less appropriate in a turbulent external environment, where age-related progression is no longer typical. However, they are still worth considering to help understand key transition points in careers and will be looked at later in this chapter.

Career anchors and career orientations

The research into career orientations undertaken by Schein and built upon by Derr has value in that it takes neither a psychological perspective (which simplistically states that a person's makeup determines their career), nor a sociological perspective (that careers shape people), but allows for both to be in evidence.

A career orientation is defined by both writers as a combination of motives, values and talents that influence an individual's career choices. An individual can therefore only gauge their true orientation after a period of work experiences. Orientations inevitably focus on the internal career and what drives the individual, but they also take account of the external career that has preceded.

The importance for organisational career management is the recognition that there are strong non-monetary factors which affect work and career satisfaction, and career orientations provide a way of understanding these motivators of career decisions. Many organisational career programmes assume that employees are motivated by the prospect of promotion, but there is considerable evidence for differences in motivation (Holland, 1985). Although, equally, there is evidence to suggest that employees promotion aspirations are often underestimated (Herriot et al., 1994).

If employees remain in a job that is not congruent with their career anchor and repress their motivations, it is argued that they seek to achieve the missing elements of their anchor through outside work interests or by withdrawing commitment, which has obvious implications for organisations.

If organisations are to use a tool for analysing employee career orientations, both Schein and Derr's models are particularly useful. Derr's model consists of five career orientations which appear to map easily onto Schein's anchors as shown in Table 8.5.

Derr suggests that organisations can benefit from analysing career orientations in order to determine which career interventions are most appropriate for each career orientation. For example, assessment centres are suited to 'Getting ahead' orientation; career counselling to 'Getting secure'; and career pathing to 'Getting high' and 'Getting free'. In addition to this, Schein puts forward the case for flexible

Table 8.5 Comparing career anchors and career orientations

Derr's orientations	Schein's career anchor
Getting ahead (i.e. seeking advancement)	General managerial
Getting secure	Security/stability
Getting free (i.e. seeking independence)	Autonomy/independence
Getting high (i.e. valuing excitement)	Pure challenge and technical competence
Getting balanced	Lifestyle

reward systems, promotion systems and recognition systems to address the differing needs of individuals. For example, people with a lifestyle anchor are likely to place a high value on flexible benefits, where people with a security/stability anchor will be more biased towards pension schemes and steady incremental pay scales. The trend towards organisations taking a portfolio approach to pay and benefits have been very helpful in this respect.

Career anchor theory was developed by Edgar Schein (1978) at the Massachusetts Institute of Technology (MIT) in the 1960s. The theory stemmed from a 10–12-year longitudinal study of 44 MBA graduates using in-depth interviews to examine job histories and the reasons behind career decisions. Career anchors emerged as a way of explaining the pattern of reasons given by the graduates as they progressed through their careers. Whilst the research was built around a study of managers, career anchors are now widely applied to all levels of employees.

Schein defines an anchor as: 'a pattern of self perceived talents, motives and values that serve to guide, constrain, stabilise and integrate individual careers'.

These three elements of the anchor are outlined more specifically as:

1. Self-perceived talents and abilities
2. Self-perceived motives and needs
3. Self-perceived attitudes and values.

Anchors are therefore broader than just values as they emphasises discovery through work experience and the importance of feedback in shaping development. They serve to explain how and why an individual interacts with the organisation, as the theory states that an individual will not give up their predominant career anchor if a choice is available (i.e. an employee will not take on a job where the needs of their career anchor are not met) if there is an alternative. This view is supported by Hall (1976) who states that an individual's values are acquired through work experience and can come to direct subsequent career behaviour and choice.

A self-scoring questionnaire has been developed containing 40 statements to which the respondent rates how true each statement is for them. Ideally, the results

Table 8.6 Schein's career anchors

Technical/functional competence
General managerial competence
Pure challenge
Autonomy/independence
Security/stability
Entrepreneurial creativity
Service/dedication to a cause
Lifestyle

are followed up by a structured interview to confirm the predominant anchor indicated. It is the availability of this easily understood tool that has helped make career anchors so prevalent in organisations. The eight anchors are shown in Table 8.6.

Technical/functional competence

This is typified by the desire to focus on the technical and functional specialisms within the role. Individuals with this anchor seek to apply their skills to specialist problems. Driver (1979) refers to these as 'steady-state' careers because success is measured in terms of expanding technical knowledge rather than promotion up a hierarchy. Where organisations have a predominance of employees anchored in this way, it would be worth considering putting in place dual career ladders to allow parallel progression for specialists. This would allow them to continue to add value to the organisation whilst maintaining their motivation and commitment.

General managerial competence

People anchored in general managerial are more interested in status, responsibility and progression, and gain satisfaction from delivering tasks through co-ordinating people's efforts. Schein identified three types of competence required for a general manager – analytical, interpersonal and emotional. This emotional competence he describes as 'the capacity to bear high levels of responsibility without becoming paralysed and the ability to exercise power without guilt or shame' (Schein, 1978, p. 136).

Driver's (1979) model of careers would describe these as 'linear' careers because success is measured in terms of upward movement. The presence of the managerial anchor has implications for organisations as career advancement within management is increasingly a difficult thing to offer. It is also possible that some of these characteristics are those defined as a measure for selection to an acceleration pool for high potentials, perhaps perpetuating the difficulties.

Pure challenge

The challenge anchor relates to people who enjoy difficult problems and solving the seemingly unsolvable. Novelty and variety are key components of this anchor.

This anchor is most closely aligned to Driver's (1979) fourth career concept – that of a 'spiral career', where development occurs in a particular field before the individual moves on to another area for development. Consultants are often anchored in pure challenge.

Autonomy/independence

People anchored in autonomy and independence seek to be free from rules and constraints and want to be able to define their work in their own way. Schein suggests that such people will turn down opportunities for promotion or advancement in order to retain autonomy. This anchor is most closely aligned to Driver's (1979) 'transitory career' where individuals move from job to job with no particular pattern.

Security/stability

With a security and stability anchor the focus in on long-term stability and the career concerns are connected with financial security (such as pension and retirement plans) and employment security. People with this anchor are less concerned with the content of their work and the position they achieve in the hierarchy.

It would be expected that individuals with a dominant security/stability anchor will seek to exert little control over their career, being largely risk averse. This was demonstrated in research by Giles and West (1995). As mentioned earlier, organisational trends towards self-management of careers would be likely to be less successful with this group of employees.

The Careers Innovation Survey mentioned earlier also highlights security as the least important career value for high flyers. The implications for organisations here occur if the company is seeking to retain a stable core of the workforce for the future, where a proportion of employees anchored in security would be valuable.

Entrepreneurial creativity

An entrepreneurial creativity anchor is concerned with self-expression and creating outcomes directly as a result of your own skills and abilities. Business startups are likely to appeal to people with this anchor and they may work for an organisation while learning and assessing other opportunities.

Unlike those with a security/stability anchor, it would be expected that those anchored in entrepreneurial creativity would exert a high level of control over their career (Bell and Straw, 1989). Like the managerial anchor, many of these characteristics are also likely to be selection criteria for high potentials, although with this group there is a chance that they will lack the commitment needed to warrant substantial investments in their development. The challenge for companies is to keep their roles exciting and new.

Service/dedication to a cause

This anchor was added in Schein's later research and is concerned with people who have strong values that drive their career choices, such as solving environmental problems and helping others. Certain types of organisations are likely to attract people anchored in this way, such as caring professions or the police force.

Lifestyle

Schein describes people who are anchored in lifestyle as people who seek to balance and integrate personal needs, family needs, and the requirements of the career and make them work as an integrated whole.

The lifestyle anchor is perhaps the most controversial of all the anchors, as most members of the workforce would advocate that they are seeking to achieve a work–life balance. Whilst the later addition of the lifestyle anchor has been cited as being causal in expanding the definition of a career to move beyond occupational choice, in a more recent survey by Schein over 50 per cent of respondents considered their anchor to be lifestyle (Schein, 1996).

If this is true, then organisations need to be paying far more attention to the employee side of the psychological contract. However, in my own experience of using the career anchor instrument, there is a tendency to focus on anchors perceived as 'good to have'. It may be the case therefore that the increased awareness of the need for work–life balance has driven people to overly focus on lifestyle and loose sight of their true drivers.

Interestingly Derr's model examines European differences and concludes that British managers are more likely to have a Getting Ahead and Getting Free orientation and a lower Getting balanced than the French and Germans (Derr and Laurent, 1989). However, possibly due to lack of further research into Derr's orientations and the limitation of only five orientations against Schein's eight, the career anchors have become much more widely used in organisations.

Schein and Derr disagree in the extent to which they believe anchors (or orientations) change over the course of a person's life. Schein has now studied 15 of the original sample group into their 40s and evidence here suggests they remain consistent throughout life. However, he argues that anchors may appear to be changed through a work experience that leads to greater self-discovery, allowing the original anchor to emerge. Derr on the other hand argues that career orientations can change with age and due to external influences.

Schein's original research has been criticised for the relatively small sample of highly educated people it drew on, who were all men in their late 20s/early 30s. The transferability to women, racial groups or less educated groups is therefore in question. The majority of the research that has gone on to follow up on the theory of career anchors has concentrated on exploring whether other anchors exist. Schein cites two potential anchors – variety and power, but claims that both of these form elements of existing anchors and are not an overriding influence in themselves.

What are the Implications of career orientations?

Understanding career orientations and anchors can have immense value both to organisations and to individuals. To summarise, the organisational benefits in understanding career orientations are:

- The ability to tailor career interventions appropriately.
- The ability to create more effective organisational design.
- Increased job satisfaction through more constructive discussions with employees.
- The ability to offer opportunities congruent with an individual's orientation.
- The ability to understanding why quality staff choose to leave the organisation.
- The design of appropriate reward systems.
- The design of appropriate promotion systems.
- More targeted recognition systems.
- An increased understanding by managers of what drives internal career satisfaction.
- A means of understanding the overriding career culture in the organisation.
- A way of helping individuals achieve a better fit with the organisation by understanding their own drivers and career goals.
- A way of structuring career discussions and particularly exit interviews.

To work effectively however, there needs to be sufficient trust in the organisation for the questionnaires or interviews to be completed honestly, to ensure that an accurate reflection of the person's anchor is determined. My own research in this area (Yarnall, 1998a) has shown that there can also be immense value in using the collective results of an organisations career anchor profile, to get a greater insight into the career culture of the company.

Career life stages

Career stages are typically defined as phases of working life. Many of the early theorists assumed career stages to be linear and stable, but the concepts have been updated to encompass modern, more varied patterns of career development. Some of the age-defined models of career stages are consequently viewed as less relevant in today's working environment. Yet, there are still benefits in understanding some of the key transitions people go through in their career.

Donald Super (1980) is one of the most famed for his life-stage work. He identified five key stages or what he called 'maxicycles': There were Growth (age 4–13 years); Exploration (14–24 years); Establishment (25–44 years); Maintenance (45–65 years) and Disengagement (65 years and over).

Other writers have further refined Super's model and the adult stages are:

- Early adulthood (18–23 years)
- Age of optimism (24–28 years)
- Transition (29–32 years)
- Age of conformity (33–38 years)
- Transition two – mid-life crisis (39–42 years)
- Age of individuality (45 years onwards).

Super suggests that not everyone progresses through these stages at fixed ages or in the same fashion, and that within each stage there are tasks whose mastery allows people to function successfully within that stage while preparing them to move on to the next task.

Before entering the later stages, for example, many individuals are in the process of asking the standard mid-life question, 'Do I want to do this job for the next 20 years?' eventually deciding to either hang on or let go. If they decide to hang on, they enter the maintenance stage. If they decide to let go and change job, company or career, they recycle back to earlier stages, crystallise new career development objectives and move forward from there. For those who hold on, they maintain what they have, update their skills and knowledge, and innovate.

In her book *Passages*, Gail Sheehy (1976) appealed to a wide audience and popularised life-stage theory. Informed by earlier research, she identified life stages as:

- Pulling Up Roots (18–22 years)
- The Trying Twenties (22–29 years)
- Catching Thirty (approaching 30 years)
- Rooting and Extending (early 30s)
- The Deadline Decade (35–45 years)
- Renewal and Resignation (mid-40s).

She describes passages as the transitional periods between life stages. Although they are difficult for most adults, they also provide the necessary impetus for growth as one gives up the securities of one stage in order to move on to the next. Shechy's life stages are highly relevant to the discussion of career stage because she marries developmental tasks with corollary career tasks, such as the duality of the search for identity and career.

Young adulthood

During this period, the most significant developmental task is establishment. Young adults experience a series of 'trial' jobs before more firmly establishing themselves in a more stable career. This process of establishing oneself is the primary task associated with young adulthood, and once stabilised, consolidation and advancement become the next developmental tasks. Several important concepts surface during this period of life, including career adaptability and career adjustment. In addition, gender differences become apparent as men and women choose whether or not to follow paths congruent with traditional gender roles.

Middle adulthood

This era is characterised by reappraisal and 'What have I done with my life?' or 'What do I truly want?' are often questions asked during this period of time. For men, state of health or career accomplishment may predominate. Levinson (1986) suggests that the reason for this fixation on re-evaluation is based on three factors that occur around this period of time: first, a modest decline in body functioning that may be interpreted as a loss of vigour as well as a reminder of one's mortality; second, an age shift that occurs as younger people regard individuals aged in the 40s to be of 'another generation'; and third, a reflection on earlier life ambitions and dreams. Women, on the other hand, may perceive this era as an opportunity: one to pursue either personal or career development goals now that their childbearing role has peaked.

Older workers

Older workers' attitudes toward career development activities and mobility relate to such factors as current employment (experience or fear of lay-offs), tenure or stage in their careers, need for achievement and need for growth. In addition, fear of stagnation, marketability perceptions, self-esteem and job-market conditions play a role in career decision making. A decision to engage in training or retraining can lead an older worker to identity growth and enhanced self-esteem which in turn may result in greater commitment to future career development goals.

Although little research exists on career stages as adults approach retirement, a developmental stage in general is implicated, which suggests a stage of self-acceptance. As workers age, they are likely to redefine what is meant by career success.

Part-time work is also an increasingly important phenomenon among older workers. More than a third of retirees want to work part time for 'interest and enjoyment' (Roper, 2002). This reflects a relatively new and increasingly common set of circumstances among late-stage workers, 'bridge jobs'. This category of jobs offers new experiences, provides flexibility, and bridges the gap between careers or before leaving the workforce permanently. Organisations with a more altruistic nature, may choose to help with this transition.

Gender differences

The majority of the work written on career stage results from studies of men, and much of that research was done prior to 1990. While the career development of women has been explored, the concept of career stage as uniquely experienced by women is not very comprehensive. One study by Roberts and Friend (1998) did find that women in high status jobs had higher scores on measures of psychological and physical well-being and these findings suggest that women's career stages may differ from men's.

Women progress through careers at different rates and in varied succession depending on a number of unique factors, such as family status. For that reason, it may be more useful when studying work/family issues to use stage theory that is independent of age rather than to use age-based stages. For example, while men typically enter and exit the career exploration stage during adolescence, women may experience this stage during mid-life for the first time, or they may re-enter exploration as childcare responsibilities decrease. Similarly, the retirement stage is based on the premise that a man has a lifelong career while women may 'retire' or intermittently leave the workforce as pregnancy or other family obligations arise. Increasingly, men are also adapting their careers to participate more fully in the parenting role and family demands are also likely to impact their career development and career stages.

What are the implications of life and career stages?

Understanding life stage theory, even if it is not an absolute, can be extremely useful for career coaches and people supporting career development. The age of transitions may vary with individuals, but understanding that particular career crisis points may occur, can be very helpful in facilitating a discussion.

Case study: *Nationwide* – a supported self-management approach to careers

Information supplied by Steve Lassman

Background

Nationwide is a mutual Building Society with 11 million members and assets of around £100 billion. The company operates across 700 branches and 200 agencies and has approximately 16,000 employees. *Nationwide* has taken a strategic approach to career development for many years and won the Personnel Today Award for innovation in career development in 2003.

Nationwide's strategic approach

Nationwide's career strategy is built on a belief that there should be careers for everyone and that whilst it is an individual's responsibility, a comprehensive range of support will be provided by the organisation to help employees to achieve this.

Nationwide has very clear statements of both organisational intent and individual responsibility for careers. At an organisational level the purpose of their career strategy is described as:

- To grow the future skills we need to support the business needs.
- Ensure we identify, develop and make the most of the talent we have in the organisation.
- Provide support to employees to make the most of their talent and use their potential to the full.
- Support individual career aspirations.

They do this through a range of supported activities as shown in the figure seen in next page.

At an individual level, responsibilities are also made clear and having a career in *Nationwide* means:

- Making the most of your talent
- Taking the most from your opportunities
- Giving the best you are able to give
- Preparing yourself today for tomorrow
- Being able to proudly say '*Nationwide* is where I want to work'.

213

Careers at *nationwide*: strategic fit

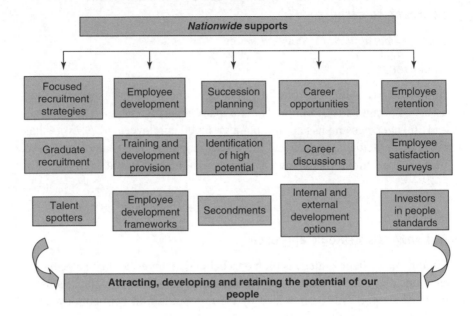

Utilising technology to widen support

In addition to career discussions and career workshops for each job family level, *Nationwide* is at the forefront of companies using Intranets to support career strategies. They have a vast range of tools and information available to all employees through their own career Intranet.

To make the most of their talent, they have a 'Development Curve' site, which helps people to self-assess aspects such as transferable skills and explore some of the options open to them.

See figure in next page.

There is also a site which focuses specifically on careers and helps people to work through a variety of tools to take them through the stages of a career planning process:

- Where am I now?
- Where do I want to be?
- How do I get there?

The career planner, which highlights these key stages, is an essential document which is used as a framework for employees' career discussions and career advice.

About the Intranet   nationwide.co.uk | Phone Book | Directory Enquiries | Log a Fault
Helping Members   You and Nationwide   How We Are Doing   Who We Are   Operating Our Business

Nationwide

Development Curve - Level 1

Which section should I do first?
Business Performance
Coaching
Employee Performance
Making the Most of My Talent
Member Experience
Help and Support
Update your Profile

Change Screen Settings >>>

Create Your Plan

Create Your Plan   View Your Plan

Making the Most of My Talent

You're on your way to creating your Training Plan for Making the Most of My Talent...

Page 1 of 4 1 2 3 4

1: Section 1		
1a: Do you understand how to take responsibility for your self development?	Yes	No
1b: Do you understand the impact your behaviour could have on others?	Yes	No
1c: Do you know how to plan your career?	Yes	No
1d: Do you understand the best way for you to learn and take in information?	Yes	No
1e: Do you understand how to carry out a SWOT and KASH analysis?	Yes	No

Save for Later   Go to page 2 of 4 >>>

Our **Help and Support** site will answer all your questions about Development Curve.   GO

Useful Links

Your Aims

Content Owner

Jeremy Wicks
Senior Manager, Retail Training
655177
Site Updated:
04/04/2006
Feedback

Nationwide

Career planner for		Date	

Whether you are looking to develop your career by staying in your present role or moving roles (either within the same Job Family or in a different Job Family) use steps 1 and 2 of this planner as a structure to prepare for your career discussion. Have it with you at the discussion to use as a guide and to make sure all the points are covered.

Step 1: Where am I now?	Step 2: Where do I want to be?
Complete this section as preparation for your career discussion. Define what you are good at and what work you enjoy. Explain how you have developed your career since your last career discussion. See 'You and Your Career' Intranet site step 1 for further advice.	Complete this section as preparation for your career discussion. What does your ideal job look like? Write down your reasons why. Define your career development goals. Describe what will you be doing, seeing and feeling when you have achieved your goal. See 'You and Your Career' Intranet site step 2 for further advice.

Summary of actions I am going to take	Step 3: How do I get there?
What actions will you take between now and my next career review? Who do you need to contact to help you achieve your goal? What other support will you need? See 'You and Your Career' Intranet site step 3 – Get Planning for further advice.	*Ask your manager to help you to consider:* What opportunities can you create or are available to help me develop my career? Think about short - and - long-term development. See 'You and Your Career' Intranet site step 3 for further advice.

Action	By when

215

Clear role boundaries

Nationwide has also established clear role definitions for all the people involved in the career strategy. Managers have a clear role in facilitating career discussions; local succession planning and spotting talent. However there is also a specialist career team who can provide career advice to individuals referred on to them and also play a role in developing career processes and tools and corporate succession planning.

Evaluating success

The long-standing nature of the career support provided has meant that *Nationwide* have been able to track progress and correlations between key indicators of success. Using their opinion survey data, they have proved a clear correlation between employee commitment and business results. They have also found length of service to be a key indicator of employee commitment.

As a result of this they now have a very clear business case for enhancing careers. If they were able to increase the average length of service by just half a year, this would expect to see £3 million more mortgages, £200 000 more in personal loans and £100 000 more in insurance business.

Ongoing challenges

Nationwide's aim is now to:

- Market its career-related tools to employees to increase awareness and usage.
- Increase take-up of career discussions facilitated by managers.
- Increase overall satisfaction with careers from the current level of 66 per cent of favourable responses, as measured by its annual employee survey.

Summary

With the 'in' strategy for careers in organisations focusing on talent management, the self-development approach to career development has shrunk away from the limelight. This chapter explored whether this move was appropriate in the current environment and which aspects of the self-development strategy are worth carrying forward into the new models.

Whilst self-development approaches did suffer from a lack on take-up if the culture was not supportive or the purpose was not clear, much of the intent behind the strategy was well thought through and the approach is particularly suited to self-motivated high potential employees and women in particular. To be effective, self-development approaches have been found to need a stimulus to encourage people to participate, such as tying the tools into other activities. The current trend towards acceleration pools is an ideal way of doing this. Particular career planning tools could be added in as part of the success criteria for attaining different levels. This may also help to overcome some of the difficulties of career resilience seen to be emerging in many high potential groups – where increasing energy is being put into developing their talent and achieving certain roles, with little thought to the longer-term consequences on health or work-life balance.

Career planning can be a difficult activity if you have never received guidance or support with it in the past. Self-development approaches can provide some useful tools to help people develop their career competences and achieve greater self-reliance with career processes. Simple frameworks, such as the 'Where am I now? Where do I want to be? How does this fit with the organisation? And How do I get there?' approach described in this chapter can be very helpful in working through the career planning process. Career theories can also add a great deal, both at an individual level, where career anchors and career life stages can help guide career coaching conversations, and also at an organisational level, where they can help diagnose and make sense of the overriding career culture.

Companies have a huge choice when it comes to deciding how to deliver self-help career planning tools such as those described in this chapter. Use of Internet and Intranet technology is growing at a rate, but for me the ability to discuss and debate the tools is vital, making career workshops and career coaching particularly valuable channels.

Overall, I would encourage organisations to put the self-development approach back at the forefront of their thinking and make steps to align some of the individual career planning tools more closely with the progression of their talent groups.

Checklist

- To what extent does your company encourage self-development as part of the career strategy?
- Are any self-help tools clearly aligned with other organisational processes?
- Do employees think of their career in terms of continually updating skills rather than upward progression?

- Is it clear to high potential employees what they stand to gain from participating in self-development initiatives?
- How much pressure is put on high potentials without taking account of their long-term personal needs?
- Does the organisational talent have the career competencies required to develop and implement effective career plans?
- Is the framework for career planning clear and appropriate for the needs of the workforce?
- Are the methods of delivery making best use of IT and support mechanisms?
- Can increased use be made of career theories to help tailor interventions more appropriately?

9

Final Reflections

When I started writing this book, I wasn't clear in my own mind whether career strategies had become old-fashioned terms that had been replaced by a newer and sexier sounding talent strategy, or whether the two things were in fact different. As my research continued, the people I talked to reinforced this confusion.

The younger generation, who started their career at a time when self-development strategies were at the fore, quite obviously saw talent management as a more managed and thought through approach to career development. Others, who had been in companies at the time of fast-track schemes and bureaucratic succession planning, saw talent management as a less managed process, with the ability to adapt to changing future circumstances.

As I conclude this book, my own opinion is that what we are seeing with the recent focus on talent management is a natural evolution of career strategies, to meet the changing demands on organisations. In the past career planning was led by the organisation and then swung to the other end of the spectrum and focused on individual-led career planning as the future of companies became less certain (see Figure 9.1). This approach had many limitations and I see the current trend as

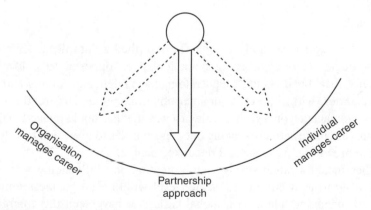

Organisation
manages career

Individual
manages career

Partnership
approach

Figure 9.1 Another swing on the spectrum?

a swing back on this spectrum to take into account more of the organisational needs and focus the individual more effectively.

Themes from the case studies

Whatever the terminology used, some strong themes emerged from the case study research for this book, highlighting the direction that companies are currently moving.

Integration with other business processes

In the past career strategies could have been accused of operating in isolation. One or two champions of the strategy would typically develop new initiatives to support careers, such as career workshops or succession planning, in the hope that it would impact career satisfaction and career development. It was unusual for selection strategies or remuneration policies to be aligned with these interventions. What is clear from the case studies is that career strategies are now being re-examined and re-positioned alongside other business processes.

There were clear examples of a lack of skill or competence being diagnosed in one area of the business and clear channels of communication to ensure that selection policies and development strategies took account of this. What was also evident, however, was a tendency for career and talent specialists to form closer allegiances with some processes than others. Some companies, for example, sat firmly within training and development and the career strategy fed clearly into initiatives in this area, whilst others were more closely aligned with selection, performance management or remuneration strategies.

Global reach

Many of the larger case study companies described a significant shift in their career strategies towards working on a global as opposed to a local scale. Historically, local business units tended to manage talent and careers within their own boundaries, with little cross-organisational planning. The trend now is for careers to be managed on a global scale in a way that has not happened in the past. Companies are more actively seeking out opportunities to grow and transfer talent in order to broaden experience and retain key people.

This has meant a much stronger co-ordinating and influencing role for HR, with the need to gain buy-in at a senior level within each business unit, to the benefits of managing talent on a global scale. We have seen the emergence of Global Talent Panels, with representatives from each part of the business as well as a greater recognition of the value of mobility and different cultural experiences as being a key component of developing global talent.

Coaching is on the increase

For virtually all the companies, coaching is playing a key role in the success of their career strategy. For talent groups, coaches are often assigned as part of a management development intervention and provide tailored support and guidance to help the individual further their development plans. For other employees, there may be access to a coach at specific career stages or events, whereas for senior managers there may be a longer-term relationship with a coach, to help their on-going development. Many companies are also working towards more of a coaching culture, where a coaching approach is embedded in all management practices.

Whilst the source of these coaches varies – some being external, some internal specialists, some from more coaching-focused management – the value of holding career conversations and focusing in on the needs of the individual has been much more widely accepted as important.

Stronger measures of success

Producing a business case for career interventions is now commonplace in organisations, in a way that was never apparent in career strategies of old. The implication of this is twofold. Companies have firstly managed to get greater involvement and buy-in to the strategy through the discussion of the business case and the options available. By engaging key stakeholders early on in the process, HR have been able to gain more commitment and leadership from management which has led to the top-level influence and buy-in which is so essential to making the strategy work.

Secondly, and perhaps more importantly, measure of success have been clearly stated up-front and the added value of career strategies can now be more readily proven. In putting the business case together, HR professionals have had to think through the financial and non-financial benefits, as well as strategies to mitigate against the potential risks. This up-front planning has helped not only to demonstrate the value of career strategies and interventions to the business, but has also helped build the credibility of those HR functions for the future.

The swing towards more managed development

As I said in the introduction to this chapter, the move to managing talent is a swing back from more recent career strategies which left the responsibility with the individual. Many of the case studies showed that they had taken control back of high potential employees, in a way not dissimilar to the fast-track schemes of old. Where this approach differs, however, is that there is a far greater interaction with the individual, and their own ideas and drivers are more likely to be taken into consideration. The growth of Personal Development Plans as a means for logging individual aspirations and intentions have been instrumental in aiding this process.

Business led activity

There was a clear sense from the case study research that operational managers are far more actively involved in career strategies and more committed to ensuring the organisation is preparing itself for its future talent needs. Senior managers were instrumental in all the case studies to help shape and progress implementation of different initiatives, often guided by newly positioned HR Business Partners taking a more consultative approach with the business. Whilst top-level ownership of career strategies has always been cited as an essential component, there is clear evidence here that this is now happening and strategies are being given the support and leadership they require to be successful.

Newly formed acceleration pools

Many of the case study companies were placing a great deal of energy into selecting the right people for newly formed acceleration pools and defining the criteria for entry and, in some cases, exit, from these pools. What was less clear for many of the companies was exactly how to fulfil the development requirements for the newly formed talent pools. Whilst many companies were working on, or had leadership development programmes in place, this was focused on training skills, rather than providing the type of growth opportunities that may develop the required skills.

It may be that this lack of focus on how acceleration pool members can gain the exposure they need was due to the fact that some of the case study organisations were in the early stages of implementing their strategy. However, there was also a strong sense that selecting the group and providing training was the easy part, whereas trying to instigate role or project opportunities was far more difficult to influence.

Issues and challenges

The trends in career strategies are not without their challenges and some of the key issues facing the case study organisations are highlighted here.

Skilling the line

As is the case with many people-focused strategies, line managers hold the key to successful implementation. This brings with it one of the difficulties facing many organisations, which is the ability to both skill the line in the required competencies to support the strategy, and motivate and get the buy-in needed for them to take on the role.

The need for perceived equity in career processes is critical and if there are groups of line managers who are not providing effective feedback, performance management or motivation to people within their teams, dissatisfaction will spread and career strategies which revolve around line manager support are likely to become discredited.

Whilst the case study organisations show that a great deal of progress is being made in this area, there are still large pools of managers who are either unwilling or unable, to play their part effectively. One of the key challenges for HR will be their ability to influence and coach these managers to take a more active part in the process.

Dealing with high potential specialists

Many of the companies researched were still unsure how to deal with specialist high potentials, who do not necessarily need the more generic approach to development or progression provided for other acceleration pools.

Organisations with larger numbers of specialists, have been able to overcome this problem by creating dual career pathways, enabling specialists to progress through the company without the need for people management. Companies with smaller numbers of specialists however need to think of appropriate ways of managing their careers, without isolating them from the generic acceleration pools and demotivating them to the point where specialists start to leave the organisation.

How far do you swing the pendulum back?

There were some definite indications in the discussions that I had, that companies were trying to regain control of employee careers and return to the managed career progression of years gone by. Whilst some made mention of career planning tools available to individuals, they often appeared as an after-thought or an add-on to their current focus on planned opportunities for high potential employees.

Whilst I am the first to admit the deficiencies of the self-development approach to careers, there are many aspects to be gained from it – not least of which is a way for the individual to structure their own thinking about their careers. As I concluded in the previous chapter, I would encourage organisations to put the self-development approach back at the forefront of their thinking and make steps to align some of the individual career planning tools more closely with the progression of their talent groups.

There is a danger if the pendulum swings too far back towards organisational-led careers, that we will start to see the more negative consequences of high-flyer schemes in the 1980s. Here, expectations were set for a core group of people that could not be met by the organisation, leading to demotivated and less productive groups of people. In addition, the excluded groups showed feelings of inequity and decreased their contribution to the organisation.

Getting the balance between people-led and role-led approaches

Career strategies can be approached by taking a people-led process, which starts by identifying the skills and competencies in the company and aims to grow pools of talent for the future; or a role-led approach, where business critical roles are identified and future scenarios are used to predict longer-term needs. Ideally, these two approaches are matched and integrated to give an overall picture of gaps. However, what tends to happen is organisations focus their strategy on one side of this analysis.

If companies over-focus on identifying and growing acceleration pools, without a thorough analysis of business critical roles and vacancy risks in the future, there is a risk that the development efforts will not position the organisation in the way that is needed for longer-term success. This may particularly be the case where the people responsible for the career strategy are closely associated with learning and development.

Equally, if the focus is too role based, there is a risk that the development will lack the flexibility and adaptability needed to attain a more uncertain future. This is more likely to be the case if the advocates of the career strategy are more closely aligned to selection processes and resource planning functions.

The ability to work with both elements of the strategy are critical to longer-term success and I see one of the challenges facing companies currently as being the ability to integrate these two aspects and ensure a common understanding of the whole picture.

Meeting and delivering on expectations for role moves and challenging development opportunities

To be successful, career strategies need to deliver on the expectations that are set. With the growing trend towards acceleration pools, there is an increased expectation amongst pool members that opportunities will be open to them, even if the message is clear that they have responsibility for initiating those opportunities. Whilst companies are able to supply training programmes and even access to support in the form of mentors and coaches, my sense is that not many of them have fully explored the implications of wider development experiences. Some smaller companies simply do not have the range of growth opportunities at their disposal and are unable to provide experiences which will grow the required sets of skills.

Sourcing and resourcing projects, assignments and short-term role requirements in a timely and effective way is a difficult task, despite the advantages which come from using talent software. Ideally, this software will match the needs with the development requirements of employees, but companies also need to ensure that people do not feel disadvantaged when opportunities come up and are filled without being openly offered to all employees. This tension is not an easy one to manage, but is not something that should be ignored in the hope that it will go away! Companies need to set realistic expectations and be clear on the implications of their approach. It is also likely that the ability to grow though experience needs to be carefully monitored as the strategy progresses.

Keeping the balance with the core population

If companies are taking a segmented approach to their career strategies, the knock-on effects on the core population need careful monitoring. Whilst it is important to grow your talent for the future, sustaining the current operation and ensuring optimum performance of your entire workforce is also critical. I have mentioned the need for equity and 'felt fair' a number of times and constantly monitoring perceptions is vital, so as not to lose sight of the overall picture. More effective career strategies of the future are likely to continue to integrate processes across the organisation at all levels. Some time spent process mapping all the components of the career strategy would be a useful way for companies to both understand and work with the consequences of career actions.

Ensuring a supportive culture

Throughout this book reference has been made to the need to develop an appropriate culture to ensure the success of your career strategy. Chapter 2 for example, highlighted the need for perceived fairness of processes and procedures, which stems from an on-going dialogue between managers and employees. Chapter 6, talked about developing a coaching culture, and the need for trust and openness for this to work effectively. These are not easy challenges for organisations, but are issues which are at the heart of successful strategies.

Companies need to be realistic about the type of culture present in their business and ensure that they don't introduce initiatives which will not suit their climate. Companies with a short-term, performance-driven culture such as the banking sector, need to think more in terms of targeted growth opportunities and changing leadership success measures, to be able to establish the longer-term focus needed for careers.

What will the future bring?

Whilst it is obviously impossible to predict the future, for me the future will bring a greater focus on some of the issues and challenges highlighted here.

If I was to suggest three particular aspects which I think will continue to be strong, these would be:

1. Integration
2. Flexibility
3. Balance

Integration needs to happen at all levels of the business, starting with a closer integration with the business strategy, through to improving links across the business and global boundaries. The HR processes and line manager role also need to be better integrated to ensure high levels of support for both individual and organisational career needs.

Career strategies will also need to be flexible, not only in adapting to changing future needs, but also to deal with the needs of a varied workforce. Specialist roles and increasing work-life balance issues highlight the need to vary your strategic approach to suit the needs of the individual. Despite this flexibility, there is also a need to balance the expectations of all the different employee groups present in the organisation, to achieve a sense of equity throughout. This issue of balance is also needed in the emphasis given to the strategy, whereby both role-led and opportunity-led development need to be balanced, as well as the emphasis between people and role requirements.

If history is anything to go by, there is also likely to be a further swing on the spectrum between organisational-led activity and individual-led approaches. I can already see high potential employees selected for career acceleration pool struggling to maintain a work-life balance without being penalised by the organisation and I wonder how long this can be sustained. As I mentioned earlier in the book, I am curious to see the effects of career pools with a strong culture of work-life balance as I believe that this would not only attract greater interest from talent within the organisation, but also lead to more sustainable performance in the longer term.

Sadly, my guess is that we still have some time to go on the swing back towards organisational-led approaches before this happens and this issue can only be addressed by changing the mindset of what careers mean in organisations, to the more life-encompassing view put forward in the introduction to this text.

Appendix: Organisations that Co-ordinate Voluntary Secondment Opportunities

Business in the Community (http://www.bitc.org.uk) was founded in 1982 to meet the responsibilities that businesses have to their communities. It has a membership of about 700 companies. Its purpose 'is to inspire, challenge, engage and support business in continually improving its positive impact on society'. The involvement of employees, supported and encouraged by their employers, is central to the work of Business In the Community.

Employees in the Community Network (www.volunteering.org.uk/managing volunteers/employeevolunteering/abouttheeitcn.htm) is for managers, including personnel and HR managers, in any organisation that has an interest in employer-supported volunteering (including secondment). It covers organisations that provide or receive volunteers. Its aims in relation to secondment are to 'promote … employer-supported volunteering as a key part of company community involvement in the public, private and voluntary sectors … and promote best practice within member organisations and more widely'. It offers various activities and services to promote this end, including network days and presentations on good practice.

Interchange (http://www.interchange.gov.uk) is a Government initiative managed by the Cabinet Office which promotes and encourages the exchange of people and good practice between the civil service and other sectors of the economy.

References

Argyris, C (1962), *Interpersonal competence and organisational effectiveness*, Irwin-Dorsey, Homewood.

Arnold, J and Mackenzie-Davey, K (1992), 'Beyond unmet expectations: a detailed analysis of graduate experiences at work during the first three years of their careers', *Personnel Review*, Vol. 21, No. 2, pp. 45–68.

Arthur, MB, Hall, DT and Lawrence, BS (eds) (1989), *Handbook of career theory*, Cambridge University Press, Cambridge.

Aryee, S and Leong, CC (1991), 'Career orientations and work outcomes among industrial and R&D professionals', *Group and Organisational Studies*, Vol. 16, No. 2, pp. 193–205.

Ashton and Lambert (2005), '*Practical talent management*', Careers Research Forum, www.crforum.co.uk

Barney, JB and Lawrence, BS (1989), '*Pin stripes, power ties, and personal relationships: the economics of career strategy*', in MB Arthur, DT Hall and Lawrence BS(eds).

Baron, JN, Davis-Blake, A and Bielby, WT (1986), 'The structure of opportunity: how promotion ladders vary within and among organisations', *Administrative Science Quarterly*, Vol. 31, pp. 248–273.

Becker, BE and Huselid, MA (1998), '*High performance work systems and firm performance*', Research in Personnel and Human Resources Management.

Beckhard, R and Harris, R (1987), *Organisational transformations: Managing complex change*, Addison-Wesley, Reading, MA.

Beeson, J (2004), 'Building bench strength: a toolkit for executive development', *Business Horizons*, November–December.

Bell, N and Straw, BM (1989), 'People as sculptors versus sculpture: the roles of personality and personal control in organisations', in MB Arthur, DT Hall and BS Lawrence (eds), *Handbook of career theory*.

Berger, LA and Berger DR (eds) (2004), *The talent management handbook: creating organistional excellence by identifying, developing and promoting your best people*, McGraw-Hill, New York.

Bergeron (2004), 'Build a talent strategy to achieve your desired business results', *Handbook of business strategy*, MCB UP Ltd, pp. 133–139.

Berney, K (1990), 'Get ready for the quality generation', *International Management*, Vol. 45, No. 6, pp. 26–31.

Bolles, RN (1988), *What colour is your parachute?*, Ten Speed Press, Berkeley.

Boston Consulting group (2000), *"Blown to bits"* Harvard Business School Press.

Boudreau, JW and Ramstad, PM (2005), 'Talentship and the new paradigm for human resource management: from professional practice to strategic talent decision science', *Human Resource Planning*, Vol. 28, No. 2.

Bourner, T and Weinstein, K (1996), 'Just another talking shop? Some of the pitfalls in action learning', *Employee Counselling Today*, Vol. 8 No. 6.

Boxall, P and Purcell, J (2003), *Strategy and human resource management*, Palgrave, London.

Bridges, W (1995), *"Jobshift: How to prosper in a workplace without jobs"* Nicholas Brealey.

Burgoyne, JG and Germain, C (1984), 'Self development and career planning: an exercise in mutual benefit', *Personnel Management*, April.

Burgoyne, JG, Pedlar, M and Boydell, T (1994), *Towards the learning company*, McGraw-Hill, Maidenhead.

Butler, P et al. (1997) 'A revolution in interactions', *McKinsey Quarterly*, No. 1.

Byham, WC, Smith, AB and Paese, MJ (2002), 'Grow your own leaders: how to identify, develop and retain leadership talent', *Financial Times*, Prentice Hall.

Cannon, JA (2006), *Making the business case*, CIPD, London.

Career Innovation Research Group (1999), *Riding the wave*, Whiteway Research International, Oxford.

Carrington, L (2005) 'A waste of talent', www.hrmagazine.co.uk

Caudron S (1994), 'HR revamps career itineraries', *Personnel Journal*, April

Caulkin, S (1995), 'The new avengers', *Management Today*, November, pp. 48–52.

Charan, R (2005), 'Ending the CEO succession crisis', *Harvard Business Review*, February.

Charan, R, Drotter, S and Noel, J (2001), *The leadership pipeline: how to build the leadership powered company*, Jossey Bass, San Francisco, CA.

Chartered Institute of Personnel and Development (CIPD) (2003a), *Understanding the people and performance link: unlocking the black box*, CIPD, London.

Chartered Institute of Personnel and Development (CIPD) (2003b), *Managing employee careers: issues, trends and prospects*, Survey Report, CIPD, London.

Chartered Institute of Personnel and Development (CIPD) (2004), *Coaching and buying coaching services*, CIPD, London.

Clark, FA (1992), *Total career management: strategies for creating management careers*, McGraw-Hill, Maidenhead.

Clutterbuck, D (2004), *Everyone needs a mentor*, CIPD, London.

Colarelli, S and Bishop, R (1990), 'Career commitment: function, correlates and management', *Group and Organisational Studies*, Vol. 15, No. 2, pp. 158–176.

Conger, J and Fulmer, R (2003), 'Developing your leadership pipeline', *Harvard Business Review*, December.

Corporate Leadership Council (2003), 'High impact succession management' www.corporateleadershipcouncil.com

Corporate Leadership Council (2005), 'Realising the full potential of rising stars' www.corporateleadershipcouncil.com

Corporate Leadership Council (2006), Web report at www.corporateleadership-council.com

Cotton, JL and Tuttle, JM (1986), 'Employee turnover: a meta analysis and review with implications for research', *Academy of Management Review*, Vol. 11, No. 1, pp. 55–70.

Defillippi, RJ and Arthur, MB (1994), 'The boundaryless career: a competency-based perspective', *Journal of Organisational Behaviour*, Vol. 15, No. 4, pp. 307–324.

Deloitte Consulting (2003), *Human Resources Magazine*.

Derr, CB (1986), *Managing the new careerists*, Jossey Bass, San Francisco, CA.

Derr, CB and Laurent (1989), 'The internal and external career: a theoretical and cross-cultural perspective', in MB Arthur, DT Hall and BS Lawrence (eds), *Handbook of career theory*.

Driver, MJ (1979), 'Career concepts and career management in organisations', in C Copper (ed.), *Behavioural problems in organisations*, Prentice Hall, NJ.

Eichinger, RW and Lonbardo, MM (2004), 'Learning ability as a prime indicator of potential', *Human Resource Planning*, pp. 12–15.

Flacharty, J (1998), *Coaching: evoking excellence in others*, Butterworth Heinemann, Oxford.

Francis, D (1985), *Managing your own career*, Fontana/Collins, London.

Garavan, TN (1990), 'Promoting strategic career development activities: some Irish experience', *Industrial and Commercial Training*, Vol. 22, No. 6, pp. 22–30.

Giles, M and West, M (1995), 'People as sculptors versus sculptures: what shape career development programmes?', *Journal of Management Development*, Vol. 14, No. 10, pp. 48–63.

Goodge, P (1994), 'Development centres: clues to effectiveness', *Management Research News*, Vol. 17, No. 5, pp. 17–22.

Gould, S (1978), 'Career planning in the organisation', *Human Resource Management*, Vol. 17, Part 1, pp. 8–11.

Granrose, CS and Portwood, JD (1987), 'Matching individual career plans and organisational career management', *Academy of Management Journal*, Vol. 30, No. 4, pp. 699–720.

Guest, D and Mackenzie, DK (1996), 'Don't write off the traditional career', *People Management*, Vol. 2, No. 4, February.

Gutteridge, TG, Leibowitz, ZB and Shore, JE (1993), 'When careers flower, organisations flourish', *Training and Development*, Vol. 47, No. 11.

Hall, DT (1976), *Careers in organisations*, Goodyear, Pacific Palisades, CA.

Hall, DT (1989), 'How top management and the organisation itself can block effective executive succession', *HRM Journal*, Vol. 28, No. 1, pp. 5–24.

Hall, DT et al. (1986), '*Career development in organisations*', Jossey Bass, San Francisco, CA.

Hamblin, AD (1974), Evaluation and control of training, McGraw-Hill, Maidenhead.

Handy, C (1985), *The future of work*, Basil Blackwell, Oxford.

Handy, C (1994), Making sense of the future, *Promoting lifelong career development*, CRAC, Hobsons Publishing, Cambridge.

Hanson, MC (1981), 'Career/life planning workshops – Are they working?' *Training and Development Journal*, July, pp. 80–90.

Harris, H (1999), 'Women in international management' in C Brewster and H Harris (eds), *International HRM: contemporary issues in Europe*, Routledge, London.

Hay Group and Human Resources (2003), 'Tap into talent' *Human Resources*, October.

Hay Group (2004), Talent Management Survey.

Herriot, P (1992), *Career management challenge: balancing individual and organisational needs*, Sage, London.

Herriot, P (1995), 'The management of careers', in S Tyson (ed.), *Strategic prospects for HRM*, Institute of Personnel and Development, London.

Herriot, P and Pemberton, C (1995), *New deals: the revolution in managerial careers*, Wiley, Chichester.

Herriot, P and Pemberton, C (1996), 'Contracting Careers' *Human Relations*, Vol. 49, No. 6, pp. 759–790.

Herriot, P, Pemberton, C and Pinder, R (1994), 'Misconceptions by managers and their bosses of each other's preferences regarding the managers' careers: a case of the blind leading the blind?', *Human Resource Management Journal*, Vol. 4, No. 2, pp. 39–51.

Herriot, P, Gibbons, P, Pemberton, C and Jackson, PR (1994), 'An empirical model of managerial careers in organisations', *British Journal of Management*, Vol. 5, No. 2, pp. 113–121.

Hirsh, Wendy, (1984), '*Career management in the organisation*', Falmer, Brighton, IMS study No. 96.

Hirsh, W (1997), 'Succession planning – current practice and future issues', IES report 184, Brighton.

Hirsh, W (2000), 'Succession planning dymstified', IES report 372, Brighton.

Hirsh, W (2004), *Leadership in organisations*, John Storey (ed), Routledge, London.

Hirsh, W and Jackson, C (1996), 'Strategies for career development: promise, practice and pretence', Report No. 305, Institute of Employment Studies, Brighton.

Hirsh, W and Jackson, C (2004), *Managing career in large organisations*, Work Foundation, London.

Hirsh, W, Jackson, C and Kidd, JM (2001), Straight talking: effective career discussions at work, NICEC/CRAC, Cambridge, June.

Holbeche, L (1995), 'Career development in flatter structures: report 2, organisational practices', July, Roffey Park, Horsham.

Holbeche, L (2001), 'Aligning human resources and business strategy', 2nd Edn. UK: Butterworth-Heinemann.

Holland, JL (1985), *Making vocational choices: a theory of vocational personalities and work environments*, Prentice Hall, Englewood Cliffs.

Hopson, B and Scally, M (1991), *Build your own rainbow: a workbook for career and life management*, Mercury Books, London.

HR Focus (2004), 'A simpler way to determine the ROI of talent management', Institute of Management and Administration, Vol. 81, No. 12.

Hurley, A (1997), 'The effects of self-esteem and source credibility on self-denying prophecies', *The Journal of Psychology*, Vol. 131, No. 6, pp. 581–594.

Hutton, W (1995), *The state we're in*, Jonathan Cope, London.

IDS Study (2006), 'Job families', January, No. 814.

Iles, P (1997), 'Sustainable high-potential career development: a resource based view', *Career Development International*, Vol. 2, No. 7, pp. 347–353.

Iles, P and Mabey, C (1993), 'Managerial career development programmes: effectiveness, availability and acceptability', *British Journal of Management*, Vol. 4, pp. 103–118.

Inkson, K (1995), 'Effects of changing economic conditions on managerial job changes and careers', *British Journal of Management*, Vol. 6, pp. 183–194.

Inkson, K and Arthur, M (2001), 'How to be a successful career capitalist', *Organisational dynamics*, Vol. 30, No. 1, pp. 48–58.

Jackson, C (1990), Careers counselling in organisations: the way forward, Falmer, Brighton, Institute of Manpower studies, Report 198.

Jones, P, Palmer, J, Osterwell, C and Whitehead, D (1996), '*Delivering exceptional performance*', Pitman, London.

Kenton, B and Yarnall, J (2005), *HR the business partner: shaping a new direction*, Elsevier, Oxford.

Kerr, SC (1989), 'AC or DC? The experience of development centres', Paper presented to *the British Psychological Society*, Windermere, January.

Kidd, JM, Hirsh, W and Jackson, C (2004), '*Straight Talking: the nature of effective career discussion at work*', *Journal of Career Development*, Vol. 30, No. 4, pp. 231–245.

King, Z (2004), *Career management. A guide*. Chartered Institute of Personnel and Development, London.

Kirkpatrick, DC (1975), *Evaluating training programmes*, American Society for Training and Development, Madison, WI.

Knight, S (1995), *NLP at work*, Nicholas Brealey, London.

Kotter, JP, Faux, UA and McArthur, CC (1978), *Self assessment and career development*, Prentice Hall, Englewood Cliffs, NJ.

Larsen, H (1997), 'Do high flyer programmes facilitate organisational learning?' *Journal of European Industrial Training*, Vol. 21, No. 9, pp. 310–317.

Leibowitz, ZB, Farren, C and Kaye, BL (1986), '*Designing career development systems*', Jossey Bass, San Francisco, CA.

Levinson, D (1986), 'A conception of adult development', *American Psychologist*, Vol. 41, No. 1, pp. 3–13.

Lewis, G (1996), *The mentoring manger: strategies for fostering talent and spreading knowledge*, Pitman, London.

Lewis, P (2006), 'Identifying and developing high potential talent: the experience of individuals and implications for people and organisation development', Roffey Park Institute, MSc 13.

Livingstone, J (1969), 'Pygmalion in management', *Harvard Business Review*, Vol. 47, No. 4, pp. 81–89.

London, M (1983), 'Towards a theory of career motivation', *Academy of Management Review*, Vol. 8, No. 4, pp. 620–630.

London, M (1993), 'Relationships between career motivation, empowerment and support for career development', *Journal of Occupational and Organisational Psychology*, Vol. 66, pp. 55–69.

Mayo, A (1991), '*Managing careers – strategies for organisations*', Institute of Personnel Management, London.

McCall, Jr MW (1998), '*High flyers: developing the next generation of leaders*', Harvard Business School Press, Boston, MA.

McCartney, C and Garrow, V (2006), *The talent management journey*, Roffey Park Institute, Horsham.

McEnrue, MP (1989), 'Self-development as a career management strategy', *Journal of Vocational Behaviour*, No. 34, pp. 57–68.

Michaels, E, Handfield-Jones, H and Axelrod, B (1998), 'War for Talent Survey', *McKinsey Quarterly*, McKinsey and Co. New York.

Michaels, E, Handfield-Jones, H and Axelrod, B (2001) *The war for talent*, Harvard Business School Press, Boston, MA.

Morton, L (2004), 'Integrated and integrative talent management', Careers research forum, www.crforum.co.uk.

Moss Kanter, RM (1994), 'Change in the global economy: an interview with Rosabeth Moss Kanter', *European Management Journal*, Vol. 12, No. 1, pp: 1–9.

Kanter, RM (1977), *Men and women of the corporation*, Basic Books, New York.

Kanter, RM (1984), *The change masters*, Unwin, London.

Mucha, T (2004), 'The art and science of talent management', *Organisatonal Development Journal*, Vol. 22, No. 4, Winter.

Nathan, R and Hill, L (2006), *Career counselling*, 2nd edition, Sage, London.

Noe, RA (1988), 'An investigation into the determinants of successful assigned mentoring relationships', *Personnel Psychology*, Vol. 39, pp. 457–523.

Noe, R, Noe, A and Bachhuber, J (1990), 'Correlates of career motivation', *Journal of Vocational Behaviour*, Vol. 37, pp. 340–356.

Novidevic, M and Harvey, M (2001), 'The changing role of the corporate HR function in global organistions of the 21st century', *International Journal of Human Resource Management*, Vol. 12, No. 8, pp. 1251–1268.

Ohlott, P (2004), 'Job assignments', in C McCauley and E VanVelsor (eds), *The center for creative leadership handbook of leadership development*, Jossey-Bass, San Francisco, CA.

Parsloe, E and Wray, M (2000), Coaching and mentoring – practical methods to improve learning, Kogan Page, London.

Pazy, A (1988), 'Joint responsibility: the relationships between organisational and individual career management and the effectiveness of careers', *Group and Organisational Studies*, Vol. 13, No. 3, pp. 311–331.

Pedlar, M, Burgoyne, J and Boydell, T (1988), *Applying self-development in organisations*, Prentice Hall, London.

Personnel Today (2006), 'Yahoo! Translate attraction into engagement', 27 June.

Petrovic, J, Harris, H and Brewster, C (2000), '*New forms of international working*', Centre for research into the management of expatriation, Cranfield School of Management, Cranfield.

Pfeffer, J (2001), 'Fighting the war for talent is hazardous to your organisation's health', *Organisational Dynamics*, Vol. 29, No. 4, pp. 248–259.

Popoff, F (1996), 'Reflections on succession', *Prism*, Third Quarter.

Reddington, M, Willianson, M and Withers, M (2005), *Transforming HR, creating value through people*, Elsevier, Oxford.

Revans, R (1982), *The origins and growth of action learning*, Chartwell-Brett.

Rice, M (2001), 'Great expectations', *Management Today*, June.

Roberts, BW and Friend, W (1998), 'Career momentum in midlife women: life context, identity, and personality correlates', *Journal of Occupational Health Psychology*, Vol.3, No. 3, pp. 195–208.

Robertson, A and Abbey, G (2003), *Managing talented people*, Pearson Education, Harlow.

Roper (2002), *Staying ahead of the curve: the AARP work and career study*, Roper Starch Worldwide & AAARP, Washington, DC.

Rothwell, WJ (2001), *Effective succession planning: ensuring leadership continuity and building talent from within*, American Management Association, New York.

Rothwell, WJ and Kazanas, HC (2003), 2nd edition, 'The strategic development of talent', HRD Press Inc., Canada.

Rousseau, D (1995), *Psychological contracts in organisations: understanding written and unwritten agreements*, Sage, London.

Russell, J (1991), 'Career development interventions in organisations', *Journal of Vocational Behaviour*, Vol. 38, pp. 237–287.

Schein, EH (1978), '*Career Dynamics: matching organisational and individual needs*', Addison-Wesley, Reading, MA.

Schein, EH (1984), 'Culture as an environmental context for careers', *Journal of Occupational Behaviour*, Vol. 5, pp. 71–81.

Schein, EH (1990), *Career anchors – discovering your real values*, Pfeiffer, Toronto.

Schein, EH (1996) 'Career anchors revisited – implications for career development in the 21st century', *Academy of Management Executive*, Vol. 10, No. 4, pp. 80–88.

Senge, PM (1990), *The fifth discipline*, Random House, London.

Sheehy, G. (1976), *Passages: Predictable crises of adult life*, Dutton, New York.

Simms, I (2003), 'The generation gap', *People Management*, February.

Smart, B (1999), *Top grading: how leading companies win by hiring, coaching and keeping the best people*, Prentice Hall, New York.

Sparrow, P, Brewster, C and Harris, H (2004), *Global Human Resource Management*, Routledge, London.

Storey, J (2004), *Leadership in organisations, current issues and key trends*, Routledge, London.

Straw, BM and Ross, J (1985), 'Stability in the midst of change: a dispositional approach to job attitudes', *Journal of Applied Psychology*, Vol. 70, pp. 469–480.

Stump, RW (1986), 'Assessing the impact of career development in organisations: a case in point', *Public Personnel Management*, Vol. 15, No. 4, pp. 399–413.

Stumpf, SA (1989), 'Towards a heuristic model of career management', *International Journal of Career Management*, Vol. 1, No. 1, 1989.

Sturges, J (2004), Storey '*Leadership in organisations, current issues and key trends*', Routledge, London.

Sullivan, J (2000), e-HR conference, September, IPQC, London.

Super, DE (1980), 'A life-span approach to career development', *Journal of Vocational Behaviour*, Vol. 16, pp. 282–298.

Super, DE (1988), *Adult career concerns inventory*, Consulting psychologists press, Palo Alto, CA.

Super, DE and Hall, DT (1978), 'Career development: exploration and planning', *Annual Review of Psychology*, Vol. 29, pp. 333–372.

Taylor, C (2004), 'The tides of talent', *Training and Development Magazine*, ASTD Press.

Thornton, GC,(1978), 'Differential effects of career planning on internals and externals', *Personnel Psychology*, Vol. 31, pp. 471–476.

Ulrich, D (1997), *Human resource champions*, Harvard University Press, Cambridge, MA.

Ulrich, D (2006), in People Management 16th June.

Veiga, JF (1983), 'Mobility influences during managerial career stages' *Academy of Management Journal*, Vol. 26, pp. 64–85.

Waterman, R, Waterman, J and Collard, BA (1994), 'Towards a career resilient workforce', *Harvard Business Review*, July/August, pp. 87–95.

Webber (2004), *Fast Company Magazine*.

Whiteley, P (2003) 'Where's the evidence?', *IRS Employment Review*, No. 787, pp. 22–24.

Williams, R (1985), 'Linking career and self-development', *The British Psychological Society*, No. 4, August.

Yapp, C (2005), 'Innovation, futures thinking and leadership', *Public Money and Management*, Vol. 25(1), pp. 57–60.

Yarnall, J (1998a), 'Career anchors: results of an organisational study in the UK', *Career Development International*, Vol. 3, No. 2, pp. 56–61.

Yarnall, J (1998b), 'Line managers as career developers: rhetoric or reality?', *Personnel Review*, Vol. 27, No. 5, pp. 378–395.

Index